Collective Action 2.0

CHANDOS
SOCIAL MEDIA SERIES

Series Editors: Geoff Walton and Woody Evans
(emails: g.l.walton@staffs.ac.uk and kdevans@gmail.com)

This series of books is aimed at practitioners and academics involved in using social media in all its forms and in any context. This includes information professionals, academics, librarians and managers, and leaders in business. Social media can enhance services, build communication channels, and create competitive advantage. The impact of these new media and decisions that surround their use in business can no longer be ignored. The delivery of education, privacy issues, logistics, political activism and research rounds out the series' coverage. As a resource to complement the understanding of issues relating to other areas of information science, teaching and related areas, books in this series respond with practical applications. If you would like a full listing of current and forthcoming titles, please visit our website www.chandospublishing.com.

New authors: we are always pleased to receive ideas for new titles; if you would like to write a book for Chandos in the area of social media, please contact George Knott, Commissioning Editor, on g.knott@elsevier.com or telephone +44 (0) 1865843114.

Collective Action 2.0
The Impact of Social Media on Collective Action

Shaked Spier

CHANDOS PUBLISHING

An imprint of Elsevier • elsevier.com

Chandos Publishing is an imprint of Elsevier
50 Hampshire Street, 5th Floor, Cambridge, MA 02139, United States
The Boulevard, Langford Lane, Kidlington, OX5 1GB, United Kingdom

Notices
Knowledge and best practice in this field are constantly changing. As new research and experience broaden our understanding, changes in research methods, professional practices, or medical treatment may become necessary.

Practitioners and researchers must always rely on their own experience and knowledge in evaluating and using any information, methods, compounds, or experiments described herein. In using such information or methods they should be mindful of their own safety and the safety of others, including parties for whom they have a professional responsibility.

To the fullest extent of the law, neither the Publisher nor the authors, contributors, or editors, assume any liability for any injury and/or damage to persons or property as a matter of products liability, negligence or otherwise, or from any use or operation of any methods, products, instructions, or ideas contained in the material herein.

Library of Congress Cataloging-in-Publication Data
A catalog record for this book is available from the Library of Congress

British Library Cataloguing-in-Publication Data
A catalogue record for this book is available from the British Library

ISBN: 978-0-08-100567-5 (print)
ISBN: 978-0-08-100579-8 (online)

For information on all Chandos Publishing publications
visit our website at https://www.elsevier.com/books-and-journals

Publisher: Glyn Jones
Acquisition Editor: George Knott
Editorial Project Manager: Anna Valutkevich
Production Project Manager: Omer Mukthar
Designer: Victoria Pearson

To my grandfathers, role models and constant inspiration;
may you rest in peace.

Contents

Biography

Shaked Spier graduated in Information Science and Gender Studies at the Humboldt University, Berlin. His research and writing includes a variety of topics related to the connection between information and communication technologies and society, information ethics, digital policies, and digital rights using interdisciplinary approaches. At present, he works as project manager in diverse information technology projects. Politically, he volunteers as spokesperson of the workgroup on Internet policy, digital society, and digital rights in the German leftwing party DIE LINKE and cooperates with various nongovernmental organizations in this field.

Acknowledgments

Work on this project was a journey that began on that Mayday 2010 in Berlin, while standing up to a Nazi march through my hometown, Berlin. It was a day that gave me the first inspiration, which led to the writing of this book.

The journey continued as I wrote my thesis on the subject. Therefore I would like to begin with expressing my appreciation to my lecturers Prof. Vivien Petras and Olaf Eigenbrodt from the Humboldt University of Berlin for enabling me to pursue a research topic somewhat outside the mainstream of our faculty.

During the writing of my thesis, I was inspired by the protesters of Tahrir Square and Rothschild Boulevard, claiming their rights of freedom, democracy, and social justice. In the years between these events and the completion of the book, I had the pleasure of participating in movements and protests that not only were academically intriguing, but also moved me as an individual with grievances and anger, with hopes and dreams. I would like to express my deepest thanks and appreciation to the many activists, protesters, and movements—from good friends to total strangers—for the conversations, ideas, insights, and inside views, especially to those with whom I had the pleasure to stand in the way of Nazi marches, demand social justice, protest against the occupation in my homeland (Israel), and spend endless days and nights preparing refugee accommodations, sorting clothing donations, serving food, and building collectives I hitherto never thought possible. This book is their accomplishment as it is my own.

I would like to thank the colleagues, friends, and fellow activists, who took the time to exchange views on the topics discussed in this book; with special thanks going to Rafael Capurro, Gad Yair, and Julia Schramm for their helpful comments and ideas. And to Mathias Stallauke, that special someone, for all the support and putting up with me during long days (and nights) of writing.

And last but not least, I thank George Knott, Harriet Clayton, Anna Valutkevich, and Omer Mukthar from Elsevier for their editorial support and input on the various stages of the work.

Acknowledgements

CHAPTER 1

Introduction

ABSTRACT

This chapter serves as an introduction to the topic of social media and collective action. The chapter stresses the importance of addressing the discourse that accompanies the topic. Furthermore, the connection between social media and collective action is regarded as part of the continuous development of the reciprocal relations between information and communication technologies (ICTs) and collective action; and in a broader sense between ICTs and society.

Keywords: Collective action; Discourse; Hype cycle; ICTs; Labor day; Social media; Social movement theory; Social networks.

CONTENTS

1.1 #1MAI_NAZIFREI

On Labor Day (May Day) 2010, the German right-wing party NPD planned to march through the Prenzlauer Berg neighborhood in Berlin. Over the years, a tradition of peaceful protests that stand in the way of these provocative right-wing demonstrations has emerged, which is supported by many civic movements, activists, political parties, and civilians. Prior to the march on May 1, 2010, several activist and antifascist groups as well as an alliance called *1. Mai Nazifrei* (May Day without Nazis) called for counterdemonstrations, publishing information regarding the Nazis' organization and their demonstration's

1

possible routes.[1] Using the gathered information, thousands of protesters tried to achieve blockades at as many strategic points as possible, to block all possible routes and thus stop the march.

The counterprotests on that day, however, have added a new dimension to the protest's on-site organization—many protesters used Twitter to communicate the developments on-site. Since there were many spots to block and the police had put up a major effort to secure the area, communication between protesters was crucial. Individuals used hashtags such as *#1Mai* or *#1Mai_Nazifrei* and delivered updates regarding developments in their current locations (about the music and cultural activities taking place in some spots; police (mis)treatment; useful breaches in the police's barricades; if the spot is occupied enough or if a certain spot is understaffed and needs reinforcement to block the Nazi march), retweeted other people's messages, and provided those who did not make it to the protests after the police sealed the area with information. Furthermore, the *1. Mai Nazifrei* alliance's Twitter account was accompanying the counterprotests, giving out important information and updates gathered from the alliance's activists on the field as well as from other activist groups and twitter users among the protesters.

As a participant and observer, I was fascinated with the new dynamics that this sort of real-time, ad hoc communication and organization has given the demonstrations—a certain spot is understaffed? Escalation with the police at a certain spot, so that other protesters should stay away? Information regarding a new alternative route that needs to be blocked? Good music and street dancing at one of the spots? A few tweets get into circulation, amplified by retweets and the official Twitter account, and many further protesters beyond those within the reach of the "classical" on-site communication channels are informed and can act accordingly. Especially, this communication has given the protesters advantage over the hierarchical, centralized manner of communication deployed by the police.

At the end of the day, the NPD groups could not march for more than several hundred meters, facing the first blockade of citizens who refused to let this kind of groups enter their neighborhoods. Since the police had to seal the surrounding area, many of the NPD sympathizers could not have reached their demonstration's starting point and the police, informed that all possible routes were being blocked, canceled the Nazi demonstration. An alternative, unregistered demonstration in a different part of town was stopped and the participants were arrested.

The communication over Twitter was not the decisive factor of the *1. Mai Nazifrei* protests and their success, but rather a supplement to weeks of preliminary

---

[1] Retrieved from: www.antifa-berlin.info/1mai2010/home.html.

research and fieldwork, on- and offline mobilization, on-site communication between activists and protesters, as well as a complex mixture of German societal and historical aspects, resentments toward the NPD Party and Nazi ideology, and a developed protest culture in the city of Berlin. Nonetheless, the new qualities that the protests gained from the additional mode of communication were visible on several levels—mobilization of participants and resources; dissemination of protest-relevant information, pictures, and videos (many of them shared on social media platforms such as YouTube); and on-site ad hoc communication, coordination, and organization.

The phenomenon that was hitherto still in emergence quickly became an integral part of a wide arsenal of tools and methods applied by social movements and activists around the world. The deployment of social media platforms has given many instances of collective action (e.g., social protests, flash mobs, political campaigns, collection of donations) new qualities that, in some cases, fundamentally affected them. On the other hand, in many cases social media usage had negative effects such as demobilization, neglect of other important sources due to an exaggerated belief in the power of social media or "the Internet," being subjected to state and/or corporate surveillance, or handing over power to those in control of the platforms and infrastructure on which they are built. Furthermore, law-enforcement and other state institutions have also adapted their methods to handle the use of social media on demonstrations. For example, in many demonstrations I visited in the past years in Berlin and elsewhere in Germany, the police force interfered with 3G cell-phone reception in the area of the demonstration, which denied cellular Internet usage by demonstrators in a certain radius.

May Day 2010 was the occasion on which I became aware of the relation between social media platforms and collective action. Over the following years, this reciprocal relation was granted a considerable amount of media, social, and academic attention. The attention to the subject peaked as the events of the Arab Spring were framed as "Twitter revolutions" or "Facebook revolutions" and continued during a wave of social protests around the world in the first half of the 2010s. As the prominent quote of the journalist Andrew Sullivan in light of the protests surrounding the Iranian 2009 elections declared: "The revolution will be twittered" (Sullivan, 2009).

Or will it?

1.2 HYPE CYCLE AND THE NEED FOR A THEORETICAL FRAMEWORK

The term *Social Media*, which describes a wide collection of technologies and practices, comprises an essential, but in most cases hidden, aspect of technologies per se, namely, being social. Technologies are designed and deployed in social contexts and therefore contain affordances and biases in their deployment. The reciprocal relation between technology, especially Information and Communication Technologies (ICTs) and social media, and society is manifold and will be critically examined from a variety of perspectives throughout the book.

Beyond its social dimension, the application of technology—the manner in which it is used, the objectives pursued by the users, etc.—is accompanied, in turn, by a discourse. Framing the discourse regarding the application of social media in the context of collective action is helpful to understand the reciprocal relation between the former as a technology with implicit and explicit social dimensions and affordances, and the latter as the social context, in which this technology is applied.

The information technology research and consulting firm Gartner has developed the Hype Cycle methodology to represent what it terms as maturity, adoption, and social application of specific technologies (Fenn and Raskino, 2008). In the Hype Cycle representation, Gartner claims that technologies go through the following five stages in the adoption and application (Fig. 1.1):

1. **Technology Trigger:** "A potential technology breakthrough kicks things off. Early proof-of-concept stories and media interest trigger significant publicity. Often no usable products exist and commercial viability is unproven."
2. **Peak of Inflated Expectations:** "Early publicity produces a number of success stories—often accompanied by scores of failures. Some companies take action; many do not."

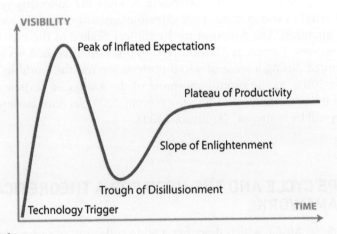

FIGURE 1.1

Gartner Hype Cycle. *From Gartner, Inc., 2015. Research Methodologies: Gartner Hype Cycle. Gartner. Retrieved from:* http://www.gartner.com/technology/research/methodologies/hype-cycle.jsp.

3. **Trough of Disillusionment:** "Interest wanes as experiments and implementations fail to deliver. Producers of the technology shake out or fail. Investments continue only if the surviving providers improve their products to the satisfaction of early adopters."

4. **Slope of Enlightenment:** "More instances of how the technology can benefit the enterprise start to crystallize and become more widely understood. Second- and third-generation products appear from technology providers. More enterprises fund pilots; conservative companies remain cautious."

5. **Plateau of Productivity:** "Mainstream adoption starts to take off. Criteria for assessing provider viability are more clearly defined. The technology's broad market applicability and relevance are clearly paying off" (Gartner, 2015).

The vocabulary used by Gartner to describe the Hype Cycle reflects the economic interests that lay behind the methodology. In fact, this methodology is often used to consult companies on the deployment of technologies, according to their "maturity," i.e., according to the extent of the technology's deployment on the market and the advantages and opportunities it might provide the company with in terms of financial profit, solving business problems, workers' productivity, public image, etc.[2]

Having said that, the five stages described in the Hype Cycle methodology also tell the story of a discourse that, according to Gartner, accompanies specific technologies (to different extents) throughout their deployment. The traditional Hype Cycle representation locates a group of tools and/or methods with a common basis in their technological or organizational utilization on a fixed "discourse axis" with the five stages mentioned earlier. The location of each specific tool, method, or utilization reflects the correlation between the expectations and promises regarding the tool and between the practical experiences gathered in different use cases.

An alternative way to look at the Hype Cycle representation is to locate the same manner of deploying a technology or a group of technologies with a common basis on the discourse axis and consider the changes, which the sociotechnological discourse experiences over time according to the Hype Cycle's five stages. Considering the utilization of social media in collective action, such a representation offers us a manner to frame the media, academic, and civic

---

[2] Gartner offers a collection of Hype Cycle representations of various technologies and fields: www.gartner.com/technology/research/methodologies/hype-cycles.jsp.
For example, Gartner offers a Hype Cycle analysis of the utilization of Social Software in corporate environments: www.gartner.com/doc/2814417.

discourse surrounding the relation between the two, which is, in turn, instructive for studying these phenomena.

1. **Technology Trigger:** Social media platforms achieve high adoption rates within different, heterogeneous groups of users. This adoption and frequent usage among users constitute a critical mass, which is in turn a basic condition for the application of specific social media platforms in small and middle-scale instances of collective actions, such as organizing fund-raisings, demonstrations, and flash mobs or locating a lost person, pet, or cell phone.

2. **Peak of Inflated Expectations:** The issue of protesters successfully deploying social media becomes a media hype in the media coverage of social protests and—for many Western recipients, surprising—revolutions around the world. Known examples of this phase are:

   a. Tehran, Iran, 2009: Protests during the elections and Andrew Sullivan's term "the revolution will be twittered."

   b. Tahrir Square, Egypt, 2010: As a central (but not first) event in the revolutionary wave known as the *Arab Spring*, the protesters' usage of Facebook and Twitter led to a media circulation of terms such as "Facebook-revolution."

3. **Trough of Disillusionment:** In face of the several revolutions leading to undesired outcomes (from other undemocratic forces taking the place of the ousted ones or a revolution ending up in a civil war) and some cases of utilization of social media backfire (e.g., tracking down activists online, shutting down internet connection or cellular reception by state authorities, or crackdowns on activists that organize online), many of the hopes pinned on social media's "revolutionary" or "democratic spirit" seem to fade. In addition, other instances of collective action, such as fund-raisings and awareness campaigns, have faced the negative effects of what Evgeny Morozov has termed as *slacktivism*.[3] Known examples of this phase are:

   a. The rather sobering, in some cases tragic, aftermath of the events of the Arab Spring as well as other events that were framed as social media protests such as the Israeli social justice protests.

   b. Sweden, 2013: The United Nations Children's Fund launches a campaign under the motto "likes don't save lives" (Murphy, 2013; Grummas, 2013; Khazan, 2013).

---

[3] Morozov (2011) uses the term *Slacktivism* to describe pseudoactivism, which serves the calming of a person's self-conscious and the maintenance of her (online) identity and image more than the engagement in influential activism.

4. **Slope of Enlightenment:** At the time of writing of this book, one can observe stabilization in the treatment of social media as means for achieving some shared goals, i.e., in collective action. On the one hand, social media is a standard component, one out of many, in the toolkit or repertoire deployed by activists and social movements. On the other hand, the scientific research of social media offers empirical, instead of mere ideological, insights on the role of social media in many cases of collective action (both for events that achieved major international coverage such as the Arab Spring and Occupy Wall Street and a significant number of further events of local scale). At the same time, media coverage and social/political discourse no longer frame events based on their social media deployment.

5. **Plateau of Productivity:** This is where we are heading, not only concerning the deployment of social media to support collective action and the achievement of common goals, but also to understanding the complex relation between the two. Reaching the Plateau of Productivity will be a result of the experience gathered by activists and movements around the world as well as critical debate regarding the chances and dangers of deploying social media, refrained from technological centrist and determinist rhetoric.

The discourse's advance through the Hype Cycle's phases, or rather, along the Hype Cycle Discourse Axis, is not strictly chronological. The experiences, both positive and negative, gathered with the usage of social media in cases of collective action vary. They happen in extremely different geographical, political, social, and technological contexts, but it is the combination of these and other aspects that constitutes the discourse.

The compatibility of the social media and collective action discourse to the Gartner Hype Cycle does not only suggest us to try and refrain from technoutopist, technocentrist, and technodeterminist rhetoric, which is a characteristic of the Technology Trigger and Peak of Inflated Expectations phases; this rhetoric was and is still present in many discussions regarding social media and collective action. It also reveals a connection between the social media–related discourses and capitalist corporation logic and interests. Given the fact that most social media platforms, especially those that are present in the discourse regarding collective action, protest, and revolution, are held by Western capitalist corporations with monetary profit interests, a technoutopist, technocentrist, and positive-determinist rhetoric or discourse serve these corporations' interests.

These two aspects (technoutopist, -centrist, and -determinist discourse as well as the capitalist nature of social media platforms) are crucial for a sincere and critical analysis of the subject and will be addressed in Chapters 2 and 11.

1.3 RECIPROCAL RELATION BETWEEN INFORMATION AND COMMUNICATION TECHNOLOGY AND COLLECTIVE ACTION

The relation between social media and collective action can and should be addressed as a technosocial relation. This relation, however, does not begin with social media. ICTs in general have been closely related to collective action across many generations of technological development and of social organization. To name a few examples: telephone and mailing lists; leaflets; the production and distribution of *samizdat* using fax machines and photocopiers during the cold war; Radio Free Europe's transmission of anticommunist messages in Eastern Europe during the same period; radio transmissions that were an integral part in effectuating the genocide in Rwanda (Li, 2004); or the Zapatistas of Chiapas pioneer use of the World Wide Web to denounce economic injustices in Mexico and strive for international mobilization (Benski et al., 2013).

In his article "Protest in an Information Society: A Review of Literature on Social Movements and New ICTs" (Garrett, 2006), R. Kelly Garrett, researcher from the Center for Research on Information Technology in Organizations at the University of California, noted that scholars from a wide range of disciplines, such as social, political, and communication science, focus their research on understanding the changes that ICTs offer in the way people communicate and collaborate for collective action. At the same time, he finds fault with the absence of a common set of organizing theoretical principles and the lack of accredited theoretical framework in which existing and new works can be located. A decade after Garrett articulated this critique, the theoretical work on the relation between ICTs and collective action has made a considerable progress, but remains somewhat fragmented. On the other hand, due to the growing popularity of the social media, as communication platforms, as entrepreneurial buzzword, as advertising platforms, and as an academic field of research, increasingly more work is being published, especially in regard to social media and collective action. Having said that, Daniel Trottier and Christian Fuchs claim that "[t]hus far, social theory foundations of social media activity have been underrepresented in scholarly literature" (Fuchs and Trottier, 2014).

To some extent, this book is a contribution to filling the void in the scholarly literature mentioned by Garrett, Trottier, and Fuchs: the first part of the book (Chapters 3–6) will examine the role of social media in instances of collective action in accordance with different theories from the broad field of Social Movement Theory (SMT). The SMT is an interdisciplinary field of research, although it is firmly anchored in the social sciences, which examines social mobilization, social movements, and collective action from various angles and academic traditions.

An overview of SMT literature reveals that the degree of emphasis on the role of ICTs in collective action varies between different models and theories. Some theories, such as the Strain and Breakdown Theories, give very little or no attention at all to the technologies used for communication and circulation of movement or action-related information. Possible reasons may include ICTs being taken for granted or overlooked, that the main focus of the theories is directed to other factors, or that there may also be a need for further research work on the subject.

In other theories, such as Resource Mobilization and several Cultural Approaches, communication and dissemination of information receive an explicit emphasis, and therefore, these theories consciously give attention to ICTs. The Resource Mobilization Theory considers (movement-related) information, knowledge, cultural objects, etc. as resources that must be (similarly to other resources) aggregated, managed, shared, and efficiently used. In this way, the resource mobilization theory acknowledges the changes that ICTs bring to these processes as they develop. Cultural Approaches on the other hand, focus on meanings that are mediated through information and cultural objects, as well as on their acceptance among the audience, i.e., the resonance/dissonance that they create with prior meanings, knowledge, and understandings (frames) on the recipient level. As ICTs often serve as a central channel through which cultural objects and information are mediated, cultural approaches tend to offer considerable attention to their role in collective action.

An examination of the above-mentioned examples using the Social Movement Theory's frameworks reveals various ways in which ICTs, and therefore also social media, support instances of collection action become visible. For example, expanding social networks, making states of relative deprivation visible and accelerating the formation of shared awareness, supporting the dissemination of frames, or supporting the aggregation and use of resources held by different group members, as well as creating access to new resources. Furthermore, these and other aspects rarely operate alone and usually intertwine with one another. That is to say, a case of collective action can be analyzed using different theoretical frameworks with the focus of analysis varying between those frameworks and also having overlapping aspects.

As ICTs facilitate different functions in collective action, the former's development influences the latter's repertoire in terms of vocabulary, resources, tools, and methods. Due to the uniqueness of each instance of collective action and the manner in which ICTs, or social media, are utilized, this reciprocal relation and the significance of certain aspects in relation to others tend to vary. In the case of social media, the implementation of decentralized, nonhierarchical methods for the organization and management of information, which are possible primarily in digital form, can in turn affect people's organization; that is, it can affect certain functions or processes of collective action. In some contexts, instead of linear and predefined hierarchies, information is organized in a network form with flexible, adaptable, and context-relevant structures. As soon as those principles are implemented in people's communication (and a critical mass of usage is achieved), the technologies at hand can support the adoption of decentralized, nonhierarchical manners of organization. As the discussion throughout the book shows, while acknowledging these new capabilities, when putting theory into practice, their limitations become clear.

Lastly, it is important to address the relation between social media and collective action as part of this broader context, to avoid the pitfall of technocentrism; or in the context of this book, to avoid the pitfall of social-media-centrism. That is to say, a research of the role of social media in collective action should be an integral part of a research of ICTs and collective action, or on a broader level, of ICTs and society.

1.4 BOOK OUTLINE

To pick up these discussions and navigate throughout the (hype cycle) discourse toward the Slope of Enlightenment and eventually Plateau of Productivity, the book is structured in two main parts. The first part of the book, Chapters 2–6, offers an examination of theoretical frameworks from the realm of collective action and social movement theory. Using case studies such as the events of the Arab Spring, social justice protests in Israel, refugee aid movements in Berlin, public debates on sexism, and more, the individual chapters will offer insights into the manner in which social media play a role in collective action, social movements, and activism. Preceding the discussion of particular theoretical frameworks, Chapter 2 offers an understanding of the concept of social media, which will serve the discussion of the reciprocal relation between social media and collective action throughout the book. To do so, this chapter will conduct a differentiation of three dimensions of social media—ICTs, institutions, and media—and discuss the unique features of social media in each of these contexts. Subsequently, common theoretical pitfalls such as technological determinism and centrism, which have proved to be counterproductive not only in theoretical, but also in practical activist work, will be discussed and critically addressed.

The second part of the book offers an in-depth discussion of the complex relation between social media from a variety of perspectives:

- the difference between actions and algorithms, an attempt to clarify the question whether algorithms can autonomously facilitate and enable collective action;

- the interplay between mass, mainstream, alternative, and social media, an interplay that is crucial for collective action/social movements and is visible in the case studies from Chapters 3–6;
- the dangers of corporate and state surveillance, both in authoritarian and democratic contexts, in the deployment of social media;
- the various dimensions of demobilization and slacktivism as well as their relation to structural elements of social media; and
- ethical considerations regarding the deployment of social media in "negative" contexts as well as the neutrality, biases, and values of social media platforms.

The book's epilogue, Chapter 12, On the Verge of the Plateau, offers a closure of the discussion in both parts of the book; coming a full circle back to the issues mentioned earlier. Additionally, Chapter 12 sketches prospects for related research subjects, which were outside the book's scope such as digital "waste disposal" labor (removal of explicit, violent, and sexual content), shaming,[4] resistance within social media platforms and their communities, and challenges of digital democracy, the notion of "postfactual" or "posttruth politics," and socially adapting to new forms of communication.[5]

References

Benski, T., Langman, L., Perugorría, I., Tejerina, B., 2013. From the streets and squares to social movement studies: what have we learned? Current Sociology 61 (4), 541–561.

Fenn, J., Raskino, M., 2008. Mastering the Hype Cycle: How to Choose the Right Innovation at the Right Time. Harvard Business Press, Boston.

Fuchs, C., Trottier, D., 2014. Theorizing social media, politics, and the state. An introduction. In: Fuchs, C., Trottier, D. (Eds.), Social Media, Politics and the State: Protests, Revolutions, Riots, Crime and Policing in the Age of Facebook, Twitter and YouTube. Routledge, New York, pp. 3–38.

Gartner, Inc, 2015. Research Methodologies: Gartner Hype Cycle. Gartner. Retrieved from: http://www.gartner.com/technology/research/methodologies/hype-cycle.jsp.

Garrett, R.K., 2006. Protest in an information society: a review of literature on social movements and new ICTs. Information, Communication and Society 9 (2), 202–224.

Grummas, E., 2013. Likes Don't Save Lives – Lessons from a Social Media Campaign. The Guardian. Retrieved from: www.theguardian.com/sustainable-business/likes-dont-save-lives-unicef-social-media.

Khazan, O., 2013. UNICEF Tells Slacktivists: Give Money, Not Facebook Likes. The Atlantic. Retrieved from: www.theatlantic.com/international/archive/2013/04/unicef-tells-slacktivists-give-money-not-facebook-likes/275429/.

---

[4] Public humiliation of a person as a form of vigilantism using social media platforms.
[5] In this regard, "tips & tricks" for the successful deployment of social media in planning and executing a campaign, demonstration, flash mob, or revolution will stay out of the book's scope as well.

Li, D., 2004. Echoes of violence: considerations on radio and genocide in Rwanda. Journal of Genocide Research 6 (1), 9–27.

Morozov, E., 2011. The Net Delusion: The Dark Side of Internet Freedom. PublicAffairs, New York.

Murphy, T., 2013. UNICEF Asks People to Stop 'Liking' Things on Facebook & Send Money. Humanosphere. Retrieved from: www.humanosphere.org/basics/2013/04/unicef-sweden-wants-your-money-not-your-likes/.

Sullivan, A., 2009. The Revolution Will Be Twittered. The Atlantic. Retrieved from: www.theatlantic.com/daily-dish/archive/2009/06/the-revolution-will-be-twittered/200478/.

PART

Theoretical Framework

1

CHAPTER 2

What Is Social Media: A Critical View

ABSTRACT

This chapter develops an understanding of the concept of social media, which will serve the discussion of the reciprocal relation between social media and collective action throughout the book. To do so, this chapter will conduct a differentiation of three dimensions of social media—information and communication technology, institutions, and media—and discuss the unique features of social media in each of these contexts. Subsequently, common theoretical pitfalls such as technological determinism, centrism, and utopianism, which have proved to be counterproductive not only in theoretical, but also in practical activist work, will be discussed and critically addressed.

Keywords: Affordance; Capitalism; ICT; Many-to-many communication; Social media; Social media platforms; Social networking sites; Social networks; Social tools; Technocentrism; Technodeterminism; Technoutopianism; Web 2.0.

CONTENTS

Social media platforms enjoy a variety of terms, concepts, interpretations, and accentuations, both in academia and in the broader social and medial discourses: Social Media, Social Media Platforms, Social Networks, Social Networking Sites, Social Software, Social Tools, and Web 2.0. The variety of concept is not merely a matter of terminology; the different terminologies symbolize the various understandings of what social media are or should be. They result from different theoretical backgrounds, disciplinary affiliations, technical aspects, the discussed issue or research question as well as social, political, or economic agenda. In the book, the term social media will

Collective Action 2.0. http://dx.doi.org/10.1016/B978-0-08-100567-5.00002-5

be used while addressing three dimensions of social media—information and communication technology (ICT), institutions, and media. Addressing these unique features of social media in each of these contexts is, in turn, instructive for applying them in the analysis of collective action and social movements.

2.1 SOCIAL MEDIA AS INFORMATION AND COMMUNICATION TECHNOLOGY

ICTs are technologies that are used as means to process and manage information and aid communication. In a broader sense they can be seen as media for storing and processing information outside the human mind as well as for communication in channels beyond the traditional vis-à-vis setting, thus replacing certain mental functions and historically grown social institutions. Although the term ICT usually refers to electronic data processing or communication devices, also "low-tech" media such as books or leaflets can be regarded as ICT. On the other hand, one major aspect of digitization is that content or certain uses of ICT are no longer bound to a certain end device or physical medium. This, in turn, means that the term ICT can be applied to intangible technologies (in contrast to physical devices) such as software or platforms with a set of distinctive functionalities.

Social media, and other, similar terms as mentioned earlier, refers to ICT-based communication platforms, which are most commonly accessed via the Internet and a variety of end devices (computers, mobile phones, tablets, smart-watches, etc.). There are, however, two exceptions to social media being a purely Internet-based technology:

- First, some social media platforms operate on a different technological infrastructure than the Internet per se. To name a few other possible environments are the anonymous and encrypted TOR (The Onion Routing) network, which in turn builds on Internet connection, or an encapsulated Intranet (e.g., a certain company's or organization's network).
- Second, there are versions of social media platforms, which require Internet connection but are used in a context that keeps them separated from further Internet usage. Projects that offer platform usage of this kind are Wikipedia Zero, Facebook Zero, and Google Free Zone. According to agreements with local Internet providers, Wikipedia, Facebook, and Google offer users in certain developing countries or regions basic access to their platforms without being charged for data (bandwidth) usage. Although these projects serve a noble cause, these practices as well as the notion of "some Internet is better than no Internet" are problematic, as they, at the least in the case of Google and Facebook, also serve the cause of binding future users in developing

countries or emerging markets as well as undermining the principle of net neutrality, which is fundamental for the Internet as we currently know it.[1]

A joint character of social media platforms such as Facebook, Twitter, Instagram, LinkedIn, Sina Weibo, Vkontakte, or diaspora* (to name a few examples) is that they integrate different functionalities, forms, and technologies of computer-mediated communication such as webpages, chat and messaging, forums, comments, virtual rooms (for building groups, sharing content, maintaining discussions etc.), connection lists ("friends" or "followers"), hyperlinks, digital images and videos, guest books, and search engines. Their existence as online platforms, rather than a physical technology or device, enables the accessibility of social media from a wide range of end devices (instead of a one designated device), usually with an Internet connection. Furthermore, some functions of Internet-based social media can be accessed without a working Internet connection, for example, publishing on Twitter via Short Message Service (Twitter, 2014). However, neither the particular functionalities nor their combination into a tool or a platform grants social media platforms a qualitatively different character that could allow us to distinguish them based on this aspect.

Being digital online platforms, social media platforms' functioning is based on the data and/or information that is produced, communicated, managed, stored, collected, and analyzed on/by them. Bruce Schneier differentiated between six types of such data (Schneier, 2015, p. 202):

- *Service data*: which a person provides the social media platform to use it. For example, name, age, email, or credit card number.
- *Disclosed data*: the content that users post and share on the platform. For example, blog entries, photographs, status updates, and comments.
- *Entrusted data*: similar to disclosed data, entrusted data are content that are actively shared by users, but refer specifically to content that is shared/posted on other people's pages or profiles. The key difference is that these data are "controlled" by another person.
- *Incidental data*: content or information that someone else posts about a person, for example, a photograph on which the person is depicted or a text paragraph in which the person is mentioned. Crucial for this type of data is that the person neither has control over it, nor did he or she create it.

---

[1] As the aspect of social media as institutions comes to show, since these markets, countries, and users will sooner or later become economically relevant for online advertising, having the individual users as well as the population as a whole accustomed to certain services is likely to become very valuable; especially when considering the fact that these services functioned as the only or most central portal to the Internet (or even substituted any other Internet usage). For these reasons—protection of net neutrality as well as resistance to infrastructural imperialism and online monopolism—some countries prohibit Google and Facebook to offer their "Zero" or "Free Zone" services; for example, India banned "discriminatory tariffs" based on content, aiming at Facebook Zero, in favor of net neutrality in 2016.

- *Behavioral data*: data the platform collects about a person's habits by monitoring his or her behavior, social interactions, platform usage, etc.
- *Derived data*: data about a person that are inferred from all the other data. For example, it can contain conclusions about the person's sexual identity, political opinion, taste in music or fashion, or eating habits, by analyzing the other types of data and combining them with data on the persons contacts.

As ICT, social media enable several communication models. Among others, social media support two-way interaction with an audience, beyond any specific recipient. This form of communication is referred to by the term *many-to-many communication* (Shirky, 2008), in which messages are broadcast to a wider audience that can then engage in an exchange. This model is different from the *one-to-one communication* (e.g., phone conversation, letter or email correspondence between two parties) and *one-to-many communication* (e.g., television or radio broadcast, newspaper article) models that are common to other ICTs. For example, the *#1mai_nazifrei* Twitter communication on Labor Day 2010 in Berlin, Listservs, or commenting functionalities on posted content (e.g., on blogs, YouTube videos, or Facebook pages) are instances of many-to-many communication. Many-to-many communication is neither unique to social media nor the only communication model available on social media, but it is implemented in the design of many social media platforms as a central usage model.

In their article *Persistence and Change in Social Media*, Hogan and Quan-Haase (2010) emphasize *social affordance*[2] as a crucial feature of social media. The idea of social media's social affordance builds on the concept of *affordance*, which refers to perceptual invocations in technological artifacts. These invocations, in turn, facilitate interaction between a person and the artifact or between the person and his or her environment, using the artifact. For example, a chair's design, height, and shape can be perceived as affording sitting. Social media as technological or ICT tools allow individuals to perceive aspects of their social environment (such as connections, who is online at the moment, what they are doing) and act/interact accordingly. The social affordance is manifested, among others, by the central role that functions such as "share," "like," and "comment" play in the design of and interaction with the platforms.

Notwithstanding the fact that (the platforms and services referred to as) social media possess central technological characteristics, it is challenging to identify the unique qualities of social media based on their technological features alone. This has two, somewhat contrasting, reasons: first, due

---

[2] For a further discussion of the affordance aspect of technology and ICT, see Chapter 11.

to the variety of available tools and platforms, the rapid pace of development of new features, functionalities, applications, and their combination
within a certain platform as well as general technological development (of
end devices, bandwidth, etc.) a strictly technological definition is destined
to be overdue at a certain point, even if other aspects of social media still
prevail. Second (and in contrast to the first aspect), as stated earlier social
media combine a variety of functionalities and technologies, which, taken
individually, neither represent a unique technological innovation nor are
they unique for social media.

In his book *Social Media is Bullshit*, which came as a reaction to his experience
as Journalist, new-media director, and the failure of a breast cancer awareness
campaign, B. J. Mendelson goes as far as to dispute social media's novelty in
terms of technological innovation and usage models. He does so by comparing
Web services that were popular in 1999—prior the social media rhetoric—with
popular Web services from 2012 with similar technological functioning and
more importantly, with equivalent usage models,[3] nonetheless acknowledging
that the 2012 services are "prettier, faster, and easier to use" (Mendelson, 2012,
pp. 21–22). The—admittedly significant—improvement in usability alone is
not sufficient to understand and define social media. It is therefore instructive
to examine the developments that took place between 1999 and 2012, to better
understand the notion of social media.

In 2005 the programmer and businessman Tim O'Reilly, who also contributed to the popularization of the term *open source*, popularized the
term "Web 2.0," which was coined several years earlier, to describe the
shift from "Web 1.0" to "Web 2.0." According to O'Reilly, this shift can be
distinguished as the move from "dumping" offline, print content, onto the
Internet, to the creation of online-only platforms that utilize the collaborative capabilities of ICT; that is, "Web 2.0" builds on collaboration and
participation (O'Reilly, 2005). According to O'Reilly, this shift manifests
itself in manifold aspect, all of which undergo a transformation: (Internet-)
usage models, methods for the organization and management of data and
information, financial models, advertising, and creation of added value.
O'Reilly characterizes these ICT-supported transformations as disruptive, so
that a "Web 2.0" emerges.

However, although this applies to different extents and plays a central role
in many social media platforms, describing these characteristics and/or

---

[3] Mendelson mentions LiveJournal, AOL Instant Messenger, RealAudio/RealPlayer, Lifecasting or Pseudo.
com, SixDgrees or Classmates.com, uBid.com or Coupons.com, ShareYourWorld.com, and Everything2
(which were popular in 1999) in comparison with their 2012, "social media" counterparts Blogs, Twitter,
Podcasts, Ustream, Facebook, Groupon, YouTube, and Wikipedia (Mendelson, 2012, pp. 21–22).

transformations with the term "Web 2.0" (which preceded the broad use of the term social media and often is used synonymously) is very problematic from a technological point of view. The term suggests a linear development (between "Web 1.0" and "Web 2.0") on the one hand and a degree of technological novelty that fundamentally, perhaps radically, changes the Web upon all its components on the other; both dimensions, when seen in a sober light, do not apply. Thus the notion of a "Web 2.0" is constructed, rather than built on a factual basis, so that there is a need to take a look at other aspects of social media to examine it as a result of developments that took place in the early 2000s. March 2000 was a constituting moment in the information technology (IT) and Internet industries—it was the month in which the Dot-com bubble burst.[4] In the aftermath of the 2000 burst, the consequences of the Dot-com crisis continued to affect the IT industry and its attractiveness for investors for several years.

As discussed earlier, Tim O'Reilly's illustration of what he terms as "Web 2.0" was not based on factual technological changes. Several authors, such as Christian Fuchs, Andrew Keen, and B. J. Mendelson, point out that the notion of "Web 2.0" was constructed in the aftermath of the Dot-com crisis with the aim to attract investors to invest financial capital in the Internet economy, including IT firms and digital media companies[5] (Fuchs, 2014a, 2014b; Keen, 2015). To do so, the "Web 2.0" notion propagated new usage models, qualities, advertising opportunities, and models of capital accumulation; a new Web, which is detached from the old one ("Web 1.0") that was wedded with the Dot-com crisis. That is to say, the "Web 2.0" notion was primarily an economic marketing tactic, rather than a technological shift based on empirical data; it was, and is, a buzzword.[6] This is a fact that O'Reilly himself acknowledged several years later (O'Reilly and Battelle, 2009). Mendelson notes further that the term social media started to pick up in usage parallel to the decline of the term "Web 2.0" on the one hand and to the financial crisis of 2007–08 on the other hand. The social media narrative was used to propagate similar ideas and ideology of "get-rich-quick" and attractive financial investments (Mendelson, 2012).

---

[4] The term *Dot-com bubble* refers to a speculative bubble that emerged in 1997 and 2000. The bubble covered the Internet sector and related fields, with a growing gap between the speculative stock value and actual revenues.

[5] For an in-depth critical view of the term Web 2.0 as a promotion of capitalist ideology see: Fuchs (2014b) and Fuchs and Trottier (2014).

[6] Furthermore, keeping in mind that Tim O'Reilly is the founder of O'Reilly Media, creator of the Web 2.0 Conference, and is involved as investor in services such as foursquare, which enjoys the status of social media or "Web 2.0" services, it is likely to assume that the notion of "Web 2.0" was not purely an altruistic one (Mendelson, 2012).

The success of this strategy lays in the adoption of the term and the ideology it stands for without suitable reflection, not only by investors, but also by the media, academics, and Internet users themselves.[7] By picking up the "Web 2.0" buzzword, the media contributed to the construction of the "Web 2.0," "Social Media," and sociality of the web narratives. In terms of a Hype Cycle Discourse, as discussed in the Introduction, this can be regarded as the development of a Technological Trigger and the beginning of the transition to the Peak of Inflated Expectations. Interestingly, the notion of "Web 2.0" as a Technological Trigger is connected to the Trough of Disillusionment from the Dot-com crisis, a fact that reaffirms "Web 2.0" being a strategy to encourage capital investments in IT and Internet industries.

In this manner, although one can dispute the novelty and coherence of the "Web 2.0" or social media notion on a technological level, a general discourse surrounding social media was established. From this point of view, the discursive practices surrounding social media played a central role in the construction of social media itself. Even when acknowledging the criticism about the lack of empirical basis or the emergence of the social media rhetoric, the existence of a social media discourse contributed to a broad agreement on the existence of social media as a set of technologies, platforms, practices, usage and communication models, financial models, and advertising models.

The emergence of the notion of "Web 2.0" and its development to social media leads us to the second dimension of social media—institutions.

---

[7] The success of rebranding IT and digital industries—and to a certain extent, the perception of the Internet itself—using the notion of "Web 2.0" had the interesting side-effect that the "Point-Zero" strategy was adopted in many further fields, to name a few examples:

Web 3.0: refers to Semantic Web.

Industry 4.0: refers to the promotion of computerization of manufacturing, the term aims to propagate a fourth industrial revolution. Considering the fact that the term was coined and promoted in cooperation between the German government and German industry, the political and financial interests behind it are obvious.

Education 3.0: refers to the integration of digital media and learning systems in the education system.

Politics 2.0: refers to E-democracy, mostly understood as participatory democracy through the mediation of ICT.

Enterprise 2.0: refers to the application of social media functionalities such as blogging, microblogging, wiki, messaging tools, social networking, and comments in corporate context.

Science 2.0: refers to the collaboration in research between scientists (and in some cases, the broader public) using ICT in general and social media functionalities in particular.

As stated earlier, in all these examples the adoption of the "Point-Zero" rhetoric fulfills a symbolic function that is primarily an issue of rebranding the field, rather than presenting change that is based on empirical facts and that is indeed fundamental and disruptive enough to argue for a second, third, or even fourth revolution in the field.

2.2 SOCIAL MEDIA AS INSTITUTIONS

As discussed earlier, without the financial interests of the firms that stand behind social media platforms as well as the interests of capitalist investors, the notion of social media as we know it (that is, as a term that encompasses more than the technological functionalities and their usage) probably would not exist. The reverse conclusion would be that the institutions behind the social media platforms are a key aspect in the overall understanding of social media.

Private, for-profit, capitalist corporations hold and operate the vast majority of social media platforms, for which advertising is the central source for generating revenues. By following a capitalist, profit-oriented logic on the one hand and being private firms on the other, the personal, political, and financial interests of the platform owners play a central role in the platform's design, the usage that the platform affords (in terms of *affordance*), the respect for users' privacy, data security, and the role of advertising in the platforms themselves.

Such a constellation has several implications. The first implication is that the corporation's—paying!—customers are the advertisers, rather than the platform's users, which leads to a commodification of the users' data (including service, disclosed, entrusted, incidental, behavioral, and derived data) and to a certain extent, the commodification of the users themselves. This, in turn, means that social media users conduct unpaid digital labor, whose product are the data that are then sold as a commodity (Fuchs, 2014a, 2014b; Keen, 2015).

The second implication is the phenomenon Eli Pariser termed as the *filter bubble*: social media platforms (as well as search engines and other online services) are designed to create personalized environments by adapting search results, news feeds, status updates, shared content, etc. in accordance with a variety of objective and subjective parameters about the individual (the user) (Pariser, 2011). The parameters, in turn, are derived from the individual's interaction with the platform and with other users (that is, from the different types of data that are collected by the platform). These personalized environments are tailored to the individual's own opinions, designed to be free of disturbance, and are filled with primarily easy to consume information. As online communication, among others using social media platforms, becomes more essential in the communication between people, the absence of deviant opinions, identities, and tastes in such personalized environments hinders critical thinking, political and public debate, acceptance of the others, etc. As Chapter 10 will discuss, this can have a demobilizing effect on collective action.

At this point, most readers of this book probably have social media platforms in mind, which are held and managed by Western institutions such as Google, Twitter, and Facebook (to name the most prominent examples according to the time of writing). In fact, most of the literature on the subject of social media aim for Western readership or address primarily such platforms, unless stated differently, even if implicitly and/or unintended. Even when taking the language barrier for Western scholars (when considering social media platforms or companies that are located and primarily used in other parts of the world) into account, the Western—more precisely US—emphasis in the literature is also a representation of global power relations, which manifest themselves in media and academic discourse; in this case, the discourse surrounding social media.

When considering the world's most accessed websites or platforms, several social media platforms, which are not based in the United States, are ranked in the first 25 places: the Chinese Baidu, QQ, and Sina Weibo as well as the Russian VK (Vkontakte) (Alexa Internet, 2015). Similar to their Western counterparts, Chinese social media platforms are privately owned by capitalist corporations and are listed on US stock markets. In his comparison of the Chinese social media platforms Baidu, Sina Weibo, and Renren with their US counterparts Google, Twitter, and Facebook, Christian Fuchs concluded striking resemblance in the corporations' financial structures, shareholding structures (as well as the connection of directors to financial investment firms), and the role of advertising in revenues (Fuchs, 2015). Also the Russian social media platform VK is privately owned by the Mail.ru Group (Reuters, 2014), which is listed on the London Stock Exchange, profit oriented with a financial model based partially on advertising.[8] This shows that as far as the institutional aspect is concerned, social media in contexts other than the Western, US-focused discourse have similar interests as their Western counterparts.

Having that said, these social media remain interesting subjects of research not only because of their high usage on international comparison, but also mainly because they are the leading social media platforms in the certain countries and societies. This makes them relevant for supporting and facilitating collective action in those societies.

There are, of course, a variety of alternative social media platforms that are not corporate social media, such as diaspora*, GNU social, Friendica, Ocupii, N-1, and Ello. These platforms offer a set of functionalities similar to mainstream, corporate social media platforms, but they also serve as an opposite pole by offering different institutional and operational structures. This difference is manifested in many respects: freedom of advertisement (which is per se a fundamental difference from corporate social media), the respect for user privacy,

---

[8] Advertising in social media is highly personalized (a fact that is presented as added value) and the personalization is based on the collection and analysis of user data. This, in turn, means that the advertising on social media relies on the surveillance of users. Therefore the fact that (personalized) advertisements constitute a central source of revenues for corporate social media is also crucial when addressing the platforms' design and corporate decisions.
  This issue was discussed by a variety of scholars, among others: Fuchs (2014b, 2015), Schneier (2015), Vaidhyanathan (2011).

user-owned and/or nonprofit structure, open source code, distributed design, and support of encryption.[9] However, according to the time of writing, these platforms are rather a niche segment in the broad spectrum of social media platforms, which means that their potential to facilitate or support instances of collective action on a broader scale is relatively limited. Although when regarded from an ICTs/media angle, these platforms offer very similar means to support collective action and when regarded from the institutional angle, perhaps even possess a more democratic and radical potential as they, for example, counter the capitalist logic and offer more protection from state and/or corporate surveillance.

In comparison with many other technologies and/or ICTs, the institutional aspect has an exceptional relevance in social media. Since social media are almost exclusively systems that are accessed and used online, rather than operate locally (e.g., a computer's operation system or locally installed software) or have physical objects as manifestations of the technology (e.g., a chair, car, or radio), institutional decisions and interests can be implemented directly into the system and immediately affect all users and their usage, thus creating a closed feedback loop between the ICT dimension and the institutional one.

2.3 SOCIAL MEDIA AS MEDIA

The third dimension of social media is, as the term itself implies, their social function as media and more importantly, the difference to other media that hitherto were not addressed as "social" ones.

Christian Fuchs, professor of social media at the University of Westminster, introduced the tripleC model, to offer such a differentiation. According to Fuchs, media and online platforms support three modes or concepts of sociality: *cognition* (related to Emile Durkheim's concept of social facts), *communication* (related to Max Weber's notion of social actions and relations), and *cooperation* (communities and collaborative work) (Fuchs, 2014b; Fuchs and Trottier, 2014). According to this framework, there are three different types of social media, of which the first two are not usually referred to as "social media":

- Social media that support *cognition*, such as websites and newspapers
- Social media that support *communication*, such as email, telephone, and chat
- Social media that support *cooperation*, such as Wikipedia and Facebook

---

[9] Not all characteristics necessarily apply for all of the mentioned platforms, but they do share a similar set of basic characteristics that appear in this list.

The emphasis in the context of this book (the relation between social media and collective action) is on social media that support cooperation and this is the manner in which the term will be used.

The design of social media platform, the combination of various technologies and functionalities that support communication, their social affordance as technological tools, and the communication models they support make social media what Fuchs and Trottier term as *Integrated Sociality* to a constitutive feature of social media: "Social media enable the convergence of the three modes of sociality (cognition, communication, cooperation) in an integrated sociality." (Fuchs and Trottier, 2014, p. 15) As the following chapters will show, all three modes of sociality, the tripleC of cognition, communication, and cooperation, are central for analyzing the relation between social media and collective action, as they are interconnected and build on one another.

As media, social media platforms also prove to be effective in the mediation not merely of "dry" information, but also of moods and emotions[10]; this can be done both implicitly and explicitly. The undertone of the textual message, deployment of positive or negative connoting words, the usage of lower- or uppercase letters (sentences with many or solely uppercase letters are usually perceived as mediating an angry, even "shouting" tone) and punctuation, or the combination of shared multimedia content and a textual message may imply the mood or the emotional state of the individual who posted the message or content on the platform. On the other hand, using emoticons (text-based icon representing a facial expression on a metacommunicative level), hashtags, or comments that express emotions and are explicitly marked as *not* being part of the informational content (e.g., *angry* or HTML-like tags such as </irony>) individuals explicitly communicate their emotions along with the (textual, multimedia, etc.) content. Furthermore, some social media platforms—as institutions—react to such developments and usages and implement them in the system. Facebook, for example, added in 2013 the option to tag shared content and status updates with moods and emotions picked out from a list offered to the user. In 2016 Facebook also enhanced its known *like* button, allowing users to mark their Facebook friends' content also with *love, haha, wow, sad,* and *angry*.

Furthermore, in 2014 Facebook conducted an experiment in cooperation with researchers from Cornell and the University of California (Kramera et al., 2014), in which the information displayed in the feeds of 689,000 users was manipulated to affect the users' emotions, making them more positive or negative.

---

[10] Scholars such as Perugorría and Tejerina (2013), Benski and Langman (2013), and Gerbaudo (2012) stress the importance of emotions in (mobilization for) collective action and pay attention to the role of social media in respective mobilization and activist processes. These aspects will be discussed in Chapters 3–5 of the book.

The process used in the experiment was termed as *emotional contagion*. By filtering the contents and communication (status updates, pictures and videos, comments and likes, links, etc.) presented to the users, exposing them to either positive or negative emotional content, an immediate influence on their emotional state was observed. As the researchers conclude: "The results show emotional contagion. […] for people who had positive content reduced in their News Feed, a larger percentage of words in people's status updates were negative and a smaller percentage were positive. When negativity was reduced, the opposite pattern occurred. These results suggest that the emotions expressed by friends, via online social networks, influence our own moods, constituting, to our knowledge, the first experimental evidence for massive-scale emotional contagion via social networks" (Kramera et al., 2014, p. 8789). Moreover, the study's worrying findings about the ease of psychological effect on and manipulation of social media users support the notion of the filter bubble and its possible social implications as well as reinforce concerns regarding the power social media institution can execute using their algorithms, power that can be used for economic and profit interest but also for political and social ones.[11]

In conclusion, a clear demarcation between social media and other types of ICT, media, or institutions as well as demarcation between the three dimensions that social media combine (ICT, institutions, and media) is hard to achieve. Each dimension offers a distinct manner to define what social media is: from a technological point of view, although some platforms, such as Facebook and Twitter, definitely account as social media, other platforms, such as online forums and chat rooms, are located in gray zone; yet other technologies, such as radio broadcast or printed media are clearly outside any definition of social media. Defining which media is social media depends on the deployed notion of sociality—cognition, communication, or cooperation. In comparison with other ICTs and media, social media platform enables individuals to mediate their emotional situations more intensively, thus supplementing the content and messages shared. Being designed, controlled, and owned by private capitalist corporations also is not distinctive to social media platforms, but this aspect is crucial for analyzing social media in a broader socioeconomic context.

Thus there is a need for a certain degree of complexity to identify the key aspects that constitute the uniqueness of social media on the one hand and the key aspects that are common for the wide spectrum of social media platforms on the other, an understanding of social media that is both inclusive and exclusive. There are, however, common theoretical pitfalls, which still prevail in many discussion and researches regarding social media.

---

[11] The publication of the study in *Proceedings of the National Academy of Sciences* was accompanied by an Editorial Expression of Concern and Correction. However, these concerns were mostly regarding the users' privacy, the data collection for the study, the issue of (lack of) informed consent, and the option to opt out of the study.

2.4 BEWARE OF SOCIAL MEDIA DETERMINISM

Philosophers deal to a great extent with issues of neutrality and embedded values in technology. Technological artifacts are shaped by society; therefore, they are value-laden and have certain affordance for their use. In other words, technological artifacts have "built-in tendencies to promote or demote the realization of particular values" (Brey, 2010, p. 43). This stands in contrast to the *neutrality thesis*, which holds that there are no consequences that are inherent to technological artifacts. The metaphysical idea of absolute built-in consequences on the other hand, employs a deterministic conception of technology. It is more accurate to claim that there are strong tendencies for particular consequences to occur in all or most of the central uses of an artifact. Furthermore, in some cases the central uses of certain artifacts may vary between contexts. Technological artifact's affordance and therefore the manner in which it is used depend not only on its design but also on the social contexts it finds itself in.

Phillip Brey uses the example of a gas-engine automobile. It can be used not only for commuter traffic, leisure driving, transfer cargo, hit jobs, auto racing, but also as a museum piece, shelter from the rain, or barricade. In all but the last three uses, gasoline is used up, greenhouse gases and other pollutants are emitted, noise is generated, and at least one person (the driver) is being moved around at high speed. These consequences are not absolute; they do not appear in all uses of the automobile (although the last three are peripheral and not central uses) and can be avoided (driving an electric car, for example) (Brey, 2010).

Turning back to ICTs, due to their complexity and often the variety of possible uses, they are probable to have biases, and therefore also values, embedded in them. These biases can be divided into three types of origin (Brey, 2010; Friedman and Nissenbaum, 1996):

1. *Preexisting biases* "arise from values and attitudes that exist prior to the design of a system. They can either be *individual*, resulting from the values of those who have a significant input into the design of the systems, or *societal*, resulting from organizations, institutions or the general culture that constitute the context in which the system is developed" (Brey, 2010, p. 49).
2. *Technical biases*, which arise from technical constraints and/or considerations.
3. *Emergent biases*, which arise "when the social context in which the system is used is not the one, intended by its designers. In the new context, the system may not adequately support the capabilities, values or interests of some user groups or the interests of other stakeholders" (Brey, 2010, p. 50).

The notion of biases can be extended to embedded values, preexisting, technical, and emergent ones. These values, however, are not necessarily intentional ones; their embedding in technological artifacts, in this case, computer systems and social media platform, can be both intentional and unintentional (Brey, 2010).

As for social media, on the one hand, many social media platforms are designed by companies based in Western countries so that one would assume democratic and free speech values to be embedded in them. On the other hand, these are also capitalist institutions driven by and for financial profit so that their choices in dilemmas between possible financial implications and standing for democratic values or their users' right for free speech are not always predictable. Furthermore, the individual values of the platform's designers are not transparent for its users by the platforms design.

Andrew Keen notes that the political and economic agendas of platform founders and/or owners such as Jeff Bezos [Amazon founder and Chief Executive Officer (CEO)], Michael Moritz (investor in Google, PayPal, Zappos, LinkedIn, and Yahoo), Reid Hoffman (LinkedIn cofounder), Kevin Systrom (Instagram founder), or Travis Kalanick (Uber cofounder and CEO) are clear capitalist, neoliberal ones (Keen, 2015). The platforms are designed not only to promote neoliberal agendas of deregulation, antiunionism, and capital (that is, money and data) accumulation but also to deploy a rhetoric that aims directly at disguising these agendas behind concepts such as sharing, community, freedom, and flexibility (Keen, 2015; Morozov, 2013).

The embodiment of *Cyber-utopianism*[12] and *Internet-centrism*[13]—special forms of technological utopianism and centrism that focus on the Internet, network technologies, and online tools or platforms—in the approach toward the Internet and social media in political and medial discourses is a clear case of a deterministic view regarding democratic values being embedded in these systems and their allegedly unavoidable revolutionary consequences.

When zooming out to the general collective action context, *cyber-utopianism*, *social media centrism* (the reframing of collective action and social change in terms of social media alone, rather than the context in which that change is to occur), and *social media determinism* (the metaphysical idea of the build-in consequence of social media to promote, even create collective action) are dangerous tendencies for the engagement in and analysis of collective action and activism.[14]

---

[12] "The idea that the Internet favors the oppressed rather than the oppressor [...] a naïve belief in the emancipatory nature of online communication that rests on stubborn refusal to acknowledge its downside" (Morozov, 2011, p. xiii).
[13] The reframing of democratic and social change in terms of the Internet rather than the context in which that change is to occur (Morozov, 2011).
[14] See Chapters 7 and 10.

In dependence on Brey's assumptions regarding the neutrality of ICTs, I argue that also social media platforms are not neutral tools. Their design contains (1) *preexisting biases/values*, such as Western norms, capitalist interests, and the political worldview of the platform founders/owners; (2) *technical biases/values* such as bandwidth and limited computing abilities and also restrictions such as the 140 characters limitation in Twitter or the algorithms that constitute the filter bubble; and (3) *emergent biases/values*, as ICTs contain affordances (e.g., social affordance as a key feature of social media) but they can also be utilized in different ways and for different goals, not always in the context meant by their developers (the social media institutions).

For these reasons an extra precaution is needed when the role of social media in collective action is addressed. Cyber-utopianism will cause disregard of negative or contra productive use of the possibilities offered by social media, which can have grave results for collective action or for the activists themselves. Social media centrism and/or determinism will concentrate mainly on social media's role while neglecting other collective action factors (without which social media will not have a collective action to facilitate in the first place) and also runs the danger of making social media a demobilizing, rather than mobilizing factor.

Furthermore, social media platforms are tools used by people who can have different goals and ways of action. This means not only that social media can be utilized for collective action goals that are not always of positive nature (for example, racism, homophobia, or proanorexia), but also that the opponents of certain social movements can utilize these tools for their own advantage as well. Therefore it is instructive to explore the reciprocal relation between social media and collective action in the specific context, in which this relation takes place, while applying existing theoretical frameworks for the analysis of collective action and social movements.

A quote often associated with the philosopher and media scholar Marshall McLuhan argues that "We become what we behold. We shape our tools and thereafter our tools shape us."[15] Although the phrase does not stem from McLuhan but from associated scholars, the premise is coherent with McLuhan's work and notion on technology, namely, that the relation between us and our tools and technologies is a reciprocal one, constantly shaping each other. In terms of social

---

[15] The phrase is often cited as part of Marshall McLuhan's book *Understanding Media*. It is, however, part of the introduction to the 1964/1994 MIT Press edition, written by Lewis H. Lapham. Lapham paraphrases Marshall McLuhan by stating that: "Beginning from the premise that 'we become what we behold', that 'we shape our tools, and thereafter our tools shape us', McLuhan examines the diktats of two technological revolutions that overthrew a settled political and aesthetic order [...]" (Lapham, 1994, p. xi).

media, this means not only that social media platforms are ICT tools and media, which are shaped by their designers, but also that these platforms, in turn, also shape and affect the individuals who use them as well as society in general. As the following chapters of the book will show, social media do not merely facilitate collective action or social change, but rather affect collective action and social movements on various levels; even shape them.

References

Alexa Internet, Inc, 2015. The Top 500 Sites on the Web. Retrieved from: www.alexa.com/topsites.

Benski, T., Langman, L., 2013. The effects of affects: the place of emotions in the mobilizations of 2011. Current Sociology 61 (4), 525–540.

Brey, P., 2010. Values in technology and disclosive computer ethics. In: Floridi, L. (Ed.), The Cambridge Handbook of Information and Computer Ethics. Cambridge University Press, Cambridge, pp. 41–58.

Friedman, B., Nissenbaum, H., 1996. Bias in computer systems. ACM Transactions on Computer Systems 14 (3), 330–347.

Fuchs, C., 2014a. Digital Labour and Karl Marx. Routledge, New York.

Fuchs, C., 2014b. Social Media: A Critical Introduction. Sage, London.

Fuchs, C., 2015. Baidu, Weibo and Renren: the global political economy of social media in China. Asian Journal of Communication 1–28. http://dx.doi.org/10.1080/01292986.2015.1041537.

Fuchs, C., Trottier, D., 2014. Theorizing social media, politics, and the state. An introduction. In: Fuchs, C., Trottier, D. (Eds.), Social Media, Politics and the State: Protests, Revolutions, Riots, Crime and Policing in the Age of Facebook, Twitter and YouTube. Routledge, New York, pp. 3–38.

Gerbaudo, P., 2012. Tweets and the Streets: Social Media and Contemporary Activism. Pluto Press, London.

Hogan, B., Quan-Haase, A., 2010. Persistence and China in social media. Bulletin of Science, Technology and Society 30, 309–315.

Keen, A., 2015. The Internet Is Not the Answer. Atlantic Monthly Press, New York.

Kramera, A.D., Guillory, J.E., Hancockb, J.T., June 17, 2014. Experimental evidence of massive-scale emotional contagion through social networks. Proceedings of the National Academy of Sciences 111 (24), 8788–8790.

Lapham, L.H., 1994. Introduction to the MIT press edition. In: McLuhan, M. (Ed.), Understanding Media: The Extensions of Man. MIT Press, Cambridge, pp. ix–xxiii.

Mendelson, B.J., 2012. Social Media Is Bullshit. St. Martin's Press, New York.

Morozov, E., 2011. The Net Delusion: The Dark Side of Internet Freedom. PublicAffairs, New York.

Morozov, E., 2013. To Save Everything, Click Here: Technology, Solutionism, and the Urge to Fix Problems that Don't Exist. Allen Lane, London.

O'Reilly, T., 2005. What Is Web 2.0? Retrieved from: www.oreilly.com/pub/a/web2/archive/what-is-web-20.html.

O'Reilly, T., Battelle, J., 2009. Web Squared: Web 2.0 Five Years on (Special Report) Retrieved from: www.assets.en.oreilly.com/1/event/28/web2009_websquared-whitepaper.pdf.

Pariser, E., 2011. The Filter Bubble. Penguin Books, London.

Perugorría, I., Tejerina, B., 2013. Politics of the encounter: cognition, emotions, and networks in the Spanish 15M. Current Sociology 61 (4), 424–442.

Reuters, 2014. Russia's Mail.Ru Buys Remaining Stake in VKontakte for $1.5 Bln. Retrieved from: www.reuters.com/article/2014/09/16/russia-mailru-group-vkontakte-idUSL6N0RH28K20140916.

Schneier, B., 2015. Data and Goliath. W. W. Norton & Company, New York.

Shirky, C., 2008. Here Comes Everybody: The Power of Organizating without Organizations. Penguin Group, London.

Twitter, Inc, 2014. Twitter Help Center: Twitter via SMS FAQs. Retrieved from: www.support.twitter.com/articles/14014-twitter-via-sms-faqs#.

Vaidhyanathan, S., 2011. The Googalization of Everything (and Why We Should Worry). University of California Press, Los Angeles.

CHAPTER 3

Tehran, Tunis, Tahrir: Social Media and the Formation of Collective Action

ABSTRACT

The events of the Arab Spring often serve as an example when addressing the role of social media in collective action. In fact, these events played a key role in the construction of the discourse regarding relation between the two. Using examples from the events of the Arab Spring, this chapter critically examines the role of social media in the formation of collective action by deploying several theories of social movements, collective behavior, and collective action and situating social media (as information and communication technology tools, institutions, and media) within these theories.

Keywords: Arab awakening; Arab Spring; Rational choice theory; Shared awareness; Social media; Social networks; Strain and breakdown theories.

CONTENTS

One of the most prominent examples when addressing the role of social media in collective action, often deploying the rhetoric of revolutions, is the spectrum of events regarded as the Arab Spring. In fact, these events played a key role in the construction of the relation between the two in the media and, to a certain extent, academic discourse. Therefore the Arab Spring is the best place to start the exploration of the complex relation, which is the subject of this book.

The term *Arab Spring* refers to a wave of uprisings in the Arab world, which began in December 2010 in Tunisia. On December 17, the Tunisian street

33

vendor Mohamed Bouazizi from the town Sidi Bouzid set himself on fire in protest of police corruption and harassment. This event served as a catalyst for civil protests that began on the following day and continued growing for several weeks, until President Zine El Abidine Ben Ali fled into exile on January 14, 2011, after 23 years in power. Following the quick success of the Tunisian uprisings, Egyptian opposition groups called for protests on January 25, 2011, known as the *Day of Anger* or *Day of Revolt*. The protests, which took place in different locations across the country turned out to be larger than expected, with the occupation of the Tahrir Square becoming the symbol of the Egyptian 2011 revolution. On February 11, Muhammad Husni Mubarak stepped down and turned power over to the army after being in power since 1981 under emergency law. The wave of protests continued to spread to Algeria, Jordan, Yemen, Bahrain, Syria, and many other countries.

The protests shared methods of civil resistance such as demonstrations, marches, occupation of public spaces, strikes, and rallies. Many of the protests faced violent responses from the state or progovernment groups as well as counterdemonstrations of government supporters.

The causes for the uprisings vary in their accentuation between the different countries, but they share common factors such as:

- regimes of dictatorship and in some cases an absolute monarchy,
- human rights violations by those regimes,
- economic decline, inflation, unemployment, and poverty,
- domestic food prices and food security (Harrigan, 2011),
- the spread of neoliberal capitalist order,[1]
- political corruption,[2]
- imperialism,
- as well as a number of further social and demographic structural factors, such as tensions between ethnic groups or between religious and secular ones.[3]

---

[1] According to Armbrust (2011), Dixon (2011) and Karatzogianni (2013), Egypt and Tunisia were considered to be examples of the neoliberal reform agenda, and there is a direct link of the revolutions occurring against regimes, which were following that agenda.

[2] The dimensions of the corruption, especially of the dictators and their extravagant lifestyle, were made public by Wikileak's diplomatic cables.

[3] Hussain and Howard (2013) offer a different approach to the causes, or variables, that contribute the uprisings. To tackle the question about the susceptibility of regimes to popular uprisings, the relative successes of some movements in relation to others, and the role of information technology in modern recipe for democratization, Hussain and Howard conducted a comparative analysis of the countries of the Arab Spring. In their analysis, they included variables such as average incomes within a country, wealth distribution, levels of unemployment, fuel-dependent economy, and demographic variables as well as the variables digital connectivity and censorship sophistication.

In other words, December 17, 2010 is not the day on which the Arab Spring started, but rather its tipping point; the dramatic change in the behavior of broad parts of the population, which manifested itself in the formation of broad civil resistance as collective action. The conditions for the Arab Spring to take place were developing over years, even decades of repression and human right violations, poverty and inequality, exploitive economical system, corruption, religious conflicts, etc., during which structures and networks of grassroots activists (with their hierarchies, leaders, and resources) were forming and operating.

The aftermath of the uprisings, on the other hand, were anything but similar. Tunisia, Egypt, Libya, and Yemen protesters succeeded in throwing over their rulers, however, with major differences in the outcome:

- In Tunisia, the Islamist Ennahda Party won the elections subsequent to the revolution.
- In Egypt, Mubarak turned power over to the military, which continued to rule until the elections in June 2012, in which the Islamist Muslim Brotherhood Party won the elections (until mass protests broke in June 2013, following a military coup in July and new elections in May 2014).
- In Yemen, Ali Abdullah Saleh signed a power-transfer agreement in November 2011 and presidential elections were held in February 2012.
- In Libya, foreign military interventions helped throwing over Muammar Gaddafi in October 2011, with the country going into a political and economic crisis that led to a second civil war in 2014.
- In other countries, such as Bahrain, violent crackdowns by the authorities (often deploying methods of Internet censorship, Internet shutdown, and online surveillance of protesters and opposition networks) managed to suppress the protests.
- The 2011 Syrian uprisings against Bashar al-Assad developed into a civil war that according to the time of writing in 2016 still persists.

While taking place as well as in their aftermath, and probably in future history books as well, the protests were not regarded solely in terms of their geopolitical significance. The discussion of the protests was conducted in terms of the effective use of social media to organize, communicate, and get information and real-time updates regarding the protests across as well as outside the country, although there are significant differences between the countries in this regard, as Media and Communication scholar Athina Karatzogianni notes: "Arab Spring countries were in different stages of digital development. The regimes involved took different steps to cut the digital lifeline from protesters. Digital networked everyday media and social media networks were used in creative ways to connect the protest both internally and externally to international players, media actors and global opinion, and to plan and accelerate protest mobilizations" (Karatzogianni, 2013, p. 160).

Media scholar and Internet activist Ethan Zukerman described the role of social media, Tunisian dissidents, and traditional broadcast media (Al Jazeera) in the development of the protests:

> Video of protests in Sidi Bouzid [the hometown of Mohamed Bouazizi], shot on mobile phones and uploaded to Facebook, reached Tunisian dissidents in Europe. They indexed and translated the footage and packaged it for distribution on sympathetic news networks such as Al Jazeera. Widely watched in Tunisia, Al Jazeera alerted citizens to protests taking place in other corners of their country. The broadcasts also acted as an invitation to participate.
>
> **Zuckerman (2013, p. 17)**

In Egypt, the role of social media in the protests was beginning to shape in June 2010 with the death of the blogger Khaled Mohamed Saeed:

> On 6 June 2010 Khaled Said, an Egyptian blogger, was dragged out of a cybercafé and beaten to death by policemen in Alexandria, Egypt. The café owner, Mr Hassan Mosbah, gave the details of this murder in a filmed interview, which was posted online, and pictures of Mr Said's shattered face appeared on social networking sites. On 14 June 2010 Issandr El Amrani posted the details on the blog site Global Voices Advocacy. A young Google executive Wael Ghonim created a Facebook page, 'We Are All Khaled Said', which enlisted 350,000 members before 14 January 2011.[4]
>
> **Khondker (2011) cited in Karatzogianni (2013, p. 161–162)**

The *We Are All Khaled Said* Facebook page had two versions, which played different roles during the protests: The Arabic version was among the opposition groups, who called for protests on the Day of Anger, and continued to be used as a mobilization and organization platform. The English version, which was launched approximately at the same time, was used for waking international awareness toward the ongoing events as well as human rights violations (Khamis and Vaughn, 2011). The Facebook page is one prominent example of many that illustrate the manner in which activists deployed social media platforms during the anti-Mubarak protests (and the following 2013 protests). As an Egyptian activist tweeted during the protests: "we use Facebook to schedule the protests, Twitter to coordinate, and YouTube to tell the world" (Global Voice Advocacy, 2011).

---

[4] There is some controversy regarding the affiliation of Ghonim to the *We Are All Khaled Said* Facebook page, as it later became apparent that the page was cocreated and coadministered by an Egyptian political activist and journalist named Abdul Rahman Mansour (Khamis and Vaughn, 2011; Herrera, 2013). Furthermore, when considering the attention to Internet companies such as Facebook and Twitter in the Arab Spring discourse, Ghonim's Google affiliation should not be underestimated in its importance for the international echo the page, it's role in the mobilization, and Ghonim's arrest have received.

Although they preceded the events of the Arab Spring—and the fact that it is a Muslim but not Arab country—the protests in light of the 2009 Iranian elections are often mentioned in this context together with their Arab Spring counterparts, due to the active deployment of social media platforms. The protests, also known as the *Green Revolution*, developed on June 12, 2009, following the announcement that President Mahmoud Ahmadinejad had won nearly 60% of the votes, whereas the opposition candidates, opposition groups, and civil organizations claimed the manipulation of votes.

At the time of protests, Western observers perceived Twitter as a key tool for their organization. As a consequence, the US government urged the company to postpone scheduled network maintenance. Twitter delayed the planned network upgrade "because events in Iran were tied directly to the growing significance of Twitter as an important communication and information network" while stressing that "the State Department does not have access to our decision making process" (Twitter, 2009). Thus without the needed empirical grounding, a discourse surrounding the central, even crucial, role of Twitter—as a platform or information and communication technology (ICT) tool and representative for social media as a whole—in the political protests with revolutionary potential was constructed. At the same time, Twitter, the company, rather than the platform, managed to present itself and its decision making as morally driven and unaffected by local US politics, while affirming the constructed "revolutionary" significance of its platform.

Although many Western observers and scholars stress the central role of Twitter during the protests, some Iranian and Western scholars argue that Twitter was scarcely used by Iranian citizens, with approximately 8900 registered users out of a 70 million population (Schectman, 2009), prior to and during the 2009 protests (Honari, 2014; Esfandyari, 2010; Rahimi, 2011). During the protests, it was the Western commentators and supporters, rather than the protesters themselves, who contributed to Twitter threads using the hashtag #IranElection. This led *The Economist* to the conclusion that the most comprehensive sources of information in English were neither Twitter nor the mainstream news outlets, which failed to report on the developments in Iran, but rather bloggers and journalists such as Nico Pitney (*Huffington Post*), Andrew Sullivan (*The Atlantic*), and Robert Mackey (*New York Times*). These journalists collected and published the useful information from the vast information that was circulating online (to the most part on social media platforms) (The Economist, 2009).

In terms of the Hype Cycle Discourse, the 2009 protests after the elections in Iran, Twitter postponing its network maintenance, and the US State Department urging it to do so are the Technology Trigger, which laid the cornerstone for the debate.[5] Subsequently, the deployment of social media in Iran and the Arab Spring can be positioned at the Peak of Inflated Expectations. The rhetoric of "social media," "Facebook," or "Twitter revolutions" is an expression of the inflated expectations from social media platforms to incite, facilitate, and foster revolutions, as if it were a *creatio ex nihilo*, while blending other crucial factors out. Moreover, it is an expression of technological—or rather, social media—centrism and determinism, constructed mostly by the Western perception of the events, as the media discourse overemphasized the role of these tools and lacked insights regarding the reasons that took protesters to streets, often under the danger of grave personal consequences. Furthermore, the fact that the protests in Tunisia and Egypt succeeded in creating a political revolution and overthrowing dictators or that the US State Department requested Twitter to postpone its network maintenance contributed to the belief in the revolutionary power of social media, thus supporting the notion of "social media revolutions." As the uprisings continued to develop and turned over to civil wars in Libya and Syria, a military coup in Egypt, and violent state crackdowns in Bahrain, mentioning the role of social media platforms in the coverage and discussion of the events significantly decreased. In fact, it was mostly mentioned with reference to the development of the protests, rather than the current situation, a Trough of Disillusionment.

According to the time of writing in 2015, broadscale protests take place in Lebanon in response to the government's failure to dispose waste that accumulates several weeks. With the garbage problem serving as a catalyzer, the protests aim at the widespread corruption, the land's political dysfunction, and unemployment and deploy protest slogans that were used during the Arab Spring. Interestingly, the news coverage in Western mainstream media focuses on the protests' context, emphasizing the garbage problem and corruption, but rarely discusses the usage of social media, although it exists at least at the same scale as it was during the events of the Arab Spring.

The question remains: to what extent, and more importantly how, do social media contribute to the emergence of collective action? To better understand the complex interplay of social media deployment and other factors in the Arab Spring protests as a case study for the posed question, it is instructive to look at several theoretical models that examine the formation of collective action.

---

[5] This does not mean that the events in Iran revealed the issue of social media deployment for the first time, but rather that they follow many further instances of such deployment on different scales and serve as a "trigger" for this deployment to become a relevant subject of theory and practice.

3.1 FROM AN INDIVIDUAL AGENT TO AN ACTIVE COLLECTIVE

3.1.1 Strain and Breakdown Theories

In the classical theories of collective action, sociologists recognized collective behavior to be irrational and/or emotional reaction of individuals to situations outside of their control. Thus forming crowds that "were theorized to act under the sway of intense emotional states generated by physical proximity; such behavior was marked as contrast to the rational and orderly behavior that prevailed in conventional social settings" (Buechler, 2004, p. 49). The notions of irrationality and the loss of individuality under the collective were later criticized, above all by the theories of rational choice and resource mobilization.[6] The main point of criticism regarding these theories is that the people who protest are often better integrated than those who do not, and that tight social networks rather than random contagion are often connecting sites of protest (Koopmans, 2004).[7]

Sociologist Herbert Blumer defined collective behavior as a primarily spontaneous, unregulated and unstructured group activity. The trigger for such collective behavior is what Blumer termed as *cultural drifts*—the tensions, disruptions, or even collapse in standard social routines. According to this view, collective behavior sets off from conventional behavior and involves elements of contagion, spontaneity, and emotionality, which in turn shape the collective behavior itself. Social unrest thus provides the conditions for the formation of collective behavior in its various forms, including crowds, masses, publics, and social movements. Furthermore, through symbolic communication and interaction, initially unstructured collective behavior can in turn promote emergent norms and incipient forms of order (Blumer, 1995; Buechler, 2004).

The concept of relative deprivation addresses collective behavior from a social-psychological perspective and views it as a result of people's assessment of their current situation against various reference groups, past situations, or an anticipated future situation; that is to say, the change in the views of individuals regarding what they believe they are entitled to. A condition of relative deprivation exists when people find a benchmark that implies a situation better for them than the current one, which could or should be achieved. This psychological strain also serves as a trigger for participation in collective action (Buechler, 2004).

---

[6] The resource mobilization theories are discussed in Chapter 6.
[7] This criticism relates to the notions of social networks and strong versus weak ties, which will be further discussed in this chapter as well as in Chapter 5.

Other sociologists and scholars of social movements, such as Perugorría and Tejerina (2013), Benski and Langman (2013), also stress the importance of emotions, an aspect that gains little attention in social movement theories. Emotions and their groupings (e.g., anger and hope, anxiety and joy) are part of the primary factors that motivate people to first participate in actions such as demonstrations and then sustain activism (Benski et al., 2013). They further argue that: "structural crises do not simply foster social movements per se. These crises need to elicit emotional reactions that in turn can be easily interpreted within existing frames of understanding, or perhaps, people can negotiate and construct new frames that resonate with actors' social/network locations, identities, character structures, and values. Thus emotions such as anger joined with powerlessness may impel actors to claim or reclaim agency by joining/creating networks where alternative visions can be negotiated and actors engage in collective struggles to work toward social change" (Benski et al., 2013, p. 545).

Based on Durkheim's analysis of modern society, which provided a major foundation for subsequent theories of collective behavior, Steven M. Buechler (2004) summarized the above-mentioned theories under the term *Strain and Breakdown Theories*. According to Buechler, the concepts of strain and breakdown as essential causes for the emergence of collective behavior (and action) are the connecting threads of an otherwise diverse group of social theorists addressing collective behavior.

Considering the conditions that led to the events of the Arab Spring, the different strain and breakdown theories deliver analytical frameworks for understanding the social and psychological factors that contributed to the formation of collectively acting groups, the motives that took people to the street.

3.1.2 Rational Choice

In contrast to some of the strain and breakdown theories and in relation to the resource mobilization theory, the Rational Choice Theory addresses individuals as rational actors, who strategically weigh the costs and benefits of joining a social movement or a collective action, rational choice being a central factor in an individual's decision if to join a social movement or take part in collective action. Compared with alternative courses of action, including the option of not taking any action at all, a decision for the course of action that is most probable to have maximal utilization is made. Such a notion, however, offers a relatively narrow account of how individuals make their decisions. Having its origins in economic theory, this narrow view of individual decisions relates to the notion of *Homo economicus*, economic (wo)men.

When addressing the Demand and Supply of Participation (in collective action), Brent Klandermans distinguishes three fundamental reasons why movement participation is appealing to people: "people may want to change their circumstances, they may want to act as members of their group, or they may want to give meaning to their world and express their views and feelings" (Klandermans, 2004, p. 361). According to Klandermans, these motives account for most of the demand for (political) collective action in society and social movements may supply the opportunity to fulfill them (Klandermans, 2004). Therefore it is important not to reduce rationality or rational choice in the context of collective action to its economical meaning, that is, not to consider individuals as *Homo economicus*, but rather to consider costs and benefits, or demand and supply, of participation also in other meanings such as social, political, and personal ones.

3.1.3 Shared Awareness

A further level in the promotion of collective action is the process of shared awareness, which is the perception among individuals that they are members of a larger group by virtue of their shared grievances or goals. According to Clay Shirky, lecturer and consultant on Internet and new media as well as author of *Here Comes Everybody: The Power of Organizing Without Organizations*, shared awareness motivates otherwise uncoordinated individuals or groups to begin cooperating more effectively, thus being a necessary step for triggering collective action (Shirky, 2008; Kelly, 2006). Shirky divided this kind of social awareness to three simplified levels (Shirky, 2008, pp. 163–164.):

1. *Everybody knows something* is a state of relative deprivation within many individuals who are not yet gathered together.
2. *Everybody knows that everybody knows* is when a shared awareness begins to form and individuals realize that the relative deprivation is spread among their close circles (such as family, friends, and coworkers).
3. *Everybody knows that everybody knows that everybody knows* describes a situation of reciprocal awareness. Individuals are aware not only of the relative deprivation (of their own and of others), but also of the fact that many others (also outside their close circles) are also aware (1) of the relative deprivation and (2) of the fact that others are also aware of it.

By addressing the link between people's individual situation and their consideration whether to participate in the movement or collective action as a social and reflective process, the concept of shared awareness offers a combined view of the Strain and Breakdown Theories and the (broad) notion of Rational Choice.

The deployment of social media (as ICT tools and as media) in collective action contributes to the development of shared awareness in different ways. This, together with further aspects of the emergence of collective action that is supported by social media, will be discussed in the following section.

3.2 A "FACEBOOK REVOLUTION" IS JUST ANOTHER REVOLUTION: SOCIAL MEDIA AND THE FORMATION OF A COLLECTIVE IN THE ARAB SPRING

As mentioned earlier, in the countries and societies of the Arab Spring, people suffered from many circumstances—human rights violations, abuse by state authorities, economic decline, inflation, unemployment and poverty, rising domestic food prices and declining food security, the spread of neoliberal capitalist order, political corruption, imperialism, as well as tensions between ethnic groups or between religious and secular ones. These aspects differ in their constellation and intensity between countries, but they certainly constituted major grievances and fueled the wish for a change of these circumstances. That is to say, there were many sufficient reasons for any kind of collective behavior and/or action to emerge.

In Tunisia and in Egypt, both cases of Mohamed Bouazizi and Khaled Said were individual fates, but they were connected to the grievances of broad parts of the population, first in their hometowns and as the events developed across the country and, to a certain extent, the Arab world. Protesters used social media platforms such as Facebook, Twitter, and YouTube to give voice to their grievances and their demands, thus deploying social media to effectively share and distribute various kinds of information—pictures and videos, updates about local developments, reports of police abuse, etc. In other words, social media's social affordance enabled the protesters to communicate and other individuals to perceive the dispersion of grievances in their social environment. As the participation grew, the circles and groups who constitute the social environments grew as well, from local protests to nationwide ones. Not only in Egypt and Tunisia, but also in many other cases of social media being involved in the emergence of collective action, the usage of social media helped making states of relative deprivation visible and accelerating the formation of shared awareness across social milieus. Thus social media constituted a factor that supported the development of the mutually reflective stage of shared awareness—everybody knows that everybody knows that everybody knows—on the one hand and made the choice of participating—partly seen as the protests ability to supply an answer to the peoples' demands—increasingly attractive on the other.

Due to the differences in their design, usage models, user demographics, and penetration rate in society, the deployment of the different social media platforms varies and so does the manner in which they support collective action.

Twitter and platforms with similar technical/medial design and functionalities, such as Sina Weibo, are by design and usage primarily a real-time medium. Twitter has a 140-character limit for each tweet, and the widespread usage of hashtags supports the horizontal communication over specific topics. Thus it is an effective tool for real-time, onsite (as well as between locations), and horizontal coordination. Through retweeting,[8] certain information can be amplified by users, who consider it to be relevant, and the use of hashtags (as long as they are not exponentially used for sharing movement-irrelevant information) supports the creation of threads that automatically assemble and concentrate the information.

In contrast to Twitter, Facebook (and platforms with similar technical/medial design and functionalities, such as Renren or diaspora*) maps and digitally outlines and reproduces people's social networks[9] from their everyday life to a great extent.[10] Although it is less compatible—not completely incompatible—than Twitter for the horizontal real-time organization and communication between strangers and groups, Facebook strength in terms of mobilization to join instances of collective action or social movements is through the users' social networks. Journalist and author Malcolm Gladwell accurately criticized the overemphasizing of Twitter's role in the Arab Spring and stressed the importance of strong ties, which are nurtured outside of social media platforms and require more than just a few clicks to emerge, for the organization of and mobilization for collective action that may contain high risk and/or personal consequences.[11] In other words, neither social media platforms alone nor the weak ties they make visible or, in some cases, strengthen, are the motor for a protest, movement, or revolution to take place. While acknowledging Gladwell's criticism, social media platforms such as Facebook that outline and reproduce a person's social network (including the network's strong ties) help people perceive the sympathy for, support of, and participation in movement or instances

---

[8] The sharing of a tweet published by another user.

[9] The term *social network* will be used throughout the book in the sociological sense of the word, rather than synonymous with social media platforms. In a nutshell, the Social Network Theory regards social relationships or connections in terms of ties and nodes, the former representing the relationships and/or connections and the latter representing the individual actors, which together build the so-called social networks. The interplay between social networks and social media in the context of collective action, especially regarding the relevance of strong ties in comparison to weak ties, is the focus of Chapter 5.

[10] Although the strength of the social ties are not represented at first glance (all Facebook connections have the same status, with the exception of family members, for which the connection can represent the particular affiliation), the strength of the relation is algorithmically calculated based on a broad array of factors—the intensity of communication (within Facebook), mutual interests and connections, mutual participation on (Facebook) events, etc., which can result with Facebook regarding the strength of ties differently from how the individuals would consider them.

[11] Gladwell (2010) criticizes that the interpretation of social media's (and particularly Twitter's) role in the Arab Spring was influenced mainly from Clay Shirky (2008) notion of social media facilitating collective action by making weak ties more relevant, since these ties give people more access to information (over social media platforms).

of collective action among their family, friends, and colleagues, thus having a mobilizing effect for joining an emerging or ongoing collective action.

Furthermore, groups and events that are organized in social media platforms are very productive for the preparation and coordination in advance and the dissemination of information regarding the event (for example, protest or flash mob). When reaching enough audience (having reached a critical mass of "fans" or "likes"), Facebook pages such as the page *We Are All Kahled Said* can effectively disseminate information in a manner similar to a one-to-many-communication, however, with the backchannel open through comments or users posting on the page's "wall." The group/event members' social networks (their "friends" or connection) perceive the member's participation in or sympathies for the group/event, both the person's own dissemination of information over the social media platform (for example, by sharing the event or status updates regarding the cause) and by the social media platform's algorithms that automatically inform the person's connections. Having said that, considering the aspect of the filter bubble, it is likely that in many cases the movement, embodied in an event, group, or page, relevant information will reach the connections, for which the platform's algorithms assume a similar interest or sympathy, thus having a demobilizing effect on other members of the person's social network.

Paolo Gerbaudo has conducted a study among activists from Egypt, Tunisia, the United Kingdom, Spain, Greece, and the United States about their deployment of social media (Gerbaudo, 2012). His study reinforces the differences in the roles that different social media platforms fulfill in collective action (in this case, in protests):

> Facebook, as we have seen, has been employed as something akin to a recruitment and training ground, to facilitate the emotional condensation and common identification of a largely un-politicised middle-class youth. Twitter, in contrast, has been mainly used as a vehicle for 'live' internal coordination within the activist elite, besides its many largely 'external' uses, including as a means for citizen journalists to document police brutality. Because of its lesser reach compared to Facebook, this medium – the most popular of social media within the core activist community – runs the risk of isolating movement leaders from the less internet-savvy sections of their constituency.
>
> **Gerbaudo (2012, p. 135)**

Interestingly, Gerbaudo's findings indicate that Twitter's strength in supporting coordination was mainly deployed within relatively small and strongly connected circles, circles that are identified with the "activist elite." This, however, is presumably the result of the study's focus on central, highly active and connected—both online and onsite—activists and the question of leadership in these movements and protests.[12]

Platforms such as YouTube, Vimeo, or Instagram are used primarily for sharing videos and images. As seen in the case of YouTube videos from protests during the Arab Spring, these platforms enable people, who take part in the protests, to publish documentation of the events that is internationally accessible, in real time, free of cost,[13] and with relatively few technical barriers. Their design as social media platforms, rather than merely video or picture archives, supports the collection and dissemination of topic-relevant content (in this case, movement or protest relevant). Aspects of this design contain the deployment of hashtags; compilation and sharing of channels or watch lists; algorithms that find similarities or contextual relevance between videos and/or pictures and automatically correlate them; and algorithms that calculate the content's relevance according to views, likes/favorites, comments, etc. and recommend it to further users.[14] Other platforms, such as Facebook and Twitter, offer the dissemination of multimedia content as well—each according to its usage models, design, and technical limitations/possibilities. The difference is that the latter are built around the interpersonal connections and communication, which make them less suitable to serve as user-generated online archives or libraries that contain event/protest/movement documentation.

The strength of social media platforms, both platforms with emphasis on images and videos and other platforms that implement images and videos to other communication models, is not the sole dissemination of such textual and/or nontextual information, but rather the ability to exhibit and mediate emotions. This aspect is present in various usages of social media—from interpersonal communication, to political communication, to self-marketing, to paid and unpaid advertisement—but can be exceptionally effective in the mobilization for collective action. The impact of Khaled Said's pictures, the interview-video with Hassan Mosbah, or the protest videos from Sidi Bouzid and Tahrir Square were not of informative nature alone, it was the emotions exhibited and mediated through them, emotions with which individuals can identify themselves and serve as a major factor of sympathy with or mobilization for the movement causes. In accordance with notions that focus on the role of emotions in mobilization (Perugorría and Tejerina, 2013; Benski and Langman, 2013), Paulo Gerbaudo argues that "Digital Activists like Wael

---

[12] The notion of leadership versus "leaderless networks" and Gerbaudo's finding on the subject are further discussed in Chapter 5.

[13] Not considering the costs for suitable end devices and Internet connection.

[14] On the other hand, the algorithms used by social media platforms also hide content from users—create a filter bubble—which can be counterproductive for the emergence of collective action or a movement.

Ghonim in Egypt, and Fabio Gandara in Spain have skillfully exploited the personal character of social media, their capacity to become channels of intimate while at the same time public conversations. They have used social media to construct an *emotional tension*, connecting the highly dispersed and individualized interactions people maintain through Facebook, Twitter and other social media to the bodily immersion of collective gatherings" (Gerbaudo, 2012, pp. 160–161).

Furthermore, even in comparison with other ICTs (e.g., email, telephone, or Short Message Service) the usage of social media—each platform according to its strengths and weaknesses—made it easier for the protesters to reach dissidents abroad and traditional media outlets, especially Al Jazeera. In the case of the Arab Spring, Al Jazeera's television broadcast helped the protesters' messages reach the populace needed to reach a nationwide or even international scale. This is not a particular feature of the events of the Arab Spring. In many other cases of collective action that reached large-scale dispersion, parallel to the formation of a collective (action), the dissemination of messages in different forms (text, pictures, videos, etc.) through social media helped people gain the attention of mainstream or broadcast media. Since more people from various demographic groups inform themselves through mainstream and broadcast media, these media, in turn, contribute to the formation of a shared awareness and to the motivation of participate.

However, when considering the role of social media—or ICTs in general—in the Arab Spring, the governments' (technological) countermeasures are just as relevant. In Egypt, for example, the government blocked Facebook and Twitter at first, expanding that measure to a complete Internet blackout that lasted 5 days, beginning on January 28, 2011. Such attempts to shutdown or censor Internet communication on different scales (from the censorship of certain websites or routes, to surveillance of activists, to complete Internet blackout) took place in most countries, in which the uprisings took place, including Libya, Syria, and Tunisia. This issue will be discussed further in Chapter 9, which discusses surveillance and the utilization of social media in authoritarian context.

3.3 CONCLUSIONS

For the image of social media corporations (and the image of their platforms), it was of course good to be affiliated with democracy-striving revolutions. Regardless of their outcome, a discourse was created, which artificially constructs a direct connection between social media platforms (and the institution) and social struggles for freedom and democracy. This discourse fosters a metaphysical belief in the powers of "social media" or "the Internet" to single-handedly make social change and even revolutions possible, thus giving the platforms a certain magical aura and the image of a socially aware, democracy-promoting capital investment.[15]

However, as it turns out, the involvement of Western information technology companies and their products in the Arab Spring did not sum up to Facebook and Twitter. For example, Gamma International, a company with branches in Germany and the United Kingdom, was reported to deliver its surveillance software FinFisher to authorities in Egypt and Bahrain, who apparently used it prior to and during the events of the Arab Spring to track down activists and lawyers (Bahrain Watch, 2014; Reißmann, 2014; Higgins, 2012). As a study by Privacy International shows, several Western firms were involved in building Syria's surveillance state under the Assad regime and prior to the Arab Spring and the outbreak of civil war (Privacy International, 2016).

The results of the uprisings in most Arab countries have somewhat faded the social-media-revolution-euphoria that prevailed over the media, political, and even academic discourse around 2011—from state crackdowns successfully suppressed protests, to undemocratic forces taking over, to counter revolutions, to civil wars. As the euphoria faded away, in the Trough of Disillusionment, the need for a differentiated and critical analysis, free of social media centrism and determinism, became clear. Athina Karatzogianni eloquently made the point that:

> In certain respects, whether social media was a crucial or just a facilitating factor is not a question worth posing. For anyone paying half attention, it is obviously a key factor in transforming how social movements operate and it has been so over a decade now. To be posing this question again, only means that commentators will be asking it every time there is a revolution or a social media movement of any description, especially in the developing countries. This is not meaningful as such for media policy or e-governance or advancing theory on the various literatures.
>
> **Karatzogianni (2013, p. 169)**

In his book *The Net Delusion*, Evgeny Morozov argues that the use of (Internet-) tools is interpreted as revolutionary by older generations, especially the baby boomers, because it fits the frameworks that were used to interpret and explain the fall of the Iron Curtain (that is, the collapse of the Soviet Union and end of the Cold War) (Morozov, 2011). Nowadays, this generation occupies positions of (discursive) power, as policymakers, as managers in media and news outlets,

---

[15] Having said that, Facebook founder Mark Zuckerberg denied the idea of a Facebook revolution. Speaking at the e-G8 Summit in May 2011 in Paris, Zuckerberg stated that "A lot has been made about the revolutions in Egypt and Tunisia and Facebook's role in them [...] It would be extremely arrogant for any specific technology company to claim credit. Facebook was neither necessary nor sufficient for any of those things to happen [...] People are now having the opportunity to communicate – that's not a Facebook thing, that's an Internet thing" (e-G8 Forum, 2011).

and as professors and researchers in the academia. The protesters who deploy social media, and smartphones, to name another ICT tool that was central in many protests, on the other hand, belong primarily to a different generation. This generation, these protesters, went to the streets as a reaction to their grievances, frustration, and lack of perspective and to voice their demands, similar to their parents' generation in these and other parts of the world. While doing so, they deployed the tools and platforms they grew up with, that they use in their everyday life, and where everybody (meaning their social networks of family, friends, and colleagues) is; for them, it is a matter of fact.[16] Thus a situation was created that while protesters deploy the tools they know to support their cause, an audience composed of policymakers, scholars, and news editors was deploying narrow-minded frameworks, misinterpreted the tools as the motor of the revolution, and had the discursive power for this interpretation to prevail.

Wolfsfeld, Segev, and Sheafer offer (and empirically reinforce) two principles for the analysis of the role of social media in collective action, which correspond to as well as complement the conclusions of this chapter. First is that politics comes first analytically; "[o]ne cannot understand the role of social media in collective action without first taking into account the political environment in which they operate" (Wolfsfeld et al., 2013, p. 119). That is to say, in places and situations in which protests emerge due to political grievances and social media is deployed, the latter "should be seen as facilitators of protest rather than causes" (Wolfsfeld et al., 2013, p. 120). The second principle, politics comes first chronologically, claims that a "significant increase in the use of the new media is much more likely to follow a significant amount of protest activity than to precede it" (Wolfsfeld et al., 2013, p. 120). This is a translation of increased usage of mainstream media when political events take place (as journalists increasingly report and the public informs itself about the events) into the deployment of social media. Political events such as protests lead to a change in the usage of social media (consumption of political and protest-related information), which in turn can lead to further changes in the political and protest environments (participation in collective action within social media and on the streets).[17]

---

[16] A fact that Mark Zuckerberg himself (obviously not a member of the baby boomers generation) seems to have noticed.

[17] Wolfsfeld, Segev, and Sheafer offer empirical data of Facebook registrations as well as Google searches for Facebook and news outlets in the different countries of the Arab Spring and divided in three periods—early, proximate, and protests periods. Their findings, which are also supported by a study of the Dubai School of Government (Salem and Mourtada, 2011), approve the second principle.

Furthermore, using social media as a generic concept while referring to a variety of platforms with differing functionalities, institutions, media, and practices is insufficient for analyzing their role in collective action. Therefore when needed in the course of the book, the role of social media will be addressed according to their functionalities, design, media, or institutional character, especially when considering the fact that some social media platforms or institutions that are widespread according to the time of writing, or were central in discussed instances of collective action, might not exist 10 years from now as other platforms/institutions have taken their place.

Keeping these important insights in mind, the following chapters of the book analyze social media as tools that certainly support, affect, and in certain cases revolutionize collective action, but do not cause it; as tools that are deployed within social, cultural, and historical contexts; and as institutions with agendas and interests that affect the tools' function as ICT and/or media.

Although this chapter focused mainly on the emergence of collective action and the role social media (can) play in it, the following chapters examine the manner in which social media support instances of collective action as they happen. Thus addressing the deployment of social media in collective action as well as social media's impact on it; considering social media as part of the social movement and collective action toolbox and repertoire. The first case study of this examination took place approx. 500 km—and a tweet—away from Tahrir Square, namely the 2010s social justice protests in Israel and their usage of cultural symbolic.

References

Armbrust, W., 2011. The Revolution Against Neoliberalism. Jadaliyya. Retrieved from: www.jadaliyya.com/pages/index/717/the-revolution-againstneoliberalism.

Bahrain Watch, 2014. Bahrain Government Hacked Lawyers and Activists with UK Spyware. Retrieved from: www.bahrainwatch.org/blog/2014/08/07/uk-spyware-used-to-hack-bahrain-lawyers-activists/.

Benski, T., Langman, L., 2013. The effects of affects: the place of emotions in the mobilizations of 2011. Current Sociology 61 (4), 525–540.

Benski, T., Langman, L., Perugorría, I., Tejerina, B., 2013. From the streets and squares to social movement studies: what have we learned? Current Sociology 61 (4), 541–561.

Blumer, H., 1995. Social movements. In: Lyman, S.M. (Ed.), Social Movements: Critiques, Concepts, Case Studies. New York University Press, New York, pp. 60–83.

Buechler, S.M., 2004. The Strange Career of strain and breakdown theories of collective action. In: Snow, D.A., Soule, S.A., Kriesi, H. (Eds.), The Blackwell Companion to Social Movements. Blackwell Publishing Ltd, Malden, MA, pp. 47–66.

Dixon, M., 2011. An Arab spring. Review of African Political Economy 28 (128), 309–316.

e-G8 Forum, 2011. Closing Conversation: Mark Zuckerberg (Founder & CEO Facebook) Talks with Maurice Lévy. Chairman & CEO Publicis Groupe. Retrieved from: www.youtube.com/watch?v=Gy0bq9FAJRs.

Esfandyari, G., 2010. The Twitter Devolution. Foreign Policy. Retrieved from: www.foreignpolicy. com/2010/06/08/the-twitter-devolution/.

Gerbaudo, P., 2012. Tweets and the Streets: Social Media and Contemporary Activism. Pluto Press, London.

Gladwell, M., 2010. Small Change: Why the Revolution Will Not Be Tweeted. Retrieved from: www. newyorker.com/magazine/2010/10/04/small-change-malcolm-gladwell.

Global Voice Advocacy, 2011. MENA Journalists & Cyber Activists: In the Line of Fire. Retrieved from: advocacy.globalvoicesonline.org/2011/04/27/mena-journalists-cyber-activists-in-the-line-of-fire/.

Harrigan, J., 2011. Did food prices plant the seeds of the Arab spring? SOAS Inaugural Lecture Series. Retrieved from: https://www.soas.ac.uk/about/events/inaugurals/28apr2011-did-food-prices-plant-the-seeds-of-the-arab-spring.html.

Herrera, L., 2013. Meet Abdel Rahman Mansour Who Made 25 January a Date to Remember. Jadaliyya. Retrieved from: www.jadaliyya.com/pages/index/9772/meet-abdelrahman-mansour-who-made-25-january-a-dat.

Higgins, P., 2012. Elusive FinFisher Spyware Identified and Analyzed. Electronic Frontier Foundation. Retrieved from: www.eff.org/deeplinks/2012/07/elusive-finfisher-spyware-identified-and-analyzed.

Honari, A., 2014. From virtual to tangible social movements in Iran. In: Aarts, P., Cavatorta, F. (Eds.), Civil Society in Syria and Iran: Activism in Authoritarian Contexts. Lynne Rienner, Boulder, CO, pp. 143–168.

Hussain, M.M., Howard, P.N., 2013. What best explains successful protest cascades? ICTs and the fuzzy causes of the Arab spring. International Studies Review 15, 48–66.

Karatzogianni, A., 2013. A Cyberconflict analysis of the 2011 Arab spring uprisings. In: Youngs, G. (Ed.), Digital World: Connectivity, Creativity and Rights. Routledge, London, pp. 159–175.

Kelly Garrett, R., 2006. Protest in an information society: a review of literature on social movements and new ICTs. Information, Communication & Society 9 (2), 202–224.

Khamis, S., Vaughn, K., July 2011. "We Are All Khaled Said": the potentials and limitations of cyberactivism in triggering public mobilization and promoting political change. Journal of Arab & Muslim Media Research 4 (2&3), 145.

Khondker, H.H., 2011. Role of the new media in the Arab spring. Globalizations 8 (5), 675–679.

Klandermans, B., 2004. The demand and supply of participation: social-psychological correlates of participation in social movement. In: Snow, D.A., Soule, S.A., Kriesi, H. (Eds.), The Blackwell Companion to Social Movements. Blackwell Publishing Ltd, Malden, MA, pp. 360–379.

Koopmans, R., 2004. Protest in time and space: the evolution of waves of contention. In: Snow, D.A., Soule, S.A., Kriesi, H. (Eds.), The Blackwell Companion to Social Movements. Blackwell Publishing Ltd, Malden, MA, pp. 19–46.

Morozov, E., 2011. The Net Delusion: The Dark Side of Internet Freedom. PublicAffairs, New York.

Perugorría, I., Tejerina, B., 2013. Politics of the encounter: cognition, emotions, and networks in the Spanish 15M. Current Sociology 61 (4), 424–442.

Privacy International, 2016. Open Season: Building Syria's Surveillance State. Retrieved from: www.privacyinternational.org/sites/default/files/OpenSeason.pdf.

Rahimi, B., 2011. The agonistic social media: cyberspace in the formation of dissent and consolidation of state power in postelection Iran. The Communication Review 14 (3), 158–178.

Reißmann, O., 2014. FinFisher-Software: Kundendienst half bei Überwachung in Bahrain. Spiegel. Retrieved from: www.spiegel.de/netzwelt/netzpolitik/gamma-gruppe-hacker-kopieren-finfisher-unterlagen-a-985098.html.

Salem, F., Mourtada, R., 2011. Arab Social Media Report. Retrieved from: http://unpan1.un.org/intradoc/groups/public/documents/dsg/unpan044212.pdf.

Schectman, J., 2009. Iran's Twitter Revolution? Maybe Not Yet. Bloomberg. Retrieved from: www.bloomberg.com/bw/technology/content/jun2009/tc20090617_803990.htm.

Shirky, C., 2008. Here Comes Everybody: The Power of Organizing Without Organizations. Penguin Group, London.

The Economist, 2009. Twitter 1, CNN 0. Retrieved from: www.economist.com/node/13856224.

Twitter, Inc., 2009. Up, Up, and Away. Retrieved from: blog.twitter.com/2009/and-away.

Wolfsfeld, G., Segev, E., Sheafer, T., 2013. Social media and the Arab Spring: politics comes first. The International Journal of Press/Politics 18 (2), 115–137.

Zuckerman, E., 2013. Rewire: Digital Cosmopolitans in the Age of Connection. W. W. Norton & Company, New York.

CHAPTER 4

Cottage, Tents, and Chocolate Pudding: The Cultural Context of the Israeli Social Justice Protests

ABSTRACT

The Israeli social justice protests of the 2010s, which reached their climax in summer 2011 and faded continually until 2014, were a set of protest movements on the issues of food and housing costs and social justice in Israeli society. The movements' deployment of social media, especially Facebook, was a constitutive element for the movements themselves as well as their perception in society, media, and politics. This chapter examines the protests as a case study for understanding social media's role in collective action in terms of cultural contexts and framing processes.

Keywords: Cultural context; Facebook; Food costs; Framing; Housing prices; Living costs; New social movement; Social justice; Social media; Social movement.

CONTENTS

4.1 SETTING UP THE FIRST TENT

On July 14, 2011, 25-year-old Daphni Leef set up a tent at the Habima Square in central Tel Aviv after being evacuated from her apartment and as a protest for the rising rent prices in the city. In support of their cause, Leef and

Collective Action 2.0. http://dx.doi.org/10.1016/B978-0-08-100567-5.00004-9

several friends opened a Facebook event page and a Facebook protest page that called other people to join. The movement grew quickly and as the tent protest became a tent encampment at the Rothschild Boulevard (which ends at the Habima Square) and the Facebook page reached several hundred members/followers, the movement started getting media attention, which in turn contributed to the movement's growth. The movement (as well as the tent encampment at the Rothschild Boulevard) grew rapidly as a variety of social and civil organizations and movements joined and diversified the movement's causes. Thus the movement momentum grew, a fact that became visible in demonstrations, tent encampments set up in other cities across the country, sit-ins in governmental buildings, media coverages, and, of course, growing social media presence such as the movement's official Facebook page *Bet Ze Ohel*[1] (paraphrasing a known children's song).[2]

The Rothschild tent encampment continued to serve as the movement's center and, although the movement avoided having an official leadership, several activists[3] were playing a central role within the movement and in its reception by the Israeli public.[4] As the number of participants in demonstrations grew, the movement organized a nationwide demonstration titled "The March of the Million"[5] on September 3, 2011, which had more than 300,000 participants in the main demonstration in Tel Aviv and approximately 100,000 participants in parallel demonstrations across the country [of a total population of nearly 8 million (Central Bureau of Statistics (Israel), 2015) Israeli citizens] (Ynet News, 2011).

Besides being a social justice, housing, or tent protest, the movement was also referred to in public discourse as a "Facebook Protest." This reference was based on the movement's success in deploying Facebook as a platform for mobilizing its first members and sympathizers, drawing first media attention to the protests, as well as the continuous usage of Facebook to organize events, communicate the movement's messages, and reach out to the public, media, and politics, thus shifting the discourse's focus from the movement's causes to the tools the movement members and sympathizers were deploying, tools that at the time were already hyped in public debate, among others due to the events of the Arab Spring, as discussed in the previous chapter and the introduction.

---

[1] www.facebook.com/j14rev and www.facebook.com/j14publici.
[2] *Bet Ze Ohel* is Hebrew for *B means Tent*, a phrase that will be discussed further in this chapter.
[3] Among others Daphni Leef, Stav Shaffir (who later became a member of Knesset, the Israeli parliament, for the *Ha'Avoda* Labor Party), and Itzik Shmuli (head of the National Union of Israeli Students and later MK for the Labor Party as well).
[4] For a discussion of the notion of "leaderless networks" in this context see Chapter 5 as well as Gerbaudo (2012).
[5] *Tse'adat Ha'Million.*

However, there is a bigger context to the 2011 Social Justice Protests in Israel, which is crucial, to better understand the movement itself and Facebook's role in it.

4.2 CHRONOLOGY OF THE 2010s ISRAELI SOCIAL JUSTICE PROTESTS

As discussed in the previous chapter, social media do not incite, facilitate, or foster collective action as if it were a *creatio ex nihilo*. Leef, her friends, and hundreds of thousands of demonstrators took their grievances to the streets; they did so using tools they know and use in their everyday lives, Facebook (and smartphones) in this case. Furthermore, Israel is a worldwide leader in the percentage of society that uses Facebook as well as in average usage time, as statistics from the time of the protests show (ComScore, 2011).

Due to shortage in available apartments as well as governmental restrictions on urban construction, rent and housing prices in Israel rose 30%–50% between the years 2007 and 2011.[6] Furthermore, neoliberal reforms in the decade prior to the protests weakened the social state, caused growing socioeconomic injustice, and erosion of the middle class. All these reflected in growing living costs and sinking real wage, a fact that helped this and other movements set a precedent in putting these issues on the public agenda.

The movement, that is, the "Tent Protest," succeeded in inducing a process or state of shared awareness regarding people's financial situation. The rising living costs, food, housing, and other consumer goods, were affecting not only the financially disadvantaged and lower economic classes, but increasingly also the Israeli middle class. For many people, the silence about their financial difficulties was broken in course of the social protests, knowing that they are not alone (and reflectively perceiving the correlating situational knowledge within their social surrounding). This gave the protests a visible middle and upper middle class character, although as the protest-movement grew, groups of people from socioeconomically weaker classes took part and helped shape the movement. The usage of social media was a contributing factor in this development. For example, social media's social affordance supported the perception of support for the movement's causes, which implies sympathy for and identification with these causes, in one's social environment; that is, friends, family, or colleagues (as Facebook friends) sharing movement content, participation on demonstrations made visible through pictures and event notifications, people expressing their opinion regarding the protests in social media, etc. Or, to state another

---

[6] Trajtenberg Committee (2011). The Trajtenberg Committee was a commission, which was appointed by the Israeli government in reaction to the social justice protests. The commission goal was to examine Israel's socioeconomic problems and propose measures to deal with these problems.

example, the movement members' and demonstrations participants' *habitus*[7] communicated through the variety of pictures and videos shared in real time and following the events.

However, public awareness for the rising living costs and the social unrest as a result did not begin the day the first test was set up. Only several weeks prior to Leef's actions, another protest occupied the Israeli public discourse—the "Cottage Cheese Boycott" or "Cottage Cheese Protest." The boycott/protest movement started a Facebook page calling for boycott of cottage cheese as a protest for the rising prices of dairy products, with the aim to broaden the boycott to further products as well.[8] Within a short time, the protest group in Facebook grew to 100,000 members. The movement, which articulated the concern of many Israeli citizens regarding food and living costs, concentrated mostly on social media (and later on mass media) communication and consumer boycotts, rather than taking its cause to the streets. It did, however, manage to draw substantial media attention and the government announced taking several measures such as reducing regulation on the import of dairy products, examination of the market concentration, and competitiveness. The boycott also succeeded in putting food corporations and chain stores under pressure to reduce prices. In addition to the specific results of the boycott on the political and market levels, it initiated a public debate on the issue of the high living costs in general.

The choice of cottage cheese as expression for the boycott's cause and subject of activism (not buying this certain type of dairy product) was not arbitrary—in Israel, cottage cheese is a very popular product and central component of many people's nutrition. Moreover, the biggest dairy products manufacturer, Tnuvah, depicts a house—a cottage, if you like—on its cottage cheese packages and uses the marketing slogan "Cottage – a cheese with a home" (symbolizing the product's homely environment or vibe). It is somewhat ironic, or perhaps reasonable, that a housing protest followed the cottage protest, as the following discussion will demonstrate.

Although the protest wave faded since 2011, there were several smaller protests and initiatives in the following years.[9] On September 2014, a young Israeli who

---

[7] The concept of Habitus, which is associated with the works of Pierre Bourdieu, refers to the embodiment of social structures, such as the gender, race, and class discrimination. That is, these structures are characterized by a set of acquired schemata, sensibilities, dispositions, and tastes, which are, in turn, expressed and communicated through the body, mimic, clothing, language, and other perceivable signs.

[8] In 2006 the Israeli government removed the price regulation from cottage cheese, which caused price increase of nearly 50% until June 2011, when one packet of cottage cheese cost 7–8 NIS (Israeli Shekel), which is approximately 2–2.3 USD).

[9] For example, a demonstration for the anniversary of the social justice protests and tent encampment in Rothschild Boulevard in July 2012 ended tragically, as the protester Moshe Silman set himself on fire in protest of his treatment by the state's welfare system.

immigrated to Berlin anonymously opened a Facebook group titled *Olim Le'Berlin*[10] and shared a picture of an invoice from a local grocery store, commenting on the low prices in comparison with similar products in Israel. In his comment, he explicitly addressed a Chocolate Pudding that is equivalent to a very popular product in Israel named *Milky*, describing it as a product that Israelis abroad especially miss and calculating the price difference—0.19 EUR, approximately 0.80 NIS in Berlin compared with 3 NIS in Israel. The invoice showed the prices of a variety of food products, all of them (with the exception of fruits and vegetables) cheaper in Berlin than in Israel. This incited a broad public debate, which stayed mostly in the media, both in social and mass media, and did not develop to a protest movement. Although in the aftermath this case caused a relatively small impact, it is deeply entwined with the social and, in the context of this chapter, cultural discourse that accompanied the wave of Israeli social justice protests.

As the cottage cheese and Milky protests show, the discourse on the subjects of living costs (as part of a broader discourse on social justice) developed and continued over several years and had various social and political implications, which in turn contributed not only to social movements and protests, but also to their cultural representation and methods of actions.

To consider the cultural aspects that played a role in this variety of instances of collective action, the following section will introduce the theoretical framework for the examination of social movements' and collective action's cultural context. Subsequently, the 2010s social justice protests in Israel will be used as a case study for the analysis of social media's role in collective action from a cultural point of view.

4.3 CULTURAL CONTEXT OF SOCIAL MOVEMENTS

The study of social movements and collective action's cultural turn has its roots in 1980s US scholarship. One interpretation of the culturalist approach, the new social movement (NSM), focuses on the movement's cultural, moral, and identity issues, rather than on economic ones. The cultural component has to do with the content of movement ideology, the concerns motivating activists, and the arena in which collective action is focused. Thus NSM shifted the focus of analysis from material interests and economic distribution, placing actors in economic classes or as ones, to cultural understandings, norms, and identities. NSM also gives explicit attention to the connection between the forms of

---

[10] Hebrew for immigrating to Berlin—however, not using the relatively neutral Hebrew verb for immigrating, but rather the term *Aliyah*, which has a deeper meaning in Hebrew as well as in Jewish (and hence to a certain extent Israeli) culture. Aliyah, literally meaning "going up," refers to the act of Jewish people immigrating from diaspora to the land of Israel and progressing toward Jerusalem (which is located on top of a mountain), thus also preforming an act of spiritual ascent.

collective action and the historical moments and societal formations in which they existed (Williams, 2004).

The second and more extensive tendency in the culturalist approach is toward the implementation of meaning into a movement. It focuses on the ways in which movements use symbols, language, discourse, identity, and other dimensions of culture to recruit, motivate, and mobilize members. Scholars of this tradition are particularly interested in the interpersonal processes through which individuals understand their own actions and how they find ideational, moral, and emotional resources to continue (Williams, 2004). Within this approach, Framing is the most prominent model (although not the only one), which is based on Erving Goffman's work and "frame"—metaphor (Goffman, 1974, 1986).

Framing focuses primarily on the deployment of symbols, claims, and identities in the pursuit of activism. In the context of social movements and collective action, the framing notion theorizes the symbolic and the meaning of work done by movement activists as they articulate grievances, generate consensus on the importance and on the forms of collective action to be pursued, and present their audience with the rationale for their actions and for the proposed solutions. The audience can include media, elites, potential recruits, sympathetic allies, and antagonists. In psychology and sociology, frames address schemes of interpretation and providing meaning. Frames can be biologically ("naturally") or culturally and socially constructed, thus varying between individuals from different social and cultural (religion, profession, class, political opinion, gender and sexuality, language, etc.) or biological (age, physical disability, biological sex, etc.) contexts. They serve as mental filters, thus the choice of frames influences the interpretation and "sense making" of the surrounding world. When articulating their positions and goals, employing phrases and symbols, and granting them with meaning, movements participate in a process of selective influence of individuals in their audience and construction of the perception (the frames used) by the same individuals. "Successful" framing can be considered when the employed frames align with the audience's frames and result in resonance (Benford and Snow, 2000; Goffman, 1974, 1986; Gamson, 2004; Johnston, 2002; Snow, 2004; Williams, 2004).

David Snow, who researches among others on crowd dynamics and framing processes and outcomes, speaks of Collective Action Frames, which "like picture frames, focus attention by punctuating or specifying what in our sensual field is relevant and what is irrelevant, what is 'in frame' and what is 'out of frame,' in relation to the object of orientation" (Snow, 2004, p. 384). However, and perhaps even more importantly, frames also function as a mechanism of articulation; that is to say, frames help punctuating various elements to promote one set of meanings rather than another. Furthermore, frames are transformative; they affect and alter the meaning of the (cultural) objects (e.g., the transformation of grievances into injustices and/or mobilization) as well as the relationship to the actors (e.g., cultural producer or receiver, activists, or sympathizers). Therefore for Snow, collective action frames do not fulfill a solely interpretative function, but rather are "more agentic and contentious in the sense of calling for action that problematizes and challenges existing authoritative views and framings of reality" (Snow, 2004, p. 385).

Based on various analytic templates for the analysis of culture, sociologist R. H. Williams offers a five-pointed "star" scheme, where each point represents a different aspect to study culture:

1. the cultural object itself;
2. cultural producers;
3. culture consumers/receivers;
4. the institutional environment in which culture is produced and used; and
5. the cultural field or environment in which cultural objects are produced and received (Williams, 2004, p. 97).

According to Williams, sociologists usually examine the connections between any two, and sometimes three, of these points. In the framing notion, it is common to examine the connections between cultural producers (e.g., movement activists on the one hand, or social elites on the other), cultural receivers (e.g., bystander publics, potential sympathizers, or movement members), and the cultural object itself (usually a public claim made by a social movement). However, when considering culture in the analysis of collective action, it is both necessary and insightful to pay attention to the institutional, cultural, political, and social environments, in which such cultural objects are produced, used, communicated, perceived, and consumed, that is, in Williams words, to "de-center" the individual social movement on the level of analysis (Williams, 2004; Gamson, 2004). As the discussion in this chapter will show, social media can be considered as such a discursive environment. The following section of the chapter will deploy a culturalist approach for understanding the 2010s social justice protests in Israel and the role social media played in the protests.[11]

4.4 SOCIAL MEDIA AND THE CULTURAL CONTEXT OF SOCIAL JUSTICE PROTESTS IN ISRAEL

4.4.1 The Cheese That Makes You Feel at Home

It is a plausible assumption that the choice of cottage cheese as the (first) product to be boycotted as a sign of protest against the rising food prices, that is,

---

[11] This is by no means derecognition of structural, economic, or political factors and aspects that played a central role in these protests, but rather a shift in the analytical focus.

against living costs in general and the high prices of dairy products in particular, was neither coincidental nor arbitrary; neither was the cottage cheese becoming the symbol of the protest movement in mass media and the broad social discourse. In Israeli culture, cottage cheese is a very popular product and central component of many people's nutrition. Furthermore, Israeli agriculture, or rather, Israeli cows, being a worldwide record holder in the yearly production of milk per cow is a source of national pride in Israeli agriculture.[12]

Nevertheless, the source of identification with cottage cheese does not end at its popularity. As mentioned earlier, the biggest Israeli dairy products manufacturer, Tnuvah,[13] depicts a house on its cottage cheese packages. Tnuvah's cottage television commercial depicts a young man coming home—from the army? from the traditional trip abroad after finishing military service?—to his mother and being served bread with cottage cheese, a family dinner with the family's cat sitting at the table licking cottage cheese, a soldier eating cottage cheese while helicopters roam in the background, and kids playing near a tree house while building their own house out of cottage cups. At the same time, the Israeli classic *Bo Ha'Baita* (Hebrew for "come home") plays in the background, thus correlating with the marketing slogan "Cottage – a cheese with a home."

Following Tnuvah's cottage price increase to 8 NIS (approximately 2.35 USD), a picture of cottage cheese covered with the text "8 Shekel???" was posted on the newly created Facebook page. It was then followed by reworked pictures of Tnuvah's cottage package with a depiction of a luxury building titled "It's not a cottage, it's a penthouse" and a supplementary movement page titled *Israel Yekara Lanu* (which is double entender in Hebrew, meaning "Israel is dear to us" as well as "Israel is too expensive for us").

Considering these aspects, Facebook was not solely an effective tool, in terms of social media as information and communication technology, to disseminate the quite straightforward message that 8 NIS is too expensive for a basic product such as cottage cheese, or that the food prices are too high for the average consumer. Facebook was used, in terms of social media as media, to disseminate this message using an array of cultural, identity, "familial," social, and to a certain extent even nationalist aspects. By sharing pictures that carry meaningful cultural symbols of homely feelings, collectiveness, "israeliness," etc. on the one hand and contrasting them with statements that express the economic grievances of

---

[12] A fact that animal rights activists also deploy and counterframe, by arguing that Israeli agriculture is "worldwide record holder in cruelty against cows."

[13] Considering Tnuvah as an "Israeli" company should be done cautiously. Founded in 1926, for over 80 years Tnuvah was an agriculture cooperative owned by collective farms and agricultural communities (known as *Kibbuzim* and *Moshavim*), but in 2008 the cooperative converted to a private limited company (Ltd.) and was sold to the British Apax Partners Worldwide LLP. In 2014 the Chinese food corporation Bright Foods bought a controlling interest (56%) in Tnuvah from Apax and other shareholders (Apax Partners, 2008; Berman, 2014).

many persons and households on the other, the initial action has achieved an extremely successful framing of the movement's claims. Furthermore, the double meaning of movement's Facebook page title embodies this contrast in a dialectic manner and gets to the heart of the movement's message (as well as to the hearts of thousands of its supporters and sympathizers).

On a broader level, this comes to show that social media are also an environment, in which claims are created, communicated, and perceived in the form of cultural objects (pictures, videos, text, pages, events, and discourse), a fact that has implications for the deployment of social media in collective action. As a (virtual) media space, in which discourse takes place, social media are still embedded within the larger cultural and societal discourse, that is, in larger institutional and cultural environments, and the frames that individuals "bring with them" as they participate in discourse on social media platforms (e.g., cottage cheese and a conception of "israeliness").

On the other hand, social media consolidate a wide variety of communication techniques (as discussed in Chapter 2); have a partially particular repertoire (e.g., like, comment, favorite, share, tweet, retweet with social-media-specific meaning for these words); constitute spaces that are conceived as somewhat private, somewhat public, as well as a combination of the two; and have some unwritten rules of conduct and communication on social media as part of cyberspace (also known as Netiquette[14]).

Thus social media platforms are spaces in which the cultural meaning of symbols and claims derive from not only discourse and culture "outside" or "surrounding" these platforms, but also rather a space in which they are constructed, shaped, and interpreted. In turn, these constructs, meanings, and interpretations influence other cultural and institutional environments, as is the case with protests that start—and therefore, construct meanings, interpretations, and frames—on social media platforms and then spread to mass media, academia, and the political arena.

From the point of view of a culturalist or framing approach, it is reasonable, rather than ironic, as stated earlier in this chapter, that a housing protest followed the "Cottage Cheese Protest." For one, issues such as living costs were already mobilizing individuals and causing pressure on political and economic stakeholders and elites, that a state of shared awareness regarding these issues was emerging, or that the success of uprising in neighboring states were affecting the whole neighborhood.[15] Moreover, the different dimensions of individual and collective identity, meaning, values, and culture were being questioned

---

[14] Netiquette, network etiquette, or Internet etiquette refers to a set of social norms that emerge in, affect, and facilitate interaction over networks, especially over the Internet.
[15] That is to say, the momentum of the Arab Spring permanently changing the Middle East as well as the role attributed to social media in this change.

(cottage or penthouse, dear vs affordable, the price of "israeliness," etc.). The consequent next step was to acknowledge that this discrepancy does not end with food security or a "cheese with a home," but it applies to the security and affordability of one's own home, be it a cottage, a penthouse, or an urban 2.5 room apartment.

4.4.2 Tents, Sushi, and Social Justice

The social justice movement that followed the initial July 2011 tent action at the Habima Square and accompanied the tent encampment in Rothschild Boulevard proved to successfully deploy social media in various ways—coordination of events, communication of movement-relevant information, drawing the attention of mass media and politics, networking within and between supportive movements and organization, and so forth. Having said that, the activists also deployed social media very creatively in terms of using cultural objects and frames:

- One of the first cultural objects transferred into a movement-related claim that confronts a person (when facing the movement's social media presence) is the movement's official Facebook page's title *Bet Ze Ohel*. The phrase, which is translatable into "B means Tent," is a paraphrase of the known children's song *Alef Bet* by the famous Israeli poet and songwriter Naomi Shemer. The song's text, which is used to teach children the Hebrew alphabet, begins with "A means Tent, B means Home" (in Hebrew *Alef Ohel, Bet ze Bait*). By stating that "B means Tent" and relying on the observer's cultural frames to recall his or her childhood—or the song they sang to their own children—the movement framed the tent protest as a housing protest using the song's text as a cultural object.
- One of the protest's symbols, which was also the Facebook page's logo, depicts a yellow tent covered with the letter *Bet* (the second letter in the Hebrew alphabet) and the phrase *ze Ohel* (means "Tent") written in punctuated letters (used mainly in the early classes, before children are capable of reading and writing without punctuation, the Hebrew *Niqqud*), thus adding a visual dimension to the usage of the song's text as a cultural object and movement-related claim.
- Furthermore, the logo's design (the minimalist combination of yellow and black, the font, and the angular shapes used to symbolize a tent) were consistently used in further communication over the movement's social media presence, thus contributing to the "branding" of the movement and its claims. The movement's logo, its "branding," and the paraphrase of the *Alef Bet* song, pulled through various movement-related and/or local movements groups in their Facebook pages and events as well as in communication outside of social media platforms (e.g., signs displayed in demonstrations, leaflets, representation of mass media).

The movement also engaged in cultural exchange with protest movement around the world. To name a few examples: the adoption of repertoire from the Egyptian Arab Spring protests; forms of organization, communication, and discourse (general assemblies, inclusive discussion culture, etc.) in common with the Spanish 15-M movement; and the hand sign language that was frequently used by the movement originate from Madrid's Puerta del Sol (Grinberg, 2013).

Social media's role in this exchange and their impact on the Israeli movement are twofold. On the one hand, the slogans, pictures presenting the hand language, and the like were disseminated among others via social media platforms (especially Facebook); some norms of discussion were also practiced in online debates. On the other hand, social media eased and even enabled such exchange with activists and movement abroad.

The cultural context of the movement extends, of course, beyond the discursive environments of social media platforms. The tent encampments were very creative and culturally active, a fact that had a profound impact both on the dynamics within the movement and between related movements.[16] Furthermore, the tent encampments were places of cultural production of cultural objects such as protest slogans, which found their way to social media. Some of the best slogans (which were paraphrasing Hebrew children's songs or Theodor Herzl's saying "If you will, it is no legend") were even up for voting on Twitter (Yair, 2011).

The movement encampments embodied another aspect of "israeliness," as political economist and sociologist Lev Luis Grinberg notes:

> While the Rothschild Boulevard encampment and the leaders of the movement were characterized as middle-class students of European descent, other encampments in other parts of the city and in peripheral areas of Israel were more representative of the Israeli class structure, including homeless families. Several encampments were also organized by Arab citizens in their neighborhoods and towns, and one in downtown Tel Aviv was populated by migrant workers. No encampment was erected in the OPT [Occupied Palestinian Territories] by either Jewish settlers or Palestinians: the protest movement clearly demarcated the borders of the Israeli sovereign state, but its leaders avoided any reference to the military occupation, the erasure of state borders, housing subsidies for Jewish settlers or house demolitions targeting Palestinians.
>
> **Grinberg (2013, p. 500)**

---

[16] Yehuda Shenhav refers to the protests' atmosphere as carnival. This attribution addresses not only the protests' and encampments' cultural characteristics, but also their apolitical attitude and the inclusive, egalitarian atmosphere. See (Shenhav, 2012).

From a culturalist point of view, and although they extend beyond the topic of this book, these aspects are a fascinating and important approach for analyzing the movement and its development.

Considering the public discourse regarding the protests and in terms of Snow's collective action frames, referring to the movement as a "Facebook protest" is an act of framing as well. Even if not always meant as deliberate counterframing, situating the protests within a "Facebook frame" not only reduces the movement, even more importantly, the movement's participants and their claims, to a limited space (Facebook), that is to say, reducing the frame to Facebook, so that everything outside of Facebook, implying Israeli individual's "real" everyday lives, is "out of frame." The "Facebook frame" is an articulation mechanism as well, promoting the meaning that the Facebook element, that is, the tool element, rather than the actual grievances and movement claims, is the central issue. In the transformative sense, the "Facebook frame" is not transforming grievances into mobilization, but rather the tool into demobilization, under the motto "it's just a Facebook thing." The terminology of "Facebook protests" was used often and without the necessary reflection, also by supportive media and movement adherents, a fact that relates to the stage of discourse surrounding social media's role in collective action. In terms of the Hype Cycle discourse and as mentioned in the Introduction, in 2011 the discourse was still at the Peak of Inflated Expectations and, as discussed in the previous chapter, some of these expectations were a result of the events of the Arab Spring; Tahrir Square being approximately 500 km—and a tweet—away from the Habima Square.

On the other hand, some of the movement opponents actively deployed counterframing strategies. For example, the Deputy Prime Minister and Minister of Foreign Affairs Avigdor Lieberman addressed the movement and its activists as "Sushi eaters" and "coffee shop protest." Thus he was framing them as spoiled middle-class and disconnected metropolitans,[17] or right-wing politicians and movements accusing the movement and activist in "striving communism," a term that has strong meaning for several hundred thousand Israeli citizens who migrated to Israel from countries of the former Union of Soviet Socialist Republics (USSR). Berlin, the place where the USSR began to end, is also a place with special cultural meanings for the 2010s Israeli social justice protests, as the following section will discuss.

4.4.3 Chocolate Pudding and the Phenomenon of Israelis in Berlin

Similar to the symbolic meaning of cottage cheese as a subject of activism or a cultural object used to articulate movement-related claims, explicitly addressing

---

[17] In certain parts in Israeli society, Tel Aviv is regarded as a disconnected city, a bubble, or even a "Tel Aviv State" (*Medinat Tel-Aviv*). A frame that Lieberman was probably referring to in his statements.

the chocolate pudding equivalent to the Israeli product Milky was neither coincidental nor arbitrary. The Israeli, who immigrated to Berlin and posted the picture of the grocery store invoice, explicitly addressed Milky of all products listed on the invoice as a product that Israelis abroad especially miss, thus constructing the product's, and hence, the movement's, symbol, "israeliness."

Similar to the other movements discussed in this chapter, the Facebook group's title *Olim Le'Berlin* correlates with frames, which are deeply anchored in Israeli culture and society. The phrase, Hebrew for "migrating to Berlin," did not deploy the relatively neutral Hebrew verb for migrating, but rather the term *Aliyah*, which has a deeper meaning in Hebrew as well as in Jewish (and hence to a certain extent Israeli) culture. Aliyah, literally meaning "going up," refers to the act of Jewish people migrating from diaspora to the land of Israel and progressing toward Jerusalem (which is located on top of a mountain), thus also preforming an act of spiritual ascent. By reverting the phrase in the meaning of progressing, even ascending, toward Berlin, the city is presented as the new place and subject of yearning for young Israelis, although migrating from Israel to Berlin would actually mean *Yerida*, that is, the leaving of Israel "downward" toward diaspora.

Furthermore, Berlin is a symbolic, rather than neutral, place in Israeli discourse for two reasons. First, one cannot ignore the role of Berlin in Nazi-Germany, World War II, and the Holocaust, all of which are constitutive and traumatic in Israeli and Jewish collective identity, memory, and history. Second and somewhat contrary, in the years prior to the "Milky Protest," Berlin, rather than Germany, became a popular destination of young Israelis who seek for life abroad. Berlin, beyond evolving to a cosmopolitan city and a center of political power in the European Union, was considered a cheap city to live in, especially in comparison with rent and food prices in Israeli cities. Thus in the period between the years 2011 and 2014, a wide public discourse regarding Berlin as a cheap and attractive city evolved in Israeli society and media, nurturing the aspiration of young Israelis to migrate to Berlin, a phenomenon that was highly controversial in Israeli society.

Interestingly, all of these aspects, the chocolate pudding as well as Berlin, were also used in the counterframing strategies that were deployed by many politicians such as the Minister of Finance Yair Lapid and members of the right-wing Likud Party. The notion of migrating (in terms of *Yerida*) to "that city" (Berlin in its historical meaning) just for a cheap portion of Milky was framed as an act of betrayal, as anything but "israeliness," even as "anti or post Zionist," thus situating the issues of social justice and living costs "out of frame," and framing the discourse as a national, even nationalist, one.

In contrast, the German reception and interpretation of the protest makes the case about the importance of (collective action) frames and understanding of cultural symbols and meanings for movement-related mobilization. As several German news outlets such as *Spiegel Online*[18] reported about the furor caused by the chocolate pudding Facebook post, there were more raised eyebrows than noddings—move to Berlin because of a chocolate pudding? Because of a Facebook post?

Even for German individuals who were aware of the social justice protests several years beforehand and who rationally understood that the people were protesting for issues such as social justice and affordable food prices, the symbolic—the Facebook, Milky, Aliyah versus Yerida, and certain aspects of the Berlin frames—were incomprehensible.

4.5 A CODE OF ISRAELINESS? CONCLUSIONS

For the Israeli sociologist and anthropologist Gad Yair (2011), the social justice protests in 2011 were culturally characterized in a significant way by what he defines as the Code of Israeliness, which contains Ten Commandments.[19] According to Yair, 6–7 of these 10 commandments, which are deeply entwined in Israeli culture, were contributing factors in the protest's motives, patterns, and discourse as well as reactions to it; in other words, the protests were, in their unique way, very much "Israeli." For example:

- The protests were deploying the rhetoric of not being "freier," a term that stems from Yiddish and is used in Hebrew slang to describe a person who lets others take advantage of him or her, to voice their grievances. Not being a "freier" is a key motif in Israeli cultural experience, which is, according to Yair, the fifth commandment in the "Code of Israeliness." As soon as the protest movement was using the rhetoric of not being a "freier," the latter was acting as a "cultural magnet" for other groups in society, which are, of course, no "freier" (Yair, 2011). Social media, in turn, proved to be an effective medium for expressing such culturally laden rhetoric.
- To name a yet different example, the Israeli affection for leaving no matter uncommented—Yair's sixth commandment—not only was visible in the course of the protests, but also enjoyed an optimal support by social media as well as social media functions on news websites such as commenting news articles. Such commenting functions are referred to—how appropriate—as "talkbacks" in Hebrew.

---

[18] www.spiegel.de/politik/ausland/israel-und-berlin-auf-facebook-starten-pudding-proteste-a-996337. html.

[19] The book's title can be translated as follows: "The Code of Israeliness: The Ten Commandments for the 21st Century."

Whether one examines the Israeli 2010s social justice protests through the lens of a "Code of Israeliness" or any other cultural lens, it is obvious that the protests were characterized and shaped by Israeli culture on various levels, and the deployment of social media has made their contribution to this aspect as well. The chapter focused on the movements and/or protests' cultural context in general and the relevance of social media in this context in particular. That is, how social media fit in collective action frames and framing processes; their impact on and relation to the cultural producers, consumers, and objects[20]; and the distinction of social media as discursive and cultural environments.

From a culturalist point of view, there is a cultural thread that connects the central movements in the 2010s Israeli social justice protests. In terms of the NSM that was discussed earlier in this chapter, they can even be seen as conditioning and presupposing each other, promoting shared awareness, discourses, symbols, and agencies that are connected beyond the traditional view of material interests and economic distribution (which certainly did play a crucial role in the movements as well).

Having said that and since this chapter did not aim to offer a general analysis of the protests (which can be done using various theoretical frameworks beyond the cultural ones), many aspects and questions regarding the protests did not find a place in the chapter. To name a few aspects:

- the complex relation between the deployment of social media (Facebook) and the role of traditional or mass media in the protests[21];
- which—geopolitical, spatial, momentum, cultural—aspects connect between the protests and the adjacent events of the Arab Spring[22];
- the relative disappointing results of the protests, both in the (lacking) impact food and housing costs as well as the inability to promote social and political change[23];

---

[20] Or in Marshall MacLuhan's words, "the Medium is the message" (McLuhan, 1994).

[21] See Lev-On (2015) for a discussion on the topic.

[22] Lev Luis Grinberg argues that the movement successfully deployed what he terms as mo(ve)ment—the intersection of the movement and moment of mass mobilization. According to Grinberg, the movement's timeframe was not dictated by the academic calendar (academic and school vacations) but by the Palestinian one: 2011 was a quiet (warless) summer and the Palestinian issue was not pressing in public debate and the movement's end (dismantling of the Rothschild tent encampment) was on September 7, a few days before the United Nations discussion of the resolution to recognize a Palestinian state. Furthermore, Grinberg suggests considering the protests as part of a greater wave of protests around the world and especially influenced by the events in Egypt, which fueled strong emotions in the Israeli media and public, as well as the Spanish 15-M movement. See (Grinberg, 2013).

[23] Left-wing and/or socialist parties did not manage to protest and social justice discourse into parliamentary majorities. On the other hand, the newly founded "centrist" party *Yesh Atid* successfully leveraged the protests' momentum and was elected based on the campaign motto "Where is the money?"; in office, the party's chairman and Minister of Finance continued the neoliberal political agenda led by the Prime Minister Benjamin Netanyahu and *Likud* Party.

- this, although it contributed a great deal to the discussed social justice protests;
- or the stress ratio between the conception of Israel as a "Start-up Nation" and an economic miracle due to its high-tech industry (Senor and Singer, 2009) (which is a frame in itself), the discrepancy between this notion and the personal experience of many Israelis that the economic miracle did not affect their lives, and the protesters' deployment of technologies such as Facebook and smartphones.

Analyzing the cultural context of collective action, with and without regard to social media, requires a deep insight into the cultural and discursive conditions surrounding the social movement, society in which the events takes place, meanings of cultural symbols, etc. On a personal note, being born and raised in Israel and living in Berlin, Germany, in the years prior and during the events described in this chapter, the chapter was not only an analysis, but also an attempt to translate these cultural and discursive aspects for the reader. A translation that is crucial to convey an understanding of how cultural symbols—be it cottage cheese, a fleeting notion of "israeliness," children songs, tents, or chocolate pudding—can bring 400,000 people to take their grievances to the streets.

References

Apax Partners, 2008. Consortium Comprising Funds Advised by Apax Partners & Mivtach Shamir Acquires Tnuva for $1.025 Billion. Retrieved from: www.apax.com/news/apax-news/2008/january/consortium-comprising-funds-advised-by-apax-partners-amp-mivtach-shamir-acquires-tnuva-for-$1025-billion/.

Benford, R.D., Snow, D.A., 2000. Framing processes and social movements: an overview and assessment. Annual Review of Sociology 26, 611–639.

Berman, L., 2014. Chinese State Company Buys Controlling Stake in Tnuva. Times of Israel. Retrieved from: www.timesofisrael.com/chinese-state-company-buys-controlling-stake-in-tnuva/.

Central Bureau of Statistics (Israel), 2015. Population & Demography. Retrieved from: cbs.gov.il/reader/?MIval=cw_usr_view_SHTML&ID=705.

ComScore, 2011. It's a Social World: Top 10 Need-to-Knows about Social Networking and Where It's Headed. Retrieved from: www.comscore.com/it_is_a_social_world.

Gamson, W.A., 2004. Bystanders, public opinion, and the media. In: Snow, D.A., Soule, S.A., Kriesi, H. (Eds.), The Blackwell Companion to Social Movements. Blackwell Publishing Ltd, Malden, pp. 242–261.

Goffman, E., 1974. Frame Analysis. Harper Colphon, New York.

Goffman, E., 1986. Frame Analysis: An Essay on the Organization of Experience. Northeastern University Press, Boston.

Gerbaudo, P., 2012. Tweets and the Streets: Social Media and Contemporary Activism. Pluto Press, London.

Grinberg, L.L., 2013. The J14 resistance mo(ve)ment: the Israeli mix of Tahrir Square and Puerta del Sol. Current Sociology 61 (4), 491–509.

Johnston, H., 2002. Verification and proof in frame and discourse analysis. In: Klandermans, B., Staggenborg, S. (Eds.), Methods of Social Movements Research. University of Minnesota Press, Minneapolis, pp. 62–69.

Lev-On, A., 2015. New Media and Activism: The Social Protest 2011 as a Case Study. Israel Internet Association. Retrieved from: www.isoc.org.il/magazine/magazine15_2.html.

McLuhan, M., 1994. Understanding Media: The Extensions of Man. MIT Press, Cambridge.

Senor, D., Singer, S., 2009. Start-up Nation: The Story of Israel's Economic Miracle. Twelve, New York.

Shenhav, Y., 2012. Carnival: Protest Without a Sting. HaOkets. Retrieved from: www.haokets.org/2012/02/20/%D7%94%D7%A7%D7%A8%D7%A0%D7%91%D7%9C-%D7%9E%D7%97%D7%90%D7%94-%D7%9C%D7%9C%D7%90-%D7%A2%D7%95%D7%A7%D7%A5/.

Snow, D.A., 2004. Framing processes, ideology and discursive fields. In: Snow, D.A., Soule, S.A., Kriesi, H. (Eds.), The Blackwell Companion to Social Movements. Blackwell Publishing Ltd, Malden, MA, pp. 380–412.

Trajtenberg Committee, 2011. Recommendations of the Trajtenberg Committee. Retrieved from: http://hidavrut.gov.il.

Williams, R.H., 2004. The cultural context of collective action: constraints, opportunities, and the symbolic life of social movements. In: Snow, D.A., Soule, S.A., Kriesi, H. (Eds.), The Blackwell Companion to Social Movements. Blackwell Publishing Ltd, Malden, MA, pp. 91–115.

Yair, G., 2011. The Code of Israeliness: The Ten Commandments for the 21st Century. Keter, Jerusalem.

Ynet News, 2011. Masses Show up for Biggest Protest in Israel's History. Retrieved from: www.ynetnews.com/articles/0, 7340,L-4117312,00.html.

CHAPTER 5

The Social Network: The Relevance of Weak and Strong Ties for Mobilization Over Social Media

ABSTRACT

The interplay between social networks, weak and strong ties, and social media in the context of collective action is a subject of controversial academic debate, especially in light of the wave of protests and related discourse around 2011. Some scholars and activists tend to stress the importance of weak ties, which mobilization through social media seems to amplify, whereas others take a critical stance toward this notion and stress the importance of strong ties. The chapter addresses this issue, while differentiating the qualities, advantages, and disadvantages of both notions.

Keywords: Leaderless networks; Small worlds; Social media; Social network theory; Social networks; Strong ties; Weak ties.

CONTENTS

The interplay between social networks—in the sociological sense of the word, rather than synonymous with social media platforms—in the context of collective action, especially regarding the relevance of weak ties in comparison with strong ties, is a subject of controversial academic debate, particularly concerning social media and in light of the wave of protests and related discourse around 2011.[1] Some scholars and activists tend to stress the importance of

---

[1] See, for example, Gladwell (2010), Keen (2015), Morozov (2013), Shirky (2008).

Collective Action 2.0. http://dx.doi.org/10.1016/B978-0-08-100567-5.00005-0

weak ties, which seem to amplify mobilization through social media, whereas others take a critical stance toward this notion and stress the importance of strong ties.

Consider the case study from the previous chapter—the Israeli housing protests in the summer of 2011. At first glance, it seems that social media, especially Facebook, enabled a broad mobilization within a short period of time by making so-called weak ties more significant by disseminating the information through such ties in the form of Facebook connections—Facebook "friends"—addressing their common grievances (growing housing/rent prices) and encouraging them to participate. This was also reinforced by mass media, which started reporting about the tent encampment even before the first tent was set up.[2]

When having a deeper look into the emergence of the tent action, the picture becomes more complex: about half of the movement's leaders were friends prior to the tent encampment and protests, some other members of the movement's leadership got to know Leef and her friends through social media as they suffered from similar problems and looked for people to join forces with. Afterward and prior to the tent action, the group met in Leef's apartment and planned their actions and protest strategies (Lev-On, 2015). Furthermore, joining forces with other movements and organizations such as the National Student Federation, the *Dror-Israel* youth movement affiliated with the *Histadrut* trade union, *Koach Laovdim* trade union, the New Israel Fund, and the already striking medical interns was crucial both for the mobilization and maintenance of the movement's momentum (Grinberg, 2013). The connections or ties between members within each of these groups are surely diverse, but they are anything but "weak."

The concepts of Social Networks and Interpersonal Ties are central for the study of collective action and social movement as well as, of course, understanding the role of social media in them.

5.1 WHAT ARE SOCIAL NETWORKS?

As individuals in society, we are all members in different groups, in different social milieus. Socioeconomical class, religion, nationality, gender, age, profession, etc. are not only such milieus, but also factors that constitute a person's identity, which is in turn enacted in different ways such as his or her habitus (Bourdieu, 1993). Different interfaces and institutions in

---

[2] Due to the mobilization of several thousand participators on the protest's Facebook event, the TV show *Zinor Layla* ("Night Pipe"), which reports about issues and trends on the Internet, broadcasted an item on the protest before the tents were set up. See (Lev-On, 2015; Zinor Layla, 2012).

these group affiliations link individuals with each other, thus constructing social networks.[3] All members of a social milieu (a religion, for example) do not necessarily create a social network, but members of an institution related to this group possibly do (e.g., a mosque, church, synagogue, or a religious or spiritual community in a small town, whose members meet on a more or less regular basis). Also, social institutions in their abstract sense, such as friend circles, coworkers, family, Facebook friends, or Twitter followers, are types of social networks. Just as a person's habitus is a mélange of social dispositions such as taste, aesthetic, and norms constructed by the person's various social milieu affiliations (Villa, 2008), a person's identity can be seen as a mélange not only of his or her group affiliation but also of his or her social network affiliations (and, of course, a variety of further factors).

When zooming out to the group level, it is not only the group members' identities that are defined among others by their group membership, but also the group's identity that is defined by the identities of its members. Furthermore, multiple memberships serve as channels for circulation of information, resources, and expertise among groups—in this case, social movements (Diani, 2004). As Mario Diani, who significantly contributed to social network approaches to the study of social movements, points out, collective action can be associated with "CATNETs, that is, with the co-presence in a given population of cat(egorical traits) and net(works). While the former provided the criteria on the basis of which recognition and identity-building would take place, the latter constituted the actual channels of communication and exchange which enabled the mobilization of resources and the emergence of collective actors" (Diani, 2004, p. 341).

The Social Network Theory regards social relationships or connections in terms of ties and nodes, the former representing the relationships and/or connections and the latter representing the individual actors. To better understand this conception of social network, we need to examine the ties that constitute such networks—interpersonal ties.

5.1.1 Interpersonal Ties

The notion of Interpersonal Ties has shown to be instructive in the study of collective action in general and the role of social media in particular, but not without controversy. The concepts of weak and strong ties as forms of interpersonal ties go back to the 1973 work of the sociologist Mark Granovetter *The Strength of Weak Ties* (Granovetter, 1973, 1983).

---

[3] The term social network is used here in its sociological meaning, rather than a synonym for a social media platform.

Interpersonal ties are theorized as information-carrying connections between individuals and are divided into three categories: strong, weak, or absent ties. A tie's "strength" is a function of various factors (such as time, emotions, intimacy, trust, and the tie's reciprocal components) as well as their combination. According to Granovetter, "[w]eak ties provide people with access to information and resources beyond those available in their own social circle; but strong ties have greater motivation to be of assistance and are typically more easily available" (Granovetter, 1973, p. 209).

That is to say, by constituting (information-carrying and interpersonal) connections between social networks with strong ties, weak ties are responsible for the majority of information that is transmitted between such networks. Thus, weak ties are crucial both for the embeddedness of social networks and for the flow of new information to individuals and social networks. On the other hand, strong ties such as close family, friends, colleagues, or fellow activists move in similar circles and have various sets of characteristics such as socialization, profession, belief, gender identity, and socioeconomic status in common. Therefore information, knowledge, experience and opinions are considerably overlapping and redundant between such ties, whereas novel information or different and contrasting opinions reach individuals (and groups) through weak ties rather than strong ones. In contrast to strong and weak ties, absent ties describe ties that lack substantial significance and where interaction is rather negligible. In other words, purely the fact that two individuals know each other does not yet qualify for a weak tie; let alone a strong one (Granovetter, 1973, 1983).

One can draw two central conclusions, or rather hypotheses, from the differentiation between weak and strong ties. The weak tie hypothesis argues that lack of weak ties causes deprivation of information from other social networks (or from distant parts of a specific social network) due to lack of information-carrying bridging ties. This means that individuals will be confined to a rather narrow variety of information, such as mainstream and/or local media and news, views and opinions of close friends, family, and colleagues.

The strong tie hypothesis, formulated by David Krackhardt (1992), stresses the importance of strong ties in cases of severe change and uncertainty: "People resist change and are uncomfortable with uncertainty. Strong ties constitute a base of trust that can reduce resistance and provide comfort in the face of uncertainty. Thus it will be argued that change is not facilitated by weak ties, but rather by a particular type of strong tie" (Krackhardt, 1992, p. 218). Krackhardt termed this particular type of strong tie as *philo* and defined the relationship *"philos"* as one that combines three necessary conditions: interaction, affection, and time. That is, for A and B to be philos, (1) they must interact with each other, (2) A must feel affection for B, and (3) they must have a history of interactions that have lasted over an extended period of time.

According to Krackhardt, a combination of these conditions or qualities of the relationship predicts trust, which is required in cases of changing status quo and related uncertainty.

Clay Shirky also uses the model of Small Worlds, which was introduced in the 1990s by the sociologist Duncan Watts and mathematician Steven Henry Strogatz, to analyze social movements (Shirky, 2008; Watts, 1999). Small world networks have two characteristics that, when balanced properly, support the circulation of information and resources[4]:

- First, small groups are densely connected. That is, the ties between members are stronger and the communication pattern within the group is that everyone is connected with virtually everyone.
- Second, large groups are sparsely connected. As groups become larger, keeping high density as in small groups becomes impractical.

Therefore, and this is the difference to the general discussion of weak and strong ties, a model of densely connected smaller groups, sparsely connected between them becomes, according to Shirky, more reasonable to foster communication and resource circulation. In this model, the multiple memberships of individuals in different small groups serve as a link between those groups. Shirky argues further, that social media are "Small Worlds networks," that is to say, tools that support these kinds of social groupings (Shirky, 2008).

In conclusion, social networks and interpersonal ties are relevant for the mobilization of movement members along the movement lifecycle, from the recruitment phase, to discouragement of leaving the movement, to support further participation in the particular and further, related movements. The strength and quality of ties and not their quantity seem to have more influence on mobilization of individuals. Smaller or denser social networks, which have a small number of strong ties, are more probable to result in mobilization as a whole, which is referred to as *Bloc Recruitment* (Diani, 2004; Gladwell, 2010). Having said that, there are aspects of mobilization that also occur outside of social networks (that are characterized by strong ties), or that do not occur despite the existence of such networks. On the other hand, weak ties tend to bridge and connect between individuals and groups, that is, between social networks characterized by high density of strong ties. Thus, weak ties (that bridge between dense social networks) also support bloc recruitment (see the above-mentioned example of the Israeli housing protest), support the dissemination of information between individuals and groups, and contribute to the introduction of novel information, experiences, and opinions into discourses.

---

[4] See Chapter 6 for discussion of the Resource Mobilization Theory.

5.2 SOCIAL MEDIA AND SOCIAL NETWORKS

From the social network theory point of view, social media [as information and communication technology (ICT) and as media] are a fascinating phenomenon. On social media platforms, individuals can construct virtual representations of their social networks with all different kinds of ties—strong, weak, and even absent—extend these networks, and operate as information-carrying and disseminating ties.

It is undeniable that social media platforms make weak ties more relevant. On such platforms, it is very easy to build weak ties—contacts, "friends," or "followers"—and fulfill the function of an information-carrying tie. Strong ties, of course, find their place on social media platforms as well—close friends, family, lovers, or fellow activists who extend their offline relationships through communication, display of affection, and joint activities over social media.[5] Furthermore, social media outline users' social networks and point out connections between different social networks [e.g., through shared contacts, mutual group memberships, revealing with whom one's own network is connected, that is, friend of a friend (FOAF), or by making communication within and between networks more visible]. In some cases, connections between social networks that were previously unknown can be revealed with the help of the platform. In contrast, social media connections, with whom the communication (beyond merely being contacts, "friends," or "followers") is negligible or even nonexistent, are a clear case of absent ties. Due to the ease of adding connections of social media, such ties are not uncommon (but tend to go under because of the filter bubble).

In a sense, this is a dimension of the integrated roles[6] described by Fuchs and Trottier: "On social media like Facebook, we act in various roles, but all of these roles become mapped onto single profiles that are observed by different people who are associated with our different social roles" (Fuchs and Trottier, 2014, p. 15). What follows the integrated roles in social media (as ICT and as media), is integrated and converging communication, which describes how different forms of communication that are traditionally related to certain roles, integrate and converge in the communication over and/or within the same social space, that is, within a social media platform (Fuchs and Trottier, 2014).

---

[5] It is important to stress that strong ties extend their relationship, their philos, using social media platforms. Since the formation, existence, and maintenance of such ties requires qualities that are very hard to achieve using solely online communication over social media.

[6] A form of sociality, in which individuals act in different social roles within the same social space.

On the surface, social media platforms do not offer much differentiation between weak and strong ties in their virtual representation on and within the platform. Regardless of whether the connections are colleagues, family, members of the same worker's union or political party, friends, or neighbors, a social media platform usually offers one type of connection—a "friend," a "follower"—one type of connection that does not yet represent the tie's strength and quality. However, social media platforms do discriminate between ties. A tie's strength or relevance is algorithmically calculated on the basis of various factors such as mutual friends, mutual group memberships, time spent on each other's content, the intensity of communication, its nature, and even its emotional tone. What the exact factors are as well as their quantity and combination are usually part of the social media corporation's—that is, social media as institution—trade secret. This is also the basis for the phenomenon and practice of filter bubble,[7] which in turn means not only that social networks are only projected into the platforms, but also that social media actively interfere and affect the strength and relevance of ties within the platforms, this mostly due and according to the institution's economic interests.

As a result, a correlation between a tie's strength within and without the social media platform does not necessarily exist. To name a few, somewhat contrasting examples:

- acquaintances who often like and share each other's content on social media (algorithmically a strong tie) but rarely communicate outside the platform (weak, perhaps absent tie), or
- by contrast, children who limit their parent's (strong tie) access to their Facebook's content (thus "degrading" the social media tie to a weak, even absent one).

Furthermore, different social media platforms are dedicated to different purposes of interpersonal communication, although the de facto usage by individuals does not always adhere to these purposes (as the concept of integrated roles argue). For example:

- LinkedIn and Xing are mostly professional, career-related platforms;
- Facebook, Vkontakte, and Renren concentrate on friends and family; whereas
- Google Plus's core feature Circles enables users to sort connections into groups that represent different types of social networks (e.g., colleagues, family, close friends).

---

[7] See Pariser (2011) as well as Chapter 2 of this book.

5.3 SOCIAL NETWORKS, INTERPERSONAL TIES, AND MOBILIZATION OVER SOCIAL MEDIA

Coming back to the subject of collective action, by making weak ties more relevant, social media (as ICT and as media) support the dissemination of movement or action-related information as well as help establishing new, at first weak ties between movements, groups, and individuals (that is, bridging between social networks). Thus social media and the social networks that are projected onto them not only help to "spread the word" but also, in some cases, support the process of individual mobilization and/or bloc recruitment.

Malcolm Gladwell voices an accurate criticism of overemphasizing social media's ability to make weak ties relevant—so relevant that they facilitate revolutions (e.g., exaggerating Twitter's role in the Arab Spring)—a criticism that is strikingly similar to the strong ties hypothesis. Gladwell stresses the importance of strong ties, which are nurtured outside of social media platforms and require more than just a few clicks to emerge, for the organization of and mobilization for collective action, especially for collective action that may contain high risk and/or personal consequences (Gladwell, 2010). The discussion in Chapter 3 uses the example of mobilization during the events of the Arab Spring to show how, among other things, social media support mobilization by making sympathy for, support of, and participation in movement or instances of collective action visible among the participants' social networks. Due to the high levels of instability and uncertainty as well as danger of personal consequences, such mobilization is not likely to succeed on such scale solely over weak ties that lack sufficient quantities and qualities of trust, emotional bonds, time, etc. However, mobilization over social media has the advantage that due to the parallel membership in various networks with a density of strong ties, various small worlds, there is a multiplication of the strong ties, over which a person or a group can be mobilized.

Furthermore, the networking over social media is no substitute for interpersonal networking outside social media (that is, building and maintaining social networks in nonvirtual, on-site environments), but rather extends, supports, and supplements it. This was visible in the occupation of public spaces in the various protests of 2010–2 (e.g., Tahrir Square, Rothschild Boulevard, Occupy Wall Street, Puerta del Sol), which were also known for their effective deployment of social media (Benski et al., 2013). Kneuer and Richter refer to the protest movements of 2011 as "hybrid phenomena" (Kneuer and Richter, 2015). As "hybrid phenomena," the protest movements extend their impact by being present on both spaces—tent encampments, demonstrations, and the streets on the one hand and virtual spaces (social media) on the other. According to Kneuer and Richter's study, the physical meeting spaces were crucial for in-depth discourses, whereas the usage of social media concentrated mainly on organizational aspects[8] and dissemination of information, on which interested individuals can follow up. In other words, spaces of face-to-face discourse and shoulder-to-shoulder activism were crucial, among other things, for building and maintaining the strong ties the movements needed. Social media discourses, on the other hand, exploited the advantages of weak ties and involved organizational aspects as well as dissemination of general information and references to in-depth movement-related discourses, and also to express and awake emotions.

Having said that, these were examples of rather exceptional instances of collective action—a political revolution and a nationwide social protest. For some instances of collective action, for some causes and levels of involvement, the mobilization over weak ties in general and over social media in particular may be sufficient. For example:

- mobilization for signing petitions,
- contacting local representatives on legislative issues,
- organization of a small or middle-scale boycott,
- help acquaintances (or FOAF) find a job or an apartment to rent,
- retrieve lost personal belongings, or
- the mere dissemination of information (e.g., regarding a lost person) for it to reach someone who can help in the particular case.

This makes weak ties as well as their realization and multiplication over social media relevant and even crucial for the success of such actions.

5.4 A LEADERLESS NETWORK?

A further notion, brought forth by discussions regarding social networks and their role in the deployment of social media in collective action, claims that some kind "leaderless networks" emerge in course of such deployment. That is to say, networks of individuals, groups, and masses, whose actions are generally uncoordinated but either they are able to coordinate themselves using solely the social media platform(s) or the platform is considered having the metaphysical ability to rid the masses of such organizational and coordination tasks. This and similar notions are supported, at least to a certain extent, not only by scholars such as Manuel Castells, Michael Hardt, Jeffrey Juris, Antonio Negri, and Clay Shirky, but also by activists in the various social and protest movements of the years 2010–2.

---

[8] The following chapter will discuss aspects of organization in terms of the resource mobilization theory.

The findings in Paolo Gerbaudo (2012) study of these social movements contrast this—somewhat technocentrist and metaphysical—notion. Gerbaudo claims that the movements had "soft leaders," a relatively small group of highly active and highly connected activists, which had a substantive amount of control on the flows of information over social media platforms (which were uncontestedly an important tool of organization and coordination), thus "constructing a *choreography of assembly*" (Gerbaudo, 2012, p. 139). According to Gerbaudo, the key Twitter tactical accounts of the Occupy Wall Street movement were managed by a core group of central movement activists and organizers, a group that also tended to be highly involved in onsite actions, general assemblies, and different commissions. These findings show striking similarities to the nonofficial leadership of the Israeli 2010 housing protests and its Facebook pages as well as to the Egyptian "We Are All Khaled Said" page during the events of the Arab Spring, which were discussed in Chapters 3 and 4.

Such control is not executed institutionally (e.g., by the social media corporation that operates the platform), but rather by the unequal distribution of social capital in social media. Social capital emerges where certain agents'—individuals or clearly distinguished groups—location in the network grants them with advantages and benefits, which are reserved from other members (and, of course, nonmembers) of the network. In social media, unequal distribution of social capital, which means unequal distribution of power, is embodied through locations in the networks that exist within the platform (number of "followers" or "likes," linking and referencing, content reach, attention, popularity, etc.) as well as through access to such centers of power in the network (official Twitter account or Facebook page).

Gerbaudo uses the term *choreography of assembly* to describe "a process of symbolic construction of public space, which revolves around an emotional 'scene-setting' and 'scripting' of participants' physical assembling. This practice is made visible in the use of social media in directing people towards specific protest events, in providing participants with suggestions and instructions about how to act, and in the construction of an emotional narration to sustain their coming together in public space" (Gerbaudo, 2012, p. 12). In other words, the term choreography comes to suggest two key insights:

- First, that actions such as protests, setting up tent encampments, sit-ins, etc. (which Gerbaudo addresses as the "reconstruction of public space") are not completely spontaneous and/or improvised.
- Second, that "despite their repeated claims to leaderlessness, contemporary social movements do have their own 'choreographers' and these choreographers are not identical with the 'dancers' or participants" (Gerbaudo, 2012, p. 159), but rather they are soft leaders, who "are for the most not visible on the stage or at least do not take center-stage as it were" (Gerbaudo, 2012, p. 159).

The ethical problem of the tension between the notion of leaderless networks, which were often propagated also by the activists themselves, and the existence of "soft leaders" or "choreographers" is the categorical denial of the existence of movement leaders (rather than their existence as such). As a result, unaccountability and lack of responsibility become common among movement leaders.

As Gerbaudo stresses, "the process of mobilisation always involves inequalities and asymmetries in which there are people who mobilise and people who are mobilised, people who lead and people who follow, and the two categories only ever partly overlap" (Gerbaudo, 2012, p. 165). Such inequalities, which are embedded in social structures and power relations in society, also operate on social media platforms. Those who are more connected than others—have more "friends" or "followers"—control centers of power—official movements page or Twitter account—and enjoy a higher level of trust—by being a public figure, a journalist, or an acknowledged movement activist—tend to have more impact than others, impact that is not purely horizontal, but also vertical.

There is an important conclusion we should draw from the tension between the belief in "self-organizing masses" on the one hand and Gerbaudo's findings on the other. Although the deployment of social media in collective action tends to strengthen the relevance of weak ties, contributes to the dissemination of information, influences the individuals' emotional involvement, and can make social networks more robust, this deployment neither generates social networks that are completely horizontal and/or movements with equality of involvement and influence nor does it guarantee spontaneous emergence of collective action by such self-organizing, leaderless collectives. This conclusion complements the discussion of the role of weak and strong ties in two aspects:

- First, being in control of or close to such a position in the network—such a center of power—in the most cases requires belonging to a group characterized by strong ties within the group and which has a substantial amount of weak ties as outside connections.
- Second, the execution of such power—affecting the *choreography*—relies heavily on a wide network of weak ties as "amplifiers" and on connections to small networks with high density of strong ties, which contribute to aspects such as trust and reliability, as well.

References

Benski, T., Langman, L., Perugorría, I., Tejerina, B., 2013. From the streets and squares to social movement studies: what have we learned? Current Sociology 61 (4), 541–561.

Bourdieu, P., 1993. Sozialer Sinn-Kritik der theoretischen Vernunft. Suhrkamp, Frankfurt am Main.

Diani, M., 2004. Networks and participation. In: Snow, D.A., Soule, S.A., Kriesi, H. (Eds.), The Blackwell Companion to Social Movements. Blackwell Publishing Ltd, Malden, MA, pp. 339–359.

Fuchs, C., Trottier, D., 2014. Theorizing social media, politics, and the state. An introduction. In: Fuchs, C., Trottier, D. (Eds.), Social Media, Politics and the State: Protests, Revolutions, Riots, Crime and Policing in the Age of Facebook, Twitter and YouTube. Routledge, New York, pp. 3–38.

Gerbaudo, P., 2012. Tweets and the Streets: Social Media and Contemporary Activism. Pluto Press, London.

Gladwell, M., 2010. Small Change: Why the Revolution Will Not Be Tweeted. The New Yorker. Retrieved from: www.newyorker.com/magazine/2010/10/04/small-change-malcolm-gladwell.

Granovetter, M., 1973. The strength of weak ties. American Journal of Sociology 78 (6), 1360–1380.

Granovetter, M., 1983. The strength of the weak tie: revisited. Sociological Theory 1, 201–233.

Grinberg, L.L., 2013. The J14 resistance mo(ve)ment: the Israeli mix of Tahrir Square and Puerta del Sol. Current Sociology 61 (4), 491–509.

Keen, A., 2015. The Internet Is Not the Answer. Atlantic Monthly Press, New York.

Kneuer, M., Richter, S., 2015. Soziale Medien in Protestbewegungen: Neue Wege für Diskurs, Organisation und Empörung? Campus Verlag, Frankfurt.

Krackhardt, D., 1992. The strength of strong ties: the importance of philos in organizations. In: Nohria, N., Eccles, R. (Eds.), Networks and Organizations: Structure, Form, and Action. Harvard Business School Press, Boston, MA, pp. 216–239.

Lev-On, A., 2015. New Media and Activism: The Social Protest 2011 as a Case Study. Israel Internet Association. Retrieved from: www.isoc.org.il/magazine/magazine15_2.html.

Morozov, E., 2013. To Save Everything, Click Here: Technology, Solutionism, and the Urge to Fix Problems That Don't Exist. Allen Lane, London.

Pariser, E., 2011. The Filter Bubble. Penguin Books, London.

Shirky, C., 2008. Here Comes Everybody: The Power of Organizating without Organizations. Penguin Group, London.

Villa, P.-I., 2008. Körper. In: Baur, N. (Ed.), Handbuch Soziologie. VS Verlag für Sozialwissenschaften, Wiesbaden, pp. 201–217.

Watts, D.J., 1999. Small Worlds: The Dynamics of Networks between Order and Randomness. Princeton University Press, Princeton.

Zinor Layla, 2012. Net News: The Housing Struggles Takes to the Streets. Retrieved from: net.nana10.co.il/Article/?ArticleID=814260.

CHAPTER 6

Berlin Helps: Resource Mobilization and Social Media Deployment in Berlin's Refugee Aid Movement

ABSTRACT

In summer 2015, as the situation of refugees in Berlin tilted into a humanitarian crisis, the city's citizens organized to help and formed a heterogenic and effective refugee aid movement. These citizen's initiatives and individual volunteers relied, among other things, on social media platforms for their organization. In terms of the resource mobilization approach, which concentrates social movements' ability to acquire resources and mobilize them toward accomplishing the movement's goals, the Berlin refugee aid movement offers many examples and insight regarding the role social media deployment plays in collective action and social movements as well as how it affects the movements themselves.

Keywords: Refugee crisis; Refugees welcome; Resource mobilization; Resource mobilization theory; Social media.

CONTENTS

6.1 ONE HOT SUMMER DAY AT #LAGESO

For many people in Berlin, Friday, August 7, 2015, is a day that symbolizes a change that took place in the city for years to come. In the first week of August, a heat wave hit the city and reached 40°C on Friday. At that time, hundreds of refugees were waiting in front of Berlin's state office for health and social issues (*Landesamt für Gesundheit und Soziales*, or in short, LaGeSo), camping days and nights without sufficient supply of food, water, beds, or medical care in the center of one of the most powerful capitals in the European Union. On Thursday, a journalist and activist in the refugee aid organization *Moabit Hilft* (German for Moabit helps), which aided the refugees camping in front of the LaGeSo offices in the city district of Moabit, twittered: "#Refugees with children in front of #Lageso #Berlin. Tomorrow 40°C and only one water tap."[1] Help was soon to come, as citizens and businesses reacted to the call and delivered water and food donations. This was one of many successful moments of mobilization during that week, through social media as well as other means of mobilization. As the word spread and the issue received media attention in traditional/mass media, the whole city became aware to the situation, which until that moment was known mostly for the residents of Moabit and activists in refugee aid organizations.

The year 2015 will probably be most remembered in association with the massive wave of refugees from crisis regions across Africa, Asia, and the Middle East, who took up a dangerous journey toward Europe to live in safety and freedom, a situation that led to social and political tension within and between the states of the European Union. The situation in front of LaGeSo and the following events was the local implication of the worldwide and Europe-wide refugee crisis.

Besides the continuously acute situation in front of LaGeSo, the authorities faced challenges of providing growing numbers of refugees with accommodation, food, clothing, and medical care as well as attending their asylum requests. Where authorities failed to provide a dignified solution, citizens voluntarily organized to fill the void: collecting, sorting, handing out donations such as clothing; helping to build up accommodations; providing food as well as medical and sanitary items; acting as interpreters between state authorities and non-English/German-speaking refugees; and being there as moral support and human proximity for the refugees. In course of time, both before and after the situation at the LaGeSo offices became widely known, local refugee aid organizations in the city's districts were emerging and taking up the tasks and welcoming refugees in their neighborhoods as well as networking with counterpart organizations from other districts.

The mobilization and organization of many volunteer helpers, on different locations across the city, in midsummer, with very limited amount of reliable information from the authorities, overcoming massive language and cultural barriers, and without central organization point or organization structures is

---

[1] www.twitter.com/KPNiko/status/629235273767870464.

by all means a challenge. Furthermore, the issue at hand included transportation of goods across the city and organizing workforce for unpopular physical tasks in short notice. In other words, a substantial amount of different kinds of resources and their mobilization was required.

In contrast to organizations such as the German Red Cross or the social welfare organization of Germany's Protestant Churches (Diakonie Deutschland), which were also engaged in the refugee aid all across Germany, local citizens' initiatives lack the variety of organizational resources and experience that large institutions have at their disposal. Facing these challenges, volunteers and their organizations relied on social media and several other online platforms to overcome many barriers, which can be regarded as resource-related ones.

Facebook groups were used for communication between volunteers, sharing relevant information, exchanging experiences and "best practices," coordinating the collection of donations and shifts in accommodations, and serving as a space of personal exchange of experience, feeling, and moral support among activists. Since most of the citizens' initiatives and volunteers were operating on a "learn as you go" modus, such spaces of exchange and support—both online and on-site—were indispensable. However, at a certain point some Facebook groups (especially those of larger organizations) were overloaded with postings, making them rather confusing than constructive and expedient; moderation on behalf of the group admins helped only partially. On the other hand, many organizations also operated Facebook pages, through which and in contrast to groups, they can unidirectionally communicate important and up-to-date information to volunteers and interested individuals. Some even established Facebook pages for single-accommodation facilities, to focus their communication on volunteers and citizens from the surrounding neighborhood.

As the following examples show, activists have deployed a variety of social media platforms and tools beyond Facebook, which offered advantages in specific use cases.

Organization of carpools and transportation:

- Using *flinc* (a smartphone app and website with a character of a social media platform that enable its users to organize carpools) volunteers organized carpools for the organization of refugee aid.[2] Individuals shared when and where (that is, to which accommodation facility or state authority) in the city they were driving to, allowing others to join them, transport donations, and help refugees reach other parts of the city or other accommodation facilities.

---

[2] www.flinc.org/groups/2394-fahrgemeinschaften-fluechtlingshilfe-berlin.

- For some time, a Facebook group and a Google Maps–based application followed similar goals—bringing drivers and volunteers together, collecting donations, etc., thus overcoming major mobility and transportation barriers.
- These improvised infrastructures have proved to be very flexible (especially in comparison with comparable state mechanisms) on the one hand, but on the other hand also unstable and difficult to control, since they rely on individual, volunteer capacities and resources (not only material such as cars and gasoline, but also cultural and moral such as motivation) (Bochow, 2015).

Coordination of on-site help in refugee accommodation—coordination of a "shift schedule":

- The platform Volunteer Planner, developed by a group of volunteer coders named *coders4help*, offered an advertisement-free and free of cost solution for the coordination of volunteer help in refugee accommodations.[3]
- On the platform's About-page, the operators mention the different manners of organization and coordination—from structured institutions to loosely connected and rather spontaneous Facebook groups—and the resulted lack of overview and high barriers for individuals who want to engage for the first time, a situation that led to the development of the platform, to ease the coordination and participation, both for volunteers and for coordinators.
- This manner of coordination made mobilization simpler as well as made more resources available for actual refugee aid instead of spending them on coordination.

Providing general information for the general public and "first steps" for new volunteers:

- The refugee aid organization ProAsyl published a Google Map that was updated on a regular basis and mapped places to which individuals can go to volunteer.[4] The map was then embedded in many websites and blogs, contributing to its distribution and serving as a starting point for interested individuals.
- "Traditional" websites provided information (lists of needed items in the different locations and accommodations, starting point for interested volunteers, organization's contact information, etc.), links

---

[3] www.volunteer-planner.org.

[4] www.proasyl.de/de/ueber-uns/foerderverein/mitmachen/ as well as www.google.com/maps/d/viewer?mid=zc6TdvfelKuY.kUvriXoSREXw.

    to coordination tools such as the ones listed earlier, or possibility to donate money.[5]

- Much of the information on the websites was also shared via social media platforms, such as the organizations' Facebook groups and pages.

Considering the operation of traditional websites versus social media pages/groups, it often happened that the information on the websites and on social media was not synchronized. On the one hand, the information on social media was usually more up-to-date than the information on the websites. On the other, since the website was maintained by a small and coordinated group of people and the information was structured, no information got lost in a sea of postings (which was common in Facebook groups and Twitter). An understandable situation, considering the fact that information on social media platforms is easier to update, more activists can have admin access to official social media accounts or pages, and other activists or volunteers can share and comment up-to-date information themselves. In contrast, maintaining and updating traditional websites require more technical knowledge and is usually confided within the hands of a small group of activists (or "admins"). However, the social media groups had the disadvantage of excluding volunteers who do not possess a Facebook account—be it due to lack of interest in social media or be it as resistance to surveillance or collection and monetization of their data.

Interestingly enough, the refugee aid movement that was operating in Vienna at the same time had deployed different methods of communication and organization over social media for very similar use cases. In Vienna, refugees arrived (and often accommodated) at the city's train stations that were also places, in which support was needed most. Since students were on a semester break at the time, many have arrived to aid in the different train stations and quickly decided to set up a communication platform. They set up the *Train of Hope* webpage[6] and Facebook page[7] as well as refugees.at,[8] where up-to-date information regarding what was needed and where was available. Furthermore, they decided to use Twitter as a platform for disseminating real-time information—when and where the next train with refugees arrives, what is needed (e.g., clothing, food, medical and sanitary items), where helping hands are needed, where the situation is under control, etc. Using corresponding hashtags, information regarding each location—each train station—was disseminated, linked, aggregated, and integrated in further Facebook pages and websites. Thus Twitter fulfilled a central function of communication from the train stations (on-site)

---

[5] For example, the website *berlin-hilft-lageso*, operated by the initiative Moabit Hilft: http://berlin-hilft-lageso.de.

[6] www.trainofhope.at.

[7] www.facebook.com/hbfvie/.

[8] www.refugees.at.

and over multiple (online) channels simultaneously and the websites (or, for those with a Twitter account, the Twitter hashtags) have offered an overview of the current situation on all train stations as well as the first and central point of information for individuals who wanted to volunteer. Moreover, the welfare association Caritas, which was also engaged in refugee aid in Vienna, also started using Twitter and the city of Vienna has published an official mobile app that gave access to the information communicated over these channels, thus joining the grassroots communication infrastructure.[9]

The bottom line is that individual volunteers as well as organized ones (citizens' initiatives and the like) were not just learning as they go. They also operated within a complex tension of scarce resources, the need of coordination, and finding the best methods of coordination that, in turn, do not require many resources and thus leaving more resources available for the work needed to be done. Thus the volunteers and their organizations deployed a variety of online tools—among which were many social media platforms—to discover, acquire, network, mobilize, and exploit different kinds of available resources while trying to increase the efficiency of such organization. The Resource Mobilization Theory/Approach is a theoretical framework that analyzes social movement and collective action from this point of view. As the above-mentioned examples indicate and the discussion in this chapter will show, the resource mobilization theory is instructive in the analysis and understanding of the deployment of online tools and social media in social movements and/or collective action.

6.2 RESOURCE MOBILIZATION THEORY

The resource mobilization theory, or resource mobilization approach, began in the 1960s and became popular in United States during the 1970s. This approach puts resources at the center of the analysis of social movement and stresses movement member's ability to acquire resources and mobilize people toward accomplishing the movement's goals (McCarthy and Zald, 1977). In contrast to several of the strain and breakdown theories as well as other theoretical frameworks, resource mobilization regards social movements as rational, goal-oriented social institutions. As such, social movements are created and

---

[9] The difference between the tools and methods that were used in Berlin and Vienna stresses once again that social media deployment (as in any deployment of ICT) should be regarded in its cultural, social, and political context. For example, Vienna is a relatively small and centered city (hence the central train station's essentiality in the refugee aid), whereas Berlin is widespread, with quite a few districts, "city centers," local administrations, and authorities, as well as alternative, leftwing, or socialist structures and groups, on which the refugee aid movements have built. These and further differences (such as the student's role of setting up the communication infrastructures in Vienna) have greatly affected the refugee aid movements themselves as well as the tools—among others ICTs and social media—they use, making a highly effective tool for one movement almost irrelevant for the other. For more on this notion, see Chapters 3, 7, and 11.

populated by social actors with certain goals. Having said that, the approach addresses social movements in the broad sense of the words, which covers a variety of actions, beliefs, opinions, and strategies for societal change. Due to aspects such as efficient use of available resources as operations logic, some theories within the resource mobilization approach stress similarities between social movements' operation and capitalist enterprises.

The resource mobilization approach is treated with a certain amount of ambiguity in literature. On the one hand, some scholars acknowledge that it became a dominant theoretical framework in the study of social movements over the past several decades (Jenkins, 1983; Gamson, 2004; Williams, 2004). On the other hand, several scholars reaffirm that there is still no agreed-upon definition or consensus regarding the theory with which social movements and collective action are to be studied (Benski etal., 2013; Taylor and Van Dyke, 2004), as scholars of sociology and behavioral sciences Benski, Langman, Perugorría, and Tejerina argue: "Since the 1980s the field of social movement studies has been characterized by an eclecticism with many theoretical strands but without a dominant paradigm(s)" (Benski etal., 2013, p. 557).

Critics of resource mobilization theories "note that the Resource Mobilization theories based on self-interested, rational actors, social movement entrepreneurs, and ever-present grievances have little explanatory value for these mobilizations and indeed they have not been used by the authors of this issue" (Benski etal., 2013, p. 557). In other words, the resource mobilization approach acknowledges that grievances are ubiquitous in society, but stresses the need of "social movement entrepreneurship" or other kinds of organizations to transform uncoordinated masses and their demands into movements with goals and strategies. Thus it does not assign sufficient weight to aspects such as grievances, identity, and culture, nor does it offer sufficient explanation to success of groups and movement with limited resources in fostering social change (Kendall, 2006). This comes to show that different theoretical frameworks offer us different manners to examine collective action and/or social movements, a notion that is explicitly followed in Chapters 2–6 of the book. When addressing the refugee aid movement in Berlin, the analysis offered in this chapter will concentrate on such goal-oriented and resource-dependent actions of the refugee aid organizations and individual volunteers in terms of resource mobilization and social media deployment. The grievances and motives of these activists—fascinating and noble as they may be for further research—will be left out of scope of this chapter (Edwards and McCarthy, 2004).

Coming back to the theories of resource mobilization, as we have seen with the example of the Berlin's refugee aid movement, the mere availability of resources is not sufficient for the emergence of collective action; coordination and strategic effort are required to transform (individually) available resources into collective ones and, in turn, utilize them for collective action. Furthermore, access to resources is deeply embedded in existing social and economic relation and thus varies greatly between social groups, an inequality in resource access and distribution. Although the efficient use of some resources can in some cases compensate for the lack of others, the likelihood of effective collective action appears to be enhanced by the availability of diverse kinds of resources (Edwards and McCarthy, 2004). Furthermore, the focus on structural factors and resources (such as membership, money, organization, human labor, and other material resources) in the study of resource mobilization is characterized by being located mostly "within" the movements themselves (Williams, 2004).

To understand what the resource mobilization theory regards as "resources" and how they accessed, coordinated, and mobilized, Edwards and McCarthy (2004), whose work was central in the articulation of a resource mobilization approach to studying social movements, distinguish a fivefold typology:[10]

1. Moral Resources include legitimacy, solidarity, and sympathetic support to the movement's goals. Those resources tend to originate outside of a social movement and are generally being granted by an external source. Therefore the source can also retract those resources. A fact that makes them less accessible and more proprietary than cultural resources.
2. Cultural Resources are artifacts and cultural products such as conceptual tools and specialized knowledge that have become widely known. These include among others understanding of the issues, collective action know-how, prior activist experience, and organizational templates. Those resources are widely available, less proprietary, and accessible for independent use (compared with moral resources). This category also includes use or issuance of relevant productions such as music, literature, magazines, films, and websites and, in the context of this chapter as well as of Chapter 4, content on social media platforms. Those products facilitate the recruitment and socialization of new agents and help maintain readiness and capacity for collective action.

---

[10] Edwards and McCarthy stress a central difference between their and Cress and Snow's (1996) typology, namely, that Edwards and McCarthy have deleted the category "informational" resources. Instead they resolved "informational" resources in social-organizational and cultural resources as separate categories. By treating "informational" resources with more details and precision (e.g., knowledge as cultural resource or individuals who command this knowledge in terms of participation and making it available as human and/or social-organizational resources), this typology is more instructive for an analysis of social media (as ICT, media, and institutions) in terms of resource mobilization.

3. Social-Organizational Resources are divided into three general forms: infrastructures, social networks,[11] and organizations. Infrastructures are mostly public goods such as postal service, transportation infrastructure, the Internet (that is, the technological information and communication network rather than the websites and commercial platforms accessible via the Internet), or sanitation. In comparison with infrastructures, the access to social networks and/or formal organizations, that is, access to the resources embedded in these networks/organizations, enjoys a great deal of social and economic control.
4. Human Resources include resources like labor, experience, skills, and expertise, which are embodied by individuals such as the movement's volunteers, staff, or leaders (i.e., the movement's human capital).
5. Material Resources refer to financial and physical capital, including monetary resources, property, office space, equipment, and supplies.

Edwards and McCarthy also identify four mechanisms of access to the defined resources:

1. Aggregation of resources held by dispersed individuals and their conversion into collective ones that can in turn be allocated by movement actors.
2. Self-production refers to mechanisms in which movement actors create or add value to resources that have been aggregated, co-opted, or provided by patrons.
3. Co-optation is the transparent, permitted borrowing of resources that have already been aggregated by other existing forms of social organization. Appropriation on the other hand, is the secret exploitation of the previously aggregated resources of other groups.
4. Patronage refers to the awarding of resources to a movement by an individual or organization. Alongside the patronage there is typically a degree of proprietary control exercised that determines how gained resources can be used, and even can attempt to influence over day-to-day operation and policy decisions.

McCarthy and Zald, pioneers of the resource mobilization approach, differentiate between different forms or stages of social movements:

- Social Movement is a set of opinions in society, which are characterized by and represent a bias toward change in social structures and/or distribution;

---

[11] For more on the aspect of social networks, see Chapter 5.

- Social Movement Organization refers to a formal organization with goals corresponding to the opinions and preferences of a social movement (or a countermovement) and which attempts to accomplish these goals;
- Social Movement Industry is the sum of all social movement organizations sharing similar goals;
- Finally, a Social Movement Sector consists of all social movement industries without regard to their social movement affiliation (McCarthy and Zald, 1980).

In the case of the Berlin refugee aid movement, social movement is the set of opinion toward welcoming refugees in Europe and the fact that the current management of the situation is unworthy. Social movement organizations are the citizens' initiatives emerged to pursue the goal of aiding refugees and welcoming them in Berlin. Social movement industry is not only the sum of these organizations and initiatives, but also the parts of other social welfare and human rights organizations that address the issue of refugee aid (e.g., ProAsyl, German Red Cross, and the Diakonie Deutschland). However, this somewhat capitalist and market-oriented terminology should be treated with caution. First, because the movements and organizations at hand do not follow an "entrepreneurial" or for-profit agenda and second, because such a terminology can be deployed by movement opponents, in this case from rightwing parties, movements, and media (e.g., by framing the volunteer/nonprofit work as tax-funded businesses).

6.3 SOCIAL MEDIA AND RESOURCE MOBILIZATION

Resource mobilization is one of the few theoretical frameworks within the wide spectrum of social movement theories, in which information and communication technology (ICT) receives explicit and conscious attention. The theory considers (movement-related) information, knowledge, and cultural objects as resources that must be aggregated, managed, shared, and efficiently used, just as other resources. The effects ICT has on such processes and on social movements' operation are acknowledged by the theory and its proponents. As with other resources, whose use-value for social movements shift between contexts and over time, as technology develops, the use-value of specific tools and resources changes (Edwards and McCarthy, 2004). Thus developments and changes in ICTs and their role in society also affect social movements, which deploy ICTs as resources and/or tool that enable mechanisms of access to other resources, as Edwards and McCarthy (2004, p. 119) note: "Shifting use-value is clearest with technology as the pace of innovation may hasten the obsolescence of once important techniques or equipment. For example, the telephone lessened the importance of participation in community organizations or events as a means of sharing movement related information, and email is rapidly replacing older techniques, like organizing 'phone trees,' as a means of contacting large numbers of people." A conclusion that gets to the heart of social media's affects collective action and social movements—especially in comparison with the usage of email, which Edwards and McCarthy mention a decade prior to the Berlin refugee aid movement. This theoretical background is a good starting point to examine the pragmatic role social media play in collective action and social movements by deploying Edwards and McCarthy's fivefold typology (Table 6.1):

6.3.1 Moral Resources

As discussed in previous chapters of the book, social media (as ICT and media) help movement activists and/or participators of collective action communicate their grievances, causes, demands, arguments, and emotions. From a resource mobilization point of view, this is regarded as deployment of social media in the self-production and aggregation of moral resources. This deployment aims at providing the movement or instance of collective action with legitimacy, solidarity, and sympathetic support, which are in turn resources that can be deployed for further purposes as well as for mobilization and acquisition of other resources.

Considering the refugee aid movement in Berlin, for example, moral resources are crucial, for the movement to be able to mobilize citizens to participate and make donations on the one hand, and reduce prejudices, resentments, and stereotypes within the local population on the other. Examples of social media uses for such goals are press statements published on initiatives' Facebook pages, the organization of solidarity demonstrations (among others using event pages of social media), and Facebook pages of local citizens' initiatives or refugee accommodation that aim at communicating with the local population and gaining its support.

6.3.2 Cultural Resources

Following on the use of culture as a resource in Chapter 4, the resource mobilization approach regards further aspects such as collective action know-how and activist experience as cultural resources (or as informational resources in other resource mobilization frameworks). As with other movements, these resources were crucial for the Berlin refugee aid movement to tackle the challenges it was facing. The aggregation, self-production (by gathering own experience and know-how as they go), co-optation, and patronage of somewhat abstract resources such as activist experience and know-how take place mainly on-site, whereas activists participate and engage in exchange.

Having said that, discussion groups as the ones the local citizens' initiatives realized using Facebook groups are a helpful tool to support such exchange while lifting many temporal and spatial limitations. These groups are spaces in which not only the exchange of experience and know-how took place, but

Table 6.1 Means of Social Movement and SMO Resource Access and Resource Type in Terms of Social Media Deployment

Resource Type/Means of Access Using Social Media (SM)	Moral	Cultural	Social-Organizational	Human	Material
Aggregation	▪ Reaching out to public figures (local politicians/celebrities) over their SM presence ▪ Lists of donors and volunteers	▪ Deploying existing social frames (e.g., cottage, "Israeli-ness," children's songs") in SM communication ▪ Know-how acquisition over SM communication	▪ Accessing social networks of movement sympathizers	▪ Mobilizing volunteers ▪ Aggregating and organizing of skilled labor, both for on-site and online tasks	▪ Up-to-date lists of needed donation items ▪ Donations from businesses over SM
Self-production	▪ Communication of grievances, causes, demands, etc. ▪ Moral authority from fulfilling social/public tasks	▪ Construction and dissemination of frames (e.g., via digital cultural objects) ▪ Know-how exchange over SM groups	▪ Building communication infrastructures such as groups and pages in SM, websites, and dedicated smartphone apps	▪ Taking over administrative tasks due to the "deprofessionalization" the operation of online presence	▪ "Grassroots" fund-raising of small contribution over SM
Co-optation/Appropriation	▪ Cross-linking and sharing of pages, posts, actions, etc. of movements from the same social movement industry	▪ Using SM to connect to other movements and organizations ▪ Sharing of movement-related information and/or digital cultural products produced by others (other movements, news outlets, etc.)	▪ Free of cost communication platform ▪ Cross-linking and sharing of pages, posts, actions, etc. of movements from the same social movement industry	▪ Mobilizing activists and volunteers from existing groups and organizations by reaching them over SM	▪ Organizing carpools and transportation over SM ▪ Free of costs communication platform
Patronage	▪ Public figures support the cause via their SM presence	▪ Public figures share movement's information and/or cultural objects via SM ▪ News outlets link movement's SM presence	▪ Receiving access/usage rights of existing communication infrastructure (e.g., public figures or alternative media lend the movement access to and usage of their SM presence)		▪ Receiving large donations from businesses, local politicians, and wealthy citizens through SM communication/fund-raising

Based on the tabular overview in Edwards, B., McCarthy, J.D., 2004. Resource and social movement mobilization. In: Snow, D.A., Soule, S.A., Kriesi, H. (Eds.), The Blackwell Companion to Social Movements. Blackwell Publishing Ltd., Malden, MA, pp. 132–133

also coordination tasks, dissemination of movement-related information, etc. In this manner, social media as platforms, which converge the three modes of sociality (cognition, communication, cooperation)[12] as well as converge different functionalities and usages within the social movement, eased and facilitated access to and exchange of these cultural resources (collective action know-how and activist experience).

Furthermore, the self-production, aggregation, and communication of cultural objects—cultural resources—as the ones discussed in Chapter 4 are actions that depend on ICTs and have significant costs embedded in them. By facilitating these functionalities and offering them free of charge, the deployment of social media platforms for these goals significantly reduce the related costs (that is, the required material and monetary resources).

6.3.3 Social-Organizational Resources

Strictly speaking, the deployment of social media relies on access to a variety of social-organizational resources—the Internet (as an infrastructure), related technological infrastructures (telephone, cable, and/or cellular networks with sufficient bandwidth, compatible end devices, and electricity),[13] and social networks as a key aspect in the deployment of social media.[14] Interestingly, access to formal organizations, as a resource, is less central in the deployment of social media; social media are even a resource or means that helps overcoming many obstacles that accompany the (need of) access to organizations such as mainstream and corporate media, political institutions, and nongovernmental organizations. However, in many cases the deployment of social media has proved to be a productive mechanism of access—even if a limited one—to such formal organizational structures, especially mainstream media.[15]

Beyond the access to technological infrastructure, which is required to use social media, social media platforms themselves are an infrastructure that is resource on the one hand and enables mechanisms of access to further resources (e.g., cultural, moral, or human resources) on the other. Considering transportation and distribution networks, the Berlin refugee aid movement demonstrated how social media could enable access to such resources. Provided that the movement and its cause has access to sufficient moral, cultural, human, and to a certain extent also material resources—in which social media can but must

---

[12] See Chapter 2 as well as Fuchs and Trottier (2014).

[13] In times in which Internet-based communication and the deployment of social media are central in collective action, many governments use measures that cut movements' access to such infrastructural social-organizational resources to make it harder for uprisings and civil resistance movements to gain momentum, pursue their goals, and access further (types of) resources.

[14] For a discussion on the topic of social networks, see Chapter 5.

[15] See Chapter 8.

not play a role—social media can be used as a mechanism to aggregate infrastructural resources that mobilized persons and organizations have at their disposal. Activists and citizens' initiatives in Berlin have used Facebook groups, flinc, and Google Maps to organize carpools for volunteers and refugees, transportation of donations, and even evacuation of refugees in need of medical care to nearby hospitals, all of which was done relying on vehicles owned or rented by volunteers and sympathizing organizations, thus making co-optation and patronage central mechanisms of access. This is one example of many, as other social movements with different causes can deploy similar mechanisms to access resources that are central for their operation. Social media's advantage in these kinds or resource mobilization is that the platforms take up and automatize much of the needed organization and coordination, which would otherwise require a considerable amount of, already scarce, human resources. Much of the remaining organization/coordination tasks are, in turn, carried out by the individuals—the platform's users, the activists—themselves.

Going off of social networks and social media in collective action context, as discussed in Chapter 5, social networks are the main resources to which one gains access by using social media in terms of resource mobilization. In turn, access to social networks (as a resources) enables access to the resources embedded within them (human, moral, cultural, or material resources), as the earlier example demonstrated. Furthermore, through social media (and the related social networks), movements can gain access to further, formal organizations. For example, in Berlin, individual activists as well as citizens' initiatives gained and maintained contact to organizations in the refugee aid movement—within the same "social movement industry"—partially through communication over social media. Nevertheless, as the example in the beginning of the chapter shows, also access to organization outside of the same "social movement industry": on many occasions, supermarkets and drugstores have sent ad hoc donations to LaGeSo or nearby refugee accommodations, after being exposed to the situation over social media communication. Nonetheless, this is dependent on the social media presence that many businesses, especially large corporations, maintain for economical and marketing interests; thus, social media are a moral as well as social-organizational resource for these organizations as well.

6.3.4 Human Resources

The access to social networks—in the context of this book, the access that is supported by social media deployment—gives movements access to a variety of human resources, which are otherwise considerably difficult to access. As the examples in this chapter demonstrate, social media were crucial in mobilizing and coordinating many volunteers and unavoidable work that needed to be done. Furthermore, by drastically reducing the needed amount of (human) resources that would otherwise be required for such mobilization and coordination, the available resources (volunteers and the time, skills, experience, and expertise at their disposal) could be used where needed most—in refugee aid.

Beyond the automation and decentralization of coordination and organization tasks, the effect on human resources manifests in a variety of ways:

- "deprofessionalizing" the operation of online presence;
- aspects of legitimacy (in terms of human resources);
- aggregation of skilled labor; and lastly,
- the decentralization of organization and coordination poses important questions regarding leadership.

Considering social media platforms' user-friendliness (in comparison with many other ICTs) and the prevalence of certain platforms, social media and their deployment (as a resource) are more accessible for individuals as well as social movements. Consider, for instance, the maintenance of websites, discussion forums, or the above-mentioned platform Volunteer Planner—beyond access to the Internet (as infrastructure), also skilled labor and time are required. Social media, on the other hand, require less technical skills and are accessible and manageable via a variety of portable and nonportable devices, which allows decentralization of the required maintenance and communication. Having said that, the maintenance of social media groups and pages also require investment of human resources, even if it can often be decentralized. For example, the admins of refugee aid initiatives' Facebook groups were occupied with replying membership requests, checking the requesters' profiles (to assure that they were not spammers, robots, or members of any racist or right-wing movements) (Bochow, 2015), or attending offending comments in group discussions. Considering the administrational tasks involved, it is clear that both social media and other forms of online tools require (different qualities and quantities of) information, Internet, and social media literacy[16]—a resource in itself that is not evenly distributed in society (both locally and globally).

Edwards and McCarthy (2004, p. 120) note on the subject: "As Internet competency becomes a marker of legitimacy, which in turn facilitates the acquisition of further resources, the mobilization potential of relatively deprived constituencies may be further constrained." This applies for social media competency/literacy as well, especially as social media play an increasingly central role in contemporary

---

[16] Social media literacy is the repertoire of competencies that enable individuals to use social media. It encompasses, among other things, the needed technical expertise as well as ability not only to perceive, evaluate, and analyze information received over social media platforms, but also to produce and communicate using these platforms.

and future social movements, and can have negative effects on social movements that lack access to this resource. In other words, legitimacy as a moral resource is to a certain extent also dependent on the technological competency of movement's human resources—its activists. Having said that, the above-mentioned difference between the deployment of social media and traditional websites by the Berlin refugee aid movement is an example of how central the role of social media is becoming in social movements, as the maintenance of traditional websites requires more skilled personnel and labor time. In terms of mobilization and legitimacy, such reliance on social media excludes movement-sympathetic individuals, who do not use social media. Furthermore, if social media competency is a source of legitimacy and certain movements are perceived as young middle-class movements—among other things because of the central role that movement leaders attributed to the deployment of social media and smartphones—then the source of legitimacy for some may become a perceived "source" of illegitimacy or demobilization for others who lack access to such resources, technology, and skills. Therefore as technology and its reciprocal relation with society develop and change, technological tools and their deployment—in this case, social media platforms—are becoming a moral resource themselves.

Another aspect of social media, as well as other online tools and the Internet in general, affecting social movements' aggregation of human resources such as skilled labor (including know-how, expertise) and labor time is making it possible for sympathizing individuals to make a contribution of their skills and labor that is not necessarily dependent on physical presence. Beyond the mere maintenance of social media presence and/or traditional websites, this can include producing, contributing, and disseminating movement-related information as well as contributing to the production of immaterial products (e.g., Wikipedia articles, open source software, or cultural objects). Furthermore, by creating a more casual context of participation, which motivates individuals to be effective without becoming highly involved activists themselves, more individuals can be reached; by aggregating their (minor) participation, an effect on collective action is possible. These small contributions also have the potential to lead to a greater sense of individual obligation; they can contribute to mobilization that is even more meaningful. For example, and in addition to the above-mentioned examples, such contributions can be small monetary donations or patronage of moral and/or cultural resources by contributing to online advocacy; in terms of social media—liking, retweeting, sharing, and disseminating movement-related information over social media platforms. In this manner, a participation distribution that resembles the long tail distribution is created.

On the other hand, such distribution of participation runs the danger of demobilization, or in Evgeny Morozov's terms, *Slacktivism* (Morozov, 2011). Although participating in collective action in its more traditional manner was attached to taking on-site actions with perceivable impact in the physical world, digital activism offers participation without leaving the comfort of one's home. However, when it comes to mobilization for more concrete, on-site rather than purely digital actions, the participation seems to decrease dramatically. Although the subject of demobilization and Slacktivism will be discussed in Chapter 10, it is important to note this imposes a substantial risk for social movements, as demobilization and Slacktivism are in fact human resource not being mobilized.

Lastly, the category of human resources also includes leadership. As mentioned in Chapter 5, Paolo Gerbaudo's discussion of social media deployment during the 2010–12 wave of social protests deals with how this deployment affects the aspect of leadership in social movements (Gerbaudo, 2012). The deployment of social media (as ICT and media) came hand in hand with the adopting ideologies of "self-regulating masses" and "wisdom of the crowd," which in turn had an ideological impact on social movements. This impact, which made many movements dismiss the need and/or existence of leadership, was in fact dismissal of leadership as a required—let alone crucial—resource by the movements that adopted these notions. In practice, the notion, and resource, of leadership did not become obsolete, but rather transformed into a form of "choreography," —a rather subtle impact on the collective action "scene," which does not take place in the center of the stage. This transformation, rather than the ideological standpoint, is social media's actual impact on social movements and collective action in terms of leadership (as a human resource). Gerbaudo's thoughts and critique of the moral aspects of this transformation make the relation between human—i.e., leadership—and moral resources visible, as the transformation of leadership results with moral implications for the movement's legitimacy and accountability.

6.3.5 Material Resources

Material resources, which play a central role in the resource mobilization approach, are generally more tangible, more proprietary, and regarding money also more fungible than other resource types. A large proportion of fungible resources enables a movement greater flexibility and money, as a highly fungible resource, is convertible to other resources and therefore compensates lack of access to those resources through other mechanisms. For example, employing paid staff and professionals can compensate shortage of human resources (Edwards and McCarthy, 2004).

The deployment of social media, which in many cases eases access to and reduces the need for other kinds of resources, contributes to the reduction of costs embedded in collective action and/or social movements' operation. For example, as mentioned earlier, the communication, aggregation, and self-production of cultural resources, and dissemination of movement-related information, are all actions that depend on ICTs and have significant costs embedded in them. By facilitating these functionalities and offering them free of charge, social media platforms contributed to reducing the costs of these aspects—in comparison with both older, nondigital technologies and other online tools such as maintaining websites. To name another example, as the case of the organization within the Berlin refugee help movement shows, by facilitating many coordination and organization tasks that otherwise would have required human resources, social media deployment can reduce the costs of paid labor (or make these human resources available for other crucial tasks). Clay Shirky notes on the subject, that the deployment of online tools (among others, social media platforms) reduces the transaction costs within social movement organizations, who deploy such tools, in comparison with other, strictly hierarchical organizations, such as big corporations or state authorities (Shirky, 2008).[17] Such transaction costs are not solely monetary, but also include aspects of human and social-organizational resources.

Beyond cost reduction, many movements and causes deploy social media in fund-raising actions, to gain access to and aggregate monetary and material resources. By reaching a wide spectrum of possible donors (among others by relying on social networks with weak and strong ties), the ease of making a donation in just a few mouse clicks, and the above-mentioned casual context of participation (which is, in this case, making a monetary donation), raising money over the Internet in general and social media in particular can be very effective. This aspect was present in the work of the Berlin refugee aid movement—social media platforms were used to reach out to the city's citizens and encourage them to make donations. In these actions, material donations of needed supplies (food, clothing, medical and sanitary items, home appliances, etc.) played a more central role than money donation, which of course were also appreciated. Prioritized needs lists were regularly published and updated on the Facebook pages (and websites) of the local citizen's initiatives, so that individuals will know which material resources are currently required in each accommodation. The wide dissemination of the needs lists over social media (in Facebook groups and pages, individuals sharing the information using their Facebook and Twitter accounts, etc.) also helped reaching scarce or rare

---

[17] Evgeny Morozov criticizes the usage of Shirky's notion of transaction costs for analyzing social movements and political uprisings as insufficient, let alone regarding the diminishing transaction costs as enablers of large-scale collective action. With reference to the 2009 political protests in Iran, Morozov claims "thinking of a Californian start-up in terms of transaction costs is much easier than pulling the same trick for, say, the Iranian society. While it seems noncontroversial to conclude that cheaper digital technologies might indeed lower most so-called transaction costs in Iran, that insight doesn't really say much, for unless we know something about Iran's culture, history, and politics, we know nothing about the contexts in which all these costs have supposedly fallen. Who are the relevant actors? What are the relevant transactions?" (Morozov, 2013, p. 43).

resources such as wheelchairs, uncommon medicines, clothing of special sizes, etc. Furthermore, the concept of "time donation" was also widely used, meaning that individuals can also come and donate some of their free time by conducting on-site volunteer work, that is, donating their own human resources.

The resource mobilization approach also acknowledges that not in every case money (although tangible, proprietary, and fungible) is the suitable means for solving the problem at hand and other resource types always play a major role. So that shifting the focus of social movements' objectives or dismissing people from taking meaningful real-life, on-site action after making a donation can result in a contraproductive effect. As Evgeny Morozov argues using the example of the popular Facebook cause Saving the Children of Africa with its over 1.7 million members, fund-raising over social media can lead to demobilization. Due to the group's—or cause's—popularity, it has raised about $12,000; 0.007% per person, which is, of course, better than making no donation at all. However, many individuals are also motivated to take the least painful sacrifice, donating a cent where they may otherwise donate a dollar or donating money where they may otherwise take part in on-site activism (Morozov, 2011). Furthermore, the ease of raising money over the Internet and social media may result in shifting the primary focus of social movements to pursue monetary objectives, that is, the aggregation and usage of material/monetary resources, instead of other objectives such as political and on-site activism; thus changing social movements themselves and not only their manner of operation and "toolbox".

6.4 CONCLUSIONS

There is an old mantra in software development and IT projects saying "Fast, Good, or Cheap. Pick Any Two." The mantra is also known in its visual form as the Project Management Triangle. The mantra's/triangle's main premise is that one cannot overcome all three constraints in one project (or in one goal-oriented activity). That is to say, to overcome two of the constraints, cutbacks in the third one must be done. This premise is nonetheless a resource-oriented one, as it addresses the balance between three central resources:

- time (e.g., the required labor-time needed for completion of a task or project);
- quality (e.g., human and material resources invested in skilled labor and quality control); and
- price (the monetary aspect of material resources).

Considering the deployment of social media in collective action and/or social movements, how does this premise apply for such deployment?

ICT's ability to accelerate and geographically extend the dissemination of social movement information is often noted in the literature. Combined with mobile end devices, the capabilities of communication over social media—the dissemination of information as well as cooperation and collaboration—have reached a new pace that was only imaginable with older generations of ICT. Social media platforms with their various functionalities also offer improved efficiency in pursuing the social movement's or collective action's goals. However, this does not mean that the deployment of social media always results in increasing quality of collective action—what are the criteria for measuring collective action's "quality"?— but rather that the deployment of social media offers social movements and collective action themselves new qualities of resource mobilization. These qualities, of course, vary according to the social movement and/or collective action at hand, the (social, political, economic, etc.) context in which they operate, and the available and required resources.

The costs and delays associated with prior ICTs have created many difficulties for the coordination and organization of geographically distant actors—from individual activists across one city to members of transnational social movement organizations. The instant and decentralized communication for low costs offered by new ICTs—Internet-based communication in general and social media in particular—is highly valuable for overcoming these difficulties. Furthermore, by reducing the—informational, social, financial, etc.—barriers individuals face in joining collective action or a social movement as well as considerably increasing social movements' ability to reach greater audience, social media deployment contributes to the aggregation of moral and human resources. In other words, the development of ICT not only increases the speed and efficiency of collective action processes, but also decreases barriers such as the embedded monetary costs or reaching movement-sympathetic audience. To put it carefully, the "winning feature" of social media for collective action and social movements lays not only in the speed and efficiency that are offered by it for little or no cost, but rather in the combination of these aspects with one's social environment (i.e., with her social networks).

Having said that, the deployment of social media also poses a variety of risks. First, when social movements' reliance on social media platforms transforms from complementing other tools, media, and forms of mobilization and organization to substituting them, the advantage of inclusion and mobilization of new resources tilts into exclusion of individuals and resource who—for a variety of reasons—do not have access to social media or intentionally avoid them.[18]

---

[18] It is important to note that this did not occur in the Berlin refugee aid movement, as other media and mechanisms of mobilization and organization were deployed parallel to social media, for example, the berlin-hilft-lageso website that was actively maintained by a team of volunteers (Keil, 2015). However, this comes to show that human resources are embedded in such maintenance of further tool and mechanisms.

Second, as privately owned, profit-oriented, corporate social media platforms become a critical infrastructure, a critical social-organizational resource, they differ from the majority of social-organizational resources that are usually public goods. When considering the example of the Berlin refugee aid movement, as well as its counterparts in other part of Germany and Europe, the state's failure to fulfill public tasks have led politicians, decision makers, public authorities, and social scientists to openly express their expectations from volunteer infrastructures to fill the void (Bochow, 2015). Such "outsourcing" of public tasks from the state to volunteer citizens' infrastructure is problematic in itself. Nevertheless, in the context of social media deployment by the citizens' infrastructures—social movements and refugee aid organizations—it cascades this "outsourcing" of infrastructure—of social-organizational resources—that is needed to fulfill these tasks to social media corporations (social media as institutions), thus making privately held technology corporations responsible for infrastructure that is critical for the fulfillment of government responsibilities. Thus promoting a neoliberal agenda, from which private corporation, in this case social media institutions, profit.[19] Besides the implicit support or neoliberal agenda, it is questionable how safe such a critical infrastructure really is when private corporations hold it; corporations with interests that often differ from the ones social movements pursue. Furthermore, social media platforms are perhaps free of charge, but movements and activists "pay" with their data—each click, each share, each organizational task, each mobilization that takes place over social media platforms are aggregated, analyzed, evaluated, and monetized. In other words, and as some scholars of critical information and media theory argue, by deploying these platforms the movements and activists conduct unpaid labor for the social media corporations.[20]

For the refugees themselves, who make their way from Asia, the Middle East, and Africa toward Europe, smartphones have become a central tool for organizing their journey, communicating with their families (that are still at home, in refugee camps, on the road, or already in Europe), communicating with other refugees, and disseminating information regarding routes, police controls, emergencies, etc. In this communication and organization, platforms and apps such as WhatsApp, Facebook, and Google Maps play a central role. Unfortunately, this deployment of ICT (and social media) for one of the decade's most massive instances of collective action—chronologically succeeding the 2010–12 wave of worldwide social protests and political uprisings, causative and historically partially connected to them, and relying on similar ICT for organization—exceeds the scope of this chapter. However, this would

---

[19] For critique on such neoliberal agenda promoted by technology firms see Morozov (2013) and Keen (2015).

[20] For more on the notion of labor in social media platforms, or "prosumer labor," see Fuchs (2014) and Spier (2016).

be a fascinating research subject that begins to gain the appropriate attention in academic, media, and activist circles. I hope that the work presented in this book will contribute to such future research.

Subsequent to the discussion in the previous chapters, which focused on theoretical models from the social movement theory in their relation to social media deployment, the chapters in the second part of the book will offer an in-depth discussion of key aspects in the deployment of social media in collective action and social movements. Aspects such as the interplay between social media and mass/mainstream media, surveillance, demobilization and slacktivism, and issues of neutrality and ethics.

References

Benski, T., Langman, L., Perugorría, I., Tejerina, B., 2013. From the streets and squares to social movement studies: what have we learned? Current Sociology 61 (4), 541–561.

Bochow, A., 2015. We Are Only Helping! "Volunteering and Social Media in Germany's New" Welcome Culture. Retrieved from: www.medizinethnologie.net/volunteering-and-social-media-in-germanys-new-welcome-culture/.

Cress, D.M., Snow, D.A., 1996. Mobilization at the margins: resources, benefactors, and the viability of homeless social movement organizations. American Sociological Review 61 (6), 1089–1109.

Edwards, B., McCarthy, J.D., 2004. Resource and social movement mobilization. In: Snow, D.A., Soule, S.A., Kriesi, H. (Eds.), The Blackwell Companion to Social Movements. Blackwell Publishing Ltd, Malden, MA, pp. 116–152.

Fuchs, C., 2014. Social Media: A Critical Introduction. Sage, London.

Fuchs, C., Trottier, D., 2014. Theorizing social media, politics, and the state. An introduction. In: Fuchs, C., Trottier, D. (Eds.), Social Media, Politics and the State: Protests, Revolutions, Riots, Crime and Policing in the Age of Facebook, Twitter and YouTube. Routledge, New York, pp. 3–38.

Gamson, W.A., 2004. Bystanders, public opinion, and the media. In: Snow, D.A., Soule, S.A., Kriesi, H. (Eds.), The Blackwell Companion to Social Movements. Blackwell Publishing Ltd, Malden, pp. 242–261.

Gerbaudo, P., 2012. Tweets and the Streets: Social Media and Contemporary Activism. Pluto Press, London.

Jenkins, J.C., 1983. Resource mobilization theory and the study of social movements. Annual Review of Sociology 9, 527–553.

Keen, A., 2015. The Internet Is Not the Answer. Atlantic Monthly Press, New York.

Keil, T., 2015. Netzwerk "Berlin Hilft". Politik Digital. Retrieved from: www.politik-digital.de/news/netzwerk-berlin-hilft-146771/.

Kendall, D.E., 2006. Sociology in Our Times. Thomson/Wadsworth, Belmont, CA.

McCarthy, J.D., Zald, M.N., 1977. Resource mobilization and social movements: a partial theory. American Journal of Sociology 82 (6), 1212–1241.

McCarthy, J.D., Zald, M.N., 1980. Social movement industries: competition and cooperation among movement organizations. In: Kriesberg, L. (Ed.). Kriesberg, L. (Ed.), Research in Social Movements, Conflicts and Change: A Research Annual, vol. 1. Jai Press, Greenwich, Conn., pp. 1–20.

Morozov, E., 2011. The Net Delusion: The Dark Side of Internet Freedom. PublicAffairs, New York.

Morozov, E., 2013. To Save Everything, Click Here: Technology, Solutionism, and the Urge to Fix Problems that Don't Exist. Allen Lane, London.

Shirky, C., 2008. Here Comes Everybody: The Power of Organizating without Organizations. Penguin Group, London.

Spier, S., 2016. From culture industry to information society: how Horkheimer and Adorno's conception of the culture industry can help us examine information overload in the capitalist information society. In: Kelly, M., Bielby, J. (Eds.), Information Cultures in the Digital Age: A Festschrift in Honor of Rafael Capurro. Springer VS, Wiesbaden, 385–396.

Taylor, V., Van Dyke, N., 2004. "Get up, stand up": tactical repertoires of social movement. In: Snow, D.A., Soule, S.A., Kriesi, H. (Eds.), The Blackwell Companion to Social Movements. Blackwell Publishing Ltd, Malden, MA, pp. 262–293.

Williams, R.H., 2004. The cultural context of collective action: constrains, opportunities, and the symbolic life of social movements. In: Snow, D.A., Soule, S.A., Kriesi, H. (Eds.), The Blackwell Companion to Social Movements. Blackwell Publishing Ltd, Malden, MA, pp. 91–115.

PART

2

Discussion

Between Actions and Algorithms: How Social Media Facilitate and Enable Collective Action

ABSTRACT

Can algorithms facilitate and even enable certain types of collective action? This is a fundamental question as more aspects of life, social and political processes, the economy, etc. are affected by digitalization and informatization. Deploying several theoretical models, among others Christian Fuchs' TripleC model and Hannah Arendt's notion of Action, the chapter discusses this question in regard to social media and collective action.

Keywords: Action; Agency; Algorithm; Collective action; Collective behavior; Integrated sociality; Social media; TripleC.

CONTENTS

The role social media (can) play in the formation processes of collective action was the topic of the first chapters of this book. One central conclusion from Chapter 3 is that during the prominent example of the Arab Spring, people took their grievances, frustration, and lack of perspective to the streets. They did so while deploying the tools and platforms that they use in their everyday life and that offer them advantages in terms of mobilization, organization, persuasion etc., tools and platforms which, in turn, affected and transformed the movements themselves. In the words of Athina Karatzogianni: "whether social media was a crucial or just a facilitating factor [in the events of the Arab Spring] is not a question worth posing. For anyone paying half attention, it is obviously a key factor in transforming how social movements operate and it has been so over a decade now" (Karatzogianni, 2013, p. 169). The discussion, however, was made on the basis of the Arab Spring as a case study. The succeeding chapters, discussing the Israeli social justice protests and the refugee aid

Collective Action 2.0. http://dx.doi.org/10.1016/B978-0-08-100567-5.00007-4

movement in Berlin, also used case studies of relatively large-scale movements, with acute grievances, life-changing goals, a variety of resources, and ideological groundings as well as active participation beyond the borders of social media, smartphones, and the Internet.

The question remains, if and to what extent do the conclusions from Chapters 3–6 apply for instances of collective action that take place with little or no intended actions by the users of the social media platform at hand, with little or no human agency? In other words, can algorithms enable and even completely facilitate certain types of collective action? This is a fundamental question as more aspects of life, social and political processes, the economy, etc. are affected by digitalization and informatization, a question that requires consideration also in regard to social media [especially, but not solely as information and communication technology (ICT)] and collective action.

7.1 BETWEEN FLICKR AND THE GOOGLE INDEX

When considering small-scale instances of collective action that rely on relatively little human agency and more on the social media platform itself, collective behavior with its noninstitutional character is a type of collective action, which is most probable to profit or emerge from the ability of such social media–supported and decentralized organization. As the definitions presented in Chapter 3 argue, instances of collective behavior, which pursue short-term goals, need less complex strategies of action and rely mainly on the quantity of participants. Collective behavior is primarily spontaneous, unregulated, and unstructured group activity. However, through symbolic communication and interaction, initially unstructured collective behavior can in turn promote emergent norms and incipient forms of order. Having said that, collective behavior also requires what scholars termed as cultural drifts, relative deprivation, strain and breakdown, or grievances. In other words, collective behavior, although spontaneous, short term, and mostly unstructured, comes as reaction to some needs or motivations.

Clay Shirky (2008) addressed the issue by stressing the difference between the picture-sharing platform Flickr and Google: as Flickr users use hashtags to label their uploaded pictures, the platform offers them related hashtags that have already been used by others and automatically links pictures with same or similar hashtags. In this manner, a collection of pictures, a pictured documentation of an event, for example, can be created by an otherwise uncoordinated group of people. Shirky correctly emphasizes that there is a distinction between a central coordination of people—as in the classical form of organizations—and the platform's ability—Flickr, in this case—to support groups of people to coordinate themselves: "Flickr is simply a platform; whatever coordination happens comes from the users and is projected onto the site" (Shirky, 2008, p. 46).

In other words, social media (as ICT) have in some cases the ability to facilitate a decentralized synchronization and coordination of individual actors by creating information links of their actions.[1] In this manner, the formation of (an instance of) collective action can be supported, become more efficient, or even enabled, as social media offer substitute or alternative ways of access to other mechanisms that are crucial for the formation of collective action, such as shared awareness, on-site organization and synchronization of actions, investment and mobilization of resources, social networks (with strong and/or weak ties), or institutional involvement.[2]

Even though social media can in some cases enable collective behavior and/or action that otherwise would not have been possible or even thought of, it is not a *creatio ex nihilo*, let alone a creation of the system itself. Such a facilitation or coordination requires active actions from the individuals; it requires agency[3] on behalf of the individuals, who use the platform. Furthermore, as the platform is designed and perceived as social media, its social affordance means people use it to interact, share information, communicate, perceive, and cooperate with their social environment. Thus they deliberately contribute to a collective behavior and/or action, also if in a spontaneous, unregulated, and unstructured manner and in some cases even without being unaware of its ends.

A further key aspect of social media facilitating and enabling collective behavior is that the platform supports the communication and interaction between individuals, even if in a symbolic manner. By deploying and suggesting hashtags, for example, Flickr both enables and facilitates a meta-level communication between the individuals who upload pictures onto the platform, to share them with others, and creates a connection between those pictures and individuals, connection that otherwise would not have been created.

A similar example is the usage of hashtags on further social media platforms such as Twitter and Instagram: on both platforms, individuals can mark their content—tweets and pictures—with hashtags using the hash sign "#" and receive from the platform recommendation for hashtags to use.[4] Thus not only the creation of picture collections—of events, of locations, of #selfie—is possible, but also (to name a few examples) the statement or positioning of opinion in discourse. For example:

---

[1] Decentralized synchronization is regarded at this point in terms of no central organization by people, institutions, or movements, knowing well that in such a case, the platform at hand is centralizing the organization.

[2] In this context, Shirky uses the words "ridiculously easy" ways of group forming to describe this support of the formation of collective behavior—"group effort" in Shirky's terms.

[3] The term agency refers to the individuals' socially constituted capacity to act independently and to make their own choices.

[4] Over time the usage of hash sign (hashtags) has developed to an unofficially standard in social media, to declare tags or metadata, which are searchable and linkable.

- Discussions on political and social issues as with the hashtags #proLife and #proChoice in regard to abortions[5] or
- the expression of solidarity and grief, as with the hashtags #JeSuisCharlie, #JeSuisHumain, and #JeSuisAhmed after the 2015 attack on the French satire-magazine *Charlie Hebdo*.

This comes to show that on social media, initially unstructured collective behavior—the tagging of statements, pictures, and other contents—can in many cases promote the emergence of norms and forms of order, both taking place within the respective platform and, when a critical mass is achieved, across platforms. Furthermore, it is not only that the platforms' design and algorithms support this phenomenon, the institutions behind the different social media platform react to such trends, norms, and forms of order that emerge within their own platform as well as other platforms and adjust their platform's design and functionalities accordingly.

Lastly, as mentioned earlier, collective behavior requires less complex strategies of action and rely mainly on the quantity of participants. The reliance on the quantity of participants (users) is a factor that is central for the relevance—and, regarding the institutional dimension, economical success—of social media platforms. In certain cases of collective behavior facilitated and/or enabled by social media, as in the above-mentioned examples, the platform offers individuals the means to join their actions into a collective or "group effort" without the need for strategic planning and organization on the one hand. On the other hand, such facilitation on behalf of the platform relies on the quantity of participant. For the system's algorithms to identify trends and calculate relevance, they rely on the quantity of users who act in a similar way within the platform (e.g., share pictures from the same location, use the same hashtags, share similar information and links, use similar phrasing and terminology, communicate with each other, etc.). In other words, they rely on collective behavior within the virtual (rather than spatial) spaces of the respective social media platform.

The aspects of agency and deliberate contribution distinguish social media from other ICTs or information platforms that aggregate information, which is generated by users, for a common good but without users' active participation. To stress this notion, Shirky compares Flickr with Google's search engine index: "There are also ways of unknowingly sharing your work, as when Google reads the linking preferences of hundreds of millions of Internet users. These users are helping create a communally available resource, as Flickr users are,

---

[5] Thus transferring the existing political framing of the issue (by groups supportive of abortions deploying the prochoice terminology and those who oppose abortions deploying the prolife one) into the discussion over social media. See also Yardi and Boyd (2010).

but unlike Flickr, the people whose work Google is aggregating aren't actively choosing to make their contributions" (Shirky, 2008, p. 49).

The Google Index therefore and according to Shirky is not a result of collective behavior, collective action, or "group effort." The creation of the Google Index may have some similarities to the creation of a picture database in Flickr or a themed timeline on Twitter on the level of aggregation and linking of information, but it excludes other important factors of collective action, such as the individuals'—the platform's users—agency as well as the platform's social affordance and the users' reaction to and interaction with it.

Furthermore, on social media platforms, individuals are able to perceive that their actions become part of a collective or movement through feedback they receive in real time both from other individuals on the platforms (e.g., through likes and favorites, shares, and retweets, perceiving similar content shared by other individuals, etc.) and from the platform itself (e.g., through suggestions for relevant hashtags based on the ones other individuals used as well as the presentation of other individuals' content that is related to the same subject of action).

This approach and the notion that social media can facilitate and enable some instances of collective behavior pose two crucial questions:

First, collective behavior, as with other forms of collective action and especially when leaving out the notion of irrationality, is theorized to require some motivation or needs—cultural drifts, relative deprivation, strain and breakdown, or grievances—as preconditions to take place. By arguing that social media can facilitate and enable instances of collective behavior, we need to address the question, what can be the motivations or needs for collective behavior that is facilitated by social media? And how do they connect to the individuals' agency?

The examples presented earlier show that in cases that can be considered as instances of collective behavior and/or action, needs and motivations on behalf of the individuals and their actions as agents are present, even if not always compatible with the terminology of grievances or stain and breakdown. In more clear cases of collective behavior and/or action, these are the self-expression in social and political discussions or expressions of solidarity and grief. In less clear cases, such as sharing and tagging of pictures, the motivations might be the simple desire to share one's "products" (e.g., pictures), the basic need of communicating with others, or even a somewhat narcissist desire to obtain attention, appreciation, and reputation (in form of likes, favorites, shared and retweets, etc.).[6]

---

[6] For a discussion on the issue of narcissism in social media and online communication see Keen (2015), Twenge and Campbell (2009).

Second, derived from these motivations, also the goal of the collective behavior poses—at least a theoretical—problem. On the one hand, in the Flickr example Shirky argues that individuals deliberately contribute to a collective action, also if sometimes unaware of its ends. On the other hand, further deploying the Flickr example, the documentation of the event (the ends) emerges as such not before someone searches for it (for the correlating hashtag) on the platform and perceives the results as an event documentation.

This, conjoint with the aspect of motivations and needs, comes to show the limitations of collective behavior and/or action that takes place within the borders of social media. Be it a photo collection, a political discussion, or an expression of solidarity, collective actions that are facilitated and enabled by social media—and therefore, take place within the borders of social media at first—pursue and obtain relatively moderate goals that usually have a minor or symbolic impact on the actions' broader context (e.g., fundamental political issues, war on terror, protests). In some cases, the goal pursued by the individual agent does not even have to do much with the outcomes of the algorithmic-facilitated collective action, as is the case with many forms of collective behavior. To achieve greater impact, the collective action needs to extend beyond merely communication and activities on social media or algorithmic collection and linking of information; that is to say, take the issues to the streets, draw the attention of mainstream/mass media, put pressure on political decision makers, etc.

7.2 BETWEEN ACTIONS AND ALGORITHMS

The TripleC model that was presented in Chapter 2 offers a further theoretical framework to examine the subject of this chapter. According to this model, what Fuchs and Trottier term as *Integrated Sociality*, that is, the convergence of the three modes of sociality cognition, communication, and cooperation, is a constitutive feature of social media. The concept of integrated sociality regards how social media (as ICT as well as media) enable such a convergence:

- individuals create content on the cognitive level (e.g., a picture or video, text, hashtag, or hyperlink);
- publish it so that others can like, comment, and share it (communication); and
- allow others to manipulate the content so that new content with multiple authorship can emerge (e.g., a photo collection, a broad expression of solidarity, a digitally documented and openly accessible discussion), which is the cooperative level (that is to say, collective action and/or its product) (Fuchs and Trottier, 2014).

Applying this model to the discussion in this chapter, integrated sociality is the mechanism that makes social media (as ICT as well as media) susceptible to facilitate and enable instances of collective behavior and/or action in the same manner that public spaces offer individuals and groups places to meet up, form a collective, communicate, and cooperate; in the same manner that a variety of—analog and digital—ICTs support processes of cognition and cooperation; in the same manner that more and less formal institutional and/or organizational frameworks support cooperation; and so on.

Social media's integrated sociality converges these spaces, mechanisms, and tools in one digital space—one social media platform—thus providing many of the needed conditions for the emergence of collective action and lowering its barriers. That is to say, the argument that social media facilitate and/or enable collective action refers to the manner in which social media may provide the needed conditions for collective action to emerge and support its participators in various ways (as Chapters 3–6 discuss). It is not, however, arguing that social media, or any other ICT or media for that matter, creates or produces actions—collective or not collective ones—taking action is done by human beings and their agency, i.e., by human actors.

In *The Human Condition* (Arendt, 1998, 1958), Hannah Arendt offers an instructive notion of Action as one of three fundamental human activities: "If labor for Arendt is the movement of the natural life-process of human being itself, based on biological need, and work is the movement of production that brings forth the works constituting an enduring, stable, material world, the realm of action is the movement of action and speech constituting what Arendt regards as the political realm proper" (Eldred, 2013, p. 79).[7] For Arendt, it is always a who and not a what, which acts—takes initiative, begins, sets something into motion, exerts power to bring about a change or movement. Furthermore, action, as an interplay, which is also a power play, among a plurality of players (or agents) has a dimension of unpredictability and incalculability of its further ramifications (Eldred, 2013). Lastly, Arendt argues that through actions and words "men distinguish themselves [...]; they are the modes in which human beings appear to each other, not indeed as physical objects, but *qua* men" (Arendt, 1998, 1958, p. 176).[8]

---

[7] Arendt's postulation of and differentiation between these "three fundamental human activities"—labor, work, and action—differ from the Marxist understanding of work and labor, which is deployed by Christian Fuchs and Daniel Trottier when using these termini in relation to the TripleC model. This points out that Arendt misunderstands Marx' distinction between productive and unproductive work as well as between work and labor. Having said that, at this point, Arendt's notion of action, rather than labor and work, will be used, among others relying on Michael Eldred's analysis of Arendt's insights into (the interplay that is) human action, in his successful attempt to bring them to their proper, elaborated socio-ontological concepts and, in turn, deploy it for a notion of Digital Whoness.

[8] As Eldred notes: "Arendt restricts this speaking and acting to a separate sphere of existence that she calls the public or political realm by distinguishing acting from laboring and working" (Eldred, 2013, p. 86).

Applying this notion to the question of collective action facilitated and/or enabled by social media—the dilemma between actions and algorithms—taking action and being agents is reserved to the who (the individual human actors, the platform's users, the activists who deploy social media) which act, rather than the what (the platform and its algorithms on the one hand, the digital representation of a person and one's identity in form of a social media profile and one's produced/shared content on the other). Be it an online expression of solidarity, the organization of political protests, the coordination of refugee aid, or the tagging of pictures, the ones who take initiative and act, who set something into motion, who exert power to bring about change or movement are the people who were motivated by their grievances and took action to pursuit certain goals. In the interaction between people and social media (as ICT), the platform and its algorithms do not take action, but rather react to people's actions within the platform, for example, by calculating probabilities, making information links to similar human (inter-)actions within the platform. Thus social media may support actions taken by human actors and in some cases make the conditions for collective action to emerge more favorable, but not act by themselves.

Considering action as a human activity in a social context,[9] which is, according to the mathematician, philosopher, and ethicist Michael Eldred, an interplay and a power play between a plurality of players, is instructive for understanding collective action. Collective action, in which the plurality of players means not only the interplay between individual actions but also the manner in which individuals come together to act—to set something into motion, to exert power and bring about change—thus forming a collective, the interplay within this collective, and the interplay between the collective and other agents, groups, institutions, and powers; a power play at its best, an interplay whose development, consequences, and results are neither predictable nor calculable. The latter is the exact opposite of algorithmic functioning, which is by definition calculable and predictable, as the possible outcomes are calculated by the algorithm according to different variables.

When considering social media, many variables are indeed unpredictable, since they are dependent on human actions, thus reinforcing the demarcation between human action and algorithmic functioning. Lastly, for Arendt human beings perceive each other as human beings instead of physical objects through their actions and words. Social media platforms help people perceive their social surrounding, link their actions, and coordinate them. Thus social media platform constitutes a digital space, a medium through which people perceive each other in their words and actions (in form of content creation,

---

[9] A "web of human relationships" in Arendt's words—an unavoidable connotation to social media.

sharing, and manipulation, textual and visual interaction, etc.). The interaction between the human actor and the platform is, in turn, an interplay between a person and other human actors from one's social network who use the same platform.

Consider the following example: in 2008 a company named Waze[10] introduced a navigation system as smartphone app. Waze uses a similar logic to Google Maps' navigation function, namely, inferring real-time traffic data from all users, that is, their end devices such as smartphones, using the app by tracking the car's movement (Schneier, 2015). However, Waze's functionalities go beyond the collection and analysis of traffic data (to offer drivers better routes). Suitable for the time period of Waze's market penetration and growth of user numbers between the yeas 2009 and 2012, which was the peak of the social media–oriented technical discourse—the *Peak of Inflated Expectations* in terms of the Hype Cycle discourse—the app functions as a social media platform as well: drivers can send messages to other drivers in their surrounding and report accidents, traffic jams, police controls, speed cameras, and so on. Furthermore, users can edit information regarding street courses, house numbers, dirt roads, construction sites, etc., which keeps Waze's information base in the system up to date.

For both of Waze's functionalities—navigation system based on traffic data derived from users and a social media platform for drivers—the system requires a critical mass of users, both in real time and continuously. But which of Waze's functionalities can be regarded as (products of) collective action on behalf of its users, the drivers?

The system's central functionality, the navigation system, is based on location and traffic data that are retrieved without the individuals' active participation, without their agency being involved,[11] and in most cases even without them being aware of that data collection. Although driving a car and actively using the Waze app are forms of action and agency, this case is comparable with the example of building webpages that are analyzed and integrated as data within the Google Index—it lacks many aspects that are crucial for collective action to emerge; it lacks cooperation, communication, and in a sense even cognition. Since the sharing of traffic data is not done cognitively, but rather automatically derived by the system without the individual's active decision, this functionality does not apply for any of the modes of cognition in terms of the TripleC model. Neither does it apply for being an action both because it does not "set something into motion" but rather reacts to people's actions (their driving) and because it is per se a calculation, hence calculable. Furthermore,

---

[10] Acquired by Google in 2013 and combined with Google Maps (Google, Inc., 2013).
[11] Agency in terms of the conscious and willing delivery of data/information for the system and other drivers to use.

with or without the Waze users being aware of the data collection, they are compelled to accept it via the app's Terms of Use. That is to say, the functioning of Waze's navigation system is based on a form of corporate surveillance, which is mandatory for every individual who chooses to use the app.[12]

On the other hand, the notion of integrated sociality applies for the Waze's social media functionalities, which offer more than the mere sharing of goal-related information (send messages, update the maps, or report accidents, traffic jams, police controls, and speed cameras); not only that individuals, that is, drivers, cognitively share content, they can communicate on it and allow others to manipulate and supplement it. In this manner, content with multiple authorship emerges, which serves as the product of collective action, namely, drivers act together to support their "cause" or goal—avoid traffic jams and speed cameras, reduce accidents, reduce gasoline consumption, etc. Furthermore, through their actions within Waze (as a social media platform), the individual drivers perceive each other as human actors, they have the ability to take initiative and act (by, for example, informing other drivers on accidents or police controls), and they can act to bring about change (e.g., reduce traffic jams). All of which comes down to an interplay between a plurality of players, a plurality of drivers, whose ramifications are incalculable and unpredictable, since the re-action of each individual driver is, unlike an algorithm, incalculable and unpredictable.

The example of Waze comes to show that it is a complex task to draw a clear demarcation of what (parts of a) system/platform can be regarded as social media or social media functionalities. And, based on this demarcation, what functionalities of the system/platform can enable and/or facilitate collective action by making the condition for individual human action becoming a collective one more favorable.

7.3 CONCLUSIONS

Social media are a complex combination of ICT, media, and institutional functionalities and aspects. In their embedding in a specific, data-driven platform, they have the ability to facilitate and even enable some instances of collective action. In other words, as discussed in previous chapters, social media can help people overcome difficulties of coordination, organization, and

---

[12] Having said that, one can also argue that the data-driven navigation functionality does apply for the cognitive, perhaps even communication and cooperation level, since some Waze users are aware of the way the app functions and actively support it by using the app instead of other navigation services. From this point of view, Waze's algorithms that combine and analyze traffic data and offer better routes as output facilitate collective action with the outcome of more efficient traffic.

communication in large groups; these difficulties are often the obstacles that prevent people from fulfilling their needs, motivations, and goals through collective action. In some cases, social media can also operate not only as helper, but also as enabler of collective action. The argument is, however, that by enabling/facilitating collective action, social media provide favorable conditions for collective action to emerge and support its participators in various ways; the actions themselves—taking initiative, setting something into motion, exerting power to bring about a change or movement—are done by human beings and their agency, i.e., by human agents.

When regarding behavior and/or collective action, whose facilitator and even enabler are social media platforms, one recognizes the limitations of social media's ability to do so. Such instances of collective action usually take place within the borders of the specific social media platform (and more rarely across platforms) and pursue and obtain relatively moderate goals that usually have a minor or symbolic impact on the actions broader context. To achieve greater impact, the collective action needs to extend beyond merely communication and activities on social media; that is to say, take the issues to the streets, draw the attention of mainstream/mass media, put pressure on political decision makers, etc. However, when such an extension of the collective action takes place, it is crucial to take a step back and address it within the greater context, in which it is embedded.

For example, in January 2013, following a public discussion of sexism in German political parties, the feminist activist Anna Wizorek suggested on Twitter that women will share their personal experiences of sexism and collect them under the hashtag #Aufschrei (German for outcry). Within a week, the #Aufschrei hashtag was mentioned over 49,000 and retweeted 30,000 times (Spiegel, 2013). The action also obtained the attention of mainstream/mass media and was discussed in the printed and online press as well as television talk shows. Considered as an instance of collective behavior and/or action that was enabled by thousands of individuals making their contribution and Twitter's ability to link the information behind the hashtags, the action resulted with an online collection of experiences, discussions, and opinions (and, of course, a wide social debate of the issue of sexism). Considered as an action that exceeded Twitter's "borders" and ignited discussions in mass media—and probably in many groups of friends, families, coworkers, and social movements—the #Aufschrei debate needs to be considered in the broader context of sexism, feminism, centuries of women's struggle, as well as German politics and white male dominance within it.

The following chapter will discuss the aspect that the #Aufschrei example touched upon—the relation of social media and mass or mainstream media when it comes to collective action.

References

Arendt, H., 1998, 1958. The Human Condition (Second Edition with an Introduction by Margaret Canovan). U.P., Chicago.

Eldred, M., 2013. Arendt on whoness in the world. In: Capurro, R., Eldred, M., Nagel, D. (Eds.), Digital Whoness: Identity, Privacy and Freedom in the Cyberworld. Ontos Verlag, Frankfurt, pp. 79–104.

Fuchs, C., Trottier, D., 2014. Theorizing social media, politics, and the state: an introduction. In: Fuchs, C., Trottier, D. (Eds.), Social Media, Politics and the State: Protests, Revolutions, Riots, Crime and Policing in the Age of Facebook, Twitter and YouTube. Routledge, New York, pp. 3–38.

Google, Inc., 2013. Google Maps and Waze, Outsmarting Traffic Together. Retrieved from: googleblog.blogspot.de/2013/06/google-maps-and-waze-outsmarting.html.

Karatzogianni, A., 2013. A cyberconflict analysis of the 2011 Arab Spring uprisings. In: Youngs, G. (Ed.), Digital World: Connectivity, Creativity and Rights. Routledge, London, pp. 159–175.

Keen, A., 2015. The Internet Is Not the Answer. Atlantic Monthly Press, New York.

Schneier, B., 2015. Data and Goliath. W. W. Norton & Company, New York.

Shirky, C., 2008. Here Comes Everybody: The Power of Organizing without Organizations. Penguin Group, London.

Spiegel, 2013. Sexismusdebatte: #Aufschrei führt zu Twitter-Rekord. Retrieved from: www.spiegel.de/netzwelt/web/Aufschrei-fuehrt-zu-twitter-rekord-a-882207.html.

Twenge, J.M., Campbell, W.K., 2009. The Narcissism Epidemic: Living in the Age of Entitlement. Free Press, New York.

Yardi, S., Boyd, D., 2010. Dynamic debates: an analysis of group polarization over time on Twitter. Bulletin of Science, Technology & Society 30 (5), 316–327.

CHAPTER 8

Alternative or Mainstream: The Interplay Between Social Media and Mass Media

ABSTRACT

Al Jazeera and its role in the events of the Arab Spring; *Zinor Layla*, Channel 2 News, and YNET coverage of the Israeli social justice protests; Tagesschau and Abendschau reporting over the refugee crisis in Germany/Berlin; *Fox News* and the Guardian treatment of the Occupy Wall Street Movement. When considering the interplay between social media and mass/mainstream media in the context of collective action and social movements, a complex and paradoxical relation that goes beyond the mere dissemination of collective action or movement-related information is revealed, a relation that is affected by aspects such as newsworthiness and gatekeepers, legitimacy and hegemony in discourse, political and economic agendas, framing processes, and institutional access.

Keywords: Alternative media; Framing; Mainstream media; Mass media; Newsworthiness; Social media; Traditional media.

CONTENTS

The previous chapter touched upon the limits of collective action within the borders of social media; these limits shed light on the complex and somewhat paradoxical relation between social media and mass/mainstream media[1] when considering

---

[1] The term *mass media* refers to a variety of media technologies that share the characteristic of reaching large audiences via mass communication; thus, ICTs fulfill a central role in the definition. Mass media technologies (and the respectable mass media outlets) are divers and include broadcast, digital, print, and outdoor media. Mainstream media, in contrast to alternative media, addresses (mass) media with influence on a large number of individuals and groups in society, thus, both reflecting and shaping prevailing opinions. In other words, mass media refers to the media's technological and institutional dimension, whereas mainstream media accentuates their role in society, discourse, public opinion, and hegemony.

their role in collective action. On the one hand, social media are often celebrated as an empowering medium or tool, which frees activists and movements from the constraints of institutionalized—state as well as private held—mass media, constraints that include aspects of access to these institutions and resources, economic and political interests and agendas, operation costs, legitimacy, and free speech. On the other hand, when relying solely on social media as tools, media, or spaces of action, collective action soon meets its limits. Although there are rare contradicting examples (such as the Gezi Park protests mentioned in this chapter), mass media are almost always crucial for collective action and/or social movements to gain relevance and increase their impact, as they help movements overcome disadvantages of online or social media communication (e.g., the lack of access to social media within broad groups in society or the ability of provide legitimacy within mainstream discourse). In other words, mass media constitutes a "master arena," through which social movements and actors of collective action gain access to the various players of the public arena—media outlets, political actors (parliaments, ministries, party conventions), courts, academia, etc.—as well as in which the contest over meaning (e.g., competing framing processes)[2] takes place (Gamson, 2004). Thus social media deployment often plays the double role of fostering discourses and actions, which are independent of institutionalized mass media, and at a certain point drawing the mass media's attention to these discourses and actions, thus helping social movements and/or collective actors take their issues to the public arena.

Strictly speaking, even the process of raising the awareness to certain issues for them to be picked up by mass/mainstream media, thus contributing to a larger debate on the issue, is a form of collective action. But the interplay between social media and mass/mainstream media is not unidirectional; it does not end by mass/mainstream media picking up the issues. People also share and discuss news, to which they are exposed through mass media, on social media, hence mainstream media's influence on discourse. As studies by the Pew Research Center and Reuters have shown, people increasingly share and discuss news over social media platforms as well as use and perceive social media (that is, the news shared by their social media contacts and media outlets) as a central news source (Barthel et al., 2015; Mitchell et al., 2016; Newman et al., 2016).[3] Thus issues that are raised in social media and picked up by mainstream media also find their way back to social media, however, within a broader spectrum of social networks, contexts, and frames.

---

[2] William A. Gamson (2004) mentions aspects of multiple, ambivalent, bystander frames in this context.

[3] Also in this respect, social media platforms vary drastically. According to the cited Reuters study, 44% of the study participants used Facebook as a news source, followed by YouTube with 19%, Twitter as rather specialized platform for journalists, politician, and "news-junkies" with 10%, and WhatsApp with 8%. There are, of course, also regional differences. For example, in Korea, Kakao Talk and Kakao Story are among the top four platforms used for news consumption (Newman et al., 2016).

In this respect, the case of the *#Aufschrei* debate breaching the borders of Twitter and taking the discussion of sexual harassment in German politics and society to mass and mainstream media—from online magazines such as *Spiegel Online*, to television talk shows such as *Günter Jauch*, to printed media etc.—is no exception when considering the interplay between social media and mass media in terms of collective action. The social media activity surrounding the emergence, organization, and carrying out collective action often receives the attention of mass media, which picks up the issue. This media coverage, in turn, contributes to the growth of the collective action and/or social movement, both in sympathetic and opposing circles. Consider the following examples:

- Al Jazeera and its role in the events of the Arab Spring;
- *Zinor Layla*,[4] Channel 2 News, and YNET coverage of the Israeli social justice protests;
- *Tagesschau* and *Abendschau* reporting over the refugee crisis in Germany/Berlin.

When looking into these examples as well as *#Aufschrei*, the interplay is revealed as a complex relation that goes beyond the mere dissemination of collective action or movement-related information, a relation that touches upon issues of newsworthiness and gatekeepers, access to resources, institutions, and centers of power, legitimacy and hegemony in discourse, and more.

8.1 THE MANY FACETS OF NEWSWORTHINESS

Not all issues, which are or can be of public interest, enjoy the attention of mass media. Scarce resources and publishing costs (e.g., print, distribution, or website and server maintenance) that are higher than the estimated produced economical profit, insufficient so-called newsworthiness in the eyes of the respectable media outlets that serve as "gatekeepers," and the political and economic agenda/interests of the media outlets serve as barriers that limit the access of social movements to mass media. This, in turn, means that such issues, movements, and actions often stay outside the public consciousness and interest. Social media, in contrast, help activists and movements overcome these barriers.

When the costs embedded in publishing (e.g., journalists' wage, print, distribution, broadcasting, or website-maintenance costs) are higher than the estimated economical profit they could produce, many issues will not be published, which is, in turn, an expression for the scarcity of resources in terms of mass media communication. By supporting efficient and cheap, even free-of-charge publishing, dissemination of information, and platform for discussions, social

---

[4] Late night show that handles current affairs, especially from culture, the net, and tech news. The show was the first to report the Rothschild tent encampment during the Israeli housing protests.

media enable activists and movements to disseminate information regarding the issues they want to promote without depending on access to mass media or having to carry the costs that are embedded in them.

For issues that are first published and discussed over social media platforms,[5] the public attention gained over social media eventually draws the attention of mass media to these issues, increasing their newsworthiness in the eyes of mass/mainstream media outlets. Mass media in turn increase the dissemination of the issue at hand and broadens public awareness also outside social media platforms. This means both overcoming the social network–based dissemination of information over social media and as reaching broader audiences that are not (or scarcely) using social media, or reaching individuals who use social media but are not exposed to the issue due to the filter bubble and/or their social networks being different from the ones discussing the issue. As mainstream media, this means that the discussion of the issue in these media affects mainstream discourse and public opinion, or at the very least make the issue present within them. Thus (and in accordance with the aspects discussed in Chapters 3, 4, and 6), success in drawing the attention of mass and mainstream media, that is, success in putting the issue and its "newsworthiness" on the public agenda, contributes to the emergence, mobilization, and development of collective action and social movements with their various dimensions and stages.

Generally speaking, this is a positive phenomenon for the democratization of public and political discourses, allowing individuals and movements that do not have access to the institutions behind mass media to raise issues and put them on the agenda (with implications that are sometimes crucial to help igniting large-scale protests and uprisings). Having said that, this aspect is not an egalitarian one. To achieve sufficient impact for an issue to become present and widespread enough in social media and, in turn, be picked up by mass/mainstream media, activists and movements need to have access to various resources such as:

- technology,
- time to pursue such online activism,
- information and media literacy, or rather, social media literacy, and
- ability to reach the "right" social networks to disseminate the particular issue.

These resources are anything but evenly distributed in society. Not to mention that not only the movements/activists, but also the "target audience"—potential sympathizers with the movement causes—needs to have access to the similar resources and to social media themselves; thus, such individuals and groups might often remain unreached or even excluded.

---

[5] Some of which may even have a mass, rather than mainstream, media character, such as Blogs.

For Clay Shirky, the scarcity of resources and the embedded costs of mass media stand in connection with the emergence of "professional classes" as "gatekeepers" (in this case, of newsworthiness) (Shirky, 2008). According to Shirky, a professional class, for example, journalism and librarianship, acquires some sort of specialization in its profession, it creates norms for the practice of the profession and acknowledges only praxis that is compatible with those norms, and the scarcity of resources plays a major role in its creation.[6] The professionals, in turn, "become gatekeepers, simultaneously providing and controlling access to information, entertainment, communication, or other ephemeral goods" (Shirky, 2008, p. 57). The costs of publishing using other information and communication technologies (ICTs; print, radio, television, traditional websites) have created a scarcity that helped form the profession of journalism, but the deployment of social media, such as blogging platforms, change the equation by offering low-cost solutions, which are in certain cases more flexible and multifunctional than traditional mass media. Therefore the deployment of social media to raise issues of public interest helps undermine the role of traditional journalism as a gatekeeper of newsworthiness. By partially breaching the dichotomy between producers and audience, the changing interplay between social media and mass/mainstream media increases the chance of collective action and social movements to emerge and gain momentum as a bottom-up process.[7]

This, however, proves to be a double-edged sword. Although removing intermediates (such as professional journalists and editors) that function as "filters" for information often makes useful information available, it simultaneously poses the danger of decline in the accuracy and quality of the (social movement–related) information being circulated. Because of the ease of dissemination of information over social media platforms, individuals often exert less effort to verify information before sharing it or even deliberately disseminate false information to pursue their goals. This is deliberately used not only by some movements, which rely on misinformation for their mobilization, but also by individuals. To state a few examples:

- In the summer of 2016, the—anything other than new phenomenon of—dissemination of misinformation and rumors over social media

---

[6] This is, in terms of Foucauldian discourse analysis, an expression of discursive power. These institutions or professional classes hold power over discourse, and therefore, over knowledge in society. This power is expressed, among other things, by control over who can take part in discourse, which information is legitimate or not legitimate, which manners of expression and articulation are legitimate part of discourse, etc.

[7] In comparison with a sociomedial reality, in which mass/mainstream media, along with their technological and institutional aspects, are the dominating, perhaps only media available to the broad public.

became an acute problem during various terrorist attacks and killing spree in several European countries. In some cases, such as the July 22 killing spree in Munich, the misinformation disseminated over social media platforms even contributed to mass panics, impaired police operations, and led to unneeded restriction of several public transportation lines (ARD Tagesschau 2016).

- Following the discussion of the German refugee aid movement in Chapter 6, at the same time a peak of rumors and false reports in social media has been observed. These contained false reports on violence, crimes, and abuse of social benefits. According to an Amedeu Antonio Stiftung study, right-wing movements and individuals actively disseminate such misinformation among others to gain support for their political agenda (Baldauf et al., 2016).
- ISIL's[8] effective use of social media for Islamistic propaganda.[9,10]
- Furthermore, also governments and intelligence agencies, of both democratic and authoritarian states, are reported to actively disseminate misinformation over social media, to promote their political goals (Financial Times, 2015; Morozov, 2011; Naji, 2015).[11]

Complementing the equation of costs, resources, gatekeepers, and newsworthiness are the economic and political interests of institutionalized mass media. In privately held corporate mass/mainstream media outlets, not only the direct "return of investment" by a news piece plays a role in the decision regarding its publication, but also the piece's content and its relation to the broader interests of the media outlet (such as the political and/or economic agenda of the respectable media outlet). For example, in his research on the Occupy Wall Stress movement, David Graeber shows how different mass/mainstream media outlets have reported on the Occupy movement in a different manner; *Al Jazeera* and the progressive *Guardian* were mostly sympathetic of the movement, whereas the conservative outlet *Fox News* reported on Occupy as violent, chaotic, and criminal (Graeber, 2012; Fuchs, 2014). To state yet another example, it was reported that the owners of the Israeli newspaper *Maariv* were interfering with the reporting on the 2011 social justice protests (by forbidding the printing of the activist Daphni Leef's photos, reducing the

---

[8] Islamic State of Iraq and the Levant (ISIL), which is also known as Islamic State of Iraq and Syria (ISIS), Islamic State (IS), and its Arabic acronym *Daesh*.

[9] In his book *The Internet Is Not the Answer*, the entrepreneur and author Andrew Keen argues that "ISIS's effective use of social media highlights the core problem with the Internet. When the gatekeeper is removed and anyone can publish anything online, much of that 'content' will be either propaganda or plain lies" (Keen, 2015, p. 142).

[10] For a further discussion of ISIL's social media deployment, see Chapter 11.

[11] See also Chapter 9.

coverage of the subject, and placing it in the last pages of the paper), since these were perceived as contradicting the interests of the paper's owners IDB Group (TheMarker, 2016). Thus not only the political and economic agenda, but also the agenda and/or economic interests of institutions relate to the media outlet (such as establishing, owning, or financing institution) as well as their ties to other powerful groups may influence reporting. Furthermore, financial considerations, such as the consequences of losing advertisers and/ or readers in response to news coverage that does not correspond with their opinions or interests may influence a media outlet's coverage of a certain subject.

In relation to aspects of publishing costs and scarcity of resources, the interplay between social media deployment and mass/mainstream media's considerations of "newsworthiness" due to political agenda and related economic interests is more complex. On the one hand, social movements may experience easy access to the media and sympathizing reporting on their issues; thus exploiting the advantages of social media deployment. On the other hand, if a social movement's issues contradict the political agenda of the respectable media outlet and related power groups, the movement may face censorship and negative coverage, in spite of the movement's momentum in public and political debate and the sympathy it experiences over social media. This, however, is common for the interplay between social movements and mass/mainstream media in general, regardless of the deployment of social media (Gamson, 2004); with the difference that even when facing barriers from mass/mainstream media, social media continue to offer movements and activists alternative ways of disseminating information, mobilizing, accessing resources, etc.

8.2 SOCIAL MEDIA—ALTERNATIVE MEDIA?

The interplay of mass/mainstream media with the social media in the context of collective action and social movements reveals a complex and paradoxical relation. On the one hand, although social media often serve as means to bypass "gatekeepers" and "newsworthiness"-barriers of various kinds, mass and mainstream media still play a crucial role in many social movements, even ones with extremely effective social media deployment. On the other hand, social media often serve as an alternative to corporate or state-controlled mass media, either for putting issues on the agenda of mass media, thus being alternative in terms of bypassing gatekeepers, or (as the following example of the Gezi Park protests shows) for bypassing mass media altogether, thus being the only or one of the few alternatives that activists, protesters, and citizens actually have.

Social media also poses an alternative to mainstream media in terms of framing processes,[12] which are dependent on the flow of carefully produced movement-related information (in the form of frames). Social media platforms help create networks and spaces, over which frames can be propagated, while bypassing mainstream media and their framing of the social movement, its issues and causes; increasing the representation of activists' and nonmainstream or not biased frames (Garrett, 2006). This is crucial for social movements, since mass/ mainstream media, who pick up the movement's issues in their news coverage— both in sympathetic and opposing coverage—often do so using other frames than the ones deployed by the movement, thus offering different interpretations and meanings than the ones intended by the movement itself.

Christian Fuchs stresses that contradictions in the treatment of social movements by different media outlets are shaped by relations of power and the gap between the resources that media outlets have at their disposal. In terms of visibility and audience reach, many corporate mass/mainstream media outlets are dominant also online, whereas alternative noncorporate media are less likely to have such dominance and visibility. Fuchs gives the example of *Fox News*, ranked by Alexa. com in position 156 among the world's most viewed sites, in comparison with *Democracy Now!* that is ranked in position 17,369. According to Fuchs, due to the structures of the media landscape in capitalism, alternative media and alternative views are in disadvantage caused by structural communication inequalities (Fuchs, 2014). Although by deploying social media, alternative media or individuals and movements with alternative views can gain more access to discourse and even draw the attention of mass media to their positions, the inequalities described by Fuchs continue to exist also within social media. The privileged position of mass and mainstream media outlets reflects their visibility and reach on social media, as individuals follow their official accounts and share their content more intensively than is the case with alternative media, thus reproducing the power relations in the media landscape within social media. Even when considering regional and national differences, (the social media presence of) traditional mainstream media outlets serve as central news source over social media. This brings the authors of a Reuters study to the conclusion that on the one hand "we see publishers losing control of distribution, some consumers not noticing where content comes from, and the growing influence of platforms and algorithms. And yet at the same time we find, both in our survey data and our qualitative work, that people still want, value, and identify with traditional news brands" (Newman et al., 2016, p. 29).

Journalism scholar Emily Bell argues that due to social media, news publishers have lost control over distribution. This leads to increase in power of social media corporations with their commercial interests and the algorithms

---

[12] For a discussion of framing, see Chapter 4.

controlled by them (Bell, 2016). Bell's conclusion summarizes several aspects and implications, not only for mainstream but also for alternative media:

The institutional aspect of social media, that is, corporate social media such as Twitter or Facebook being profit oriented companies, contributes for the reproduction of the media landscape's power relations in their platforms. By posing limitations on content reach and allowing the content producers—be it private individuals, activists, social movement, alternative media, or mainstream media outlets—to pay for extending their reach and visibility, corporate media that have access to significantly more resources than alternative media or social movements are in clear advantage. Thus in a capitalist economy, social media (as institutions) reproduce the power relations in the media landscape and therefore help increase the influence of mainstream media on discourse and public opinion, rather than to pose an alternative to corporate mainstream media. Having said that, in the occasions, in which social movements do gain access to sympathetic coverage by mass media, this mechanism works for their advantage, provided that this coverage is inclusive, rather than distortive for the movement's own frames.

Furthermore, in 2014 Facebook has presented Trending, which "shows you a list of topics and hashtags that have recently spiked in popularity on Facebook. This list is personalized based on a number of factors, including Pages you've liked, your location and what's trending across Facebook" (Facebook, 2016). In 2016 it was reported that Facebook workers have tampered with the results presented in the Trending section, for example, suppressing conservative news (related to the Republican Party) or artificially placing issues such as Syria or Black Lives Matter, to avoid the negative image of prominent issues not being discussed on Facebook (Gizmodo, 2016). Facebook responded with rejecting the accusations, stating that "[p]opular topics are first surfaced by an algorithm, then audited by review team members to confirm that the topics are in fact trending news in the real world and not, for example, similar-sounding topics or misnomers" (Stocky, 2016). Several months later, Facebook has dismissed the Trending team employees, stating that from now on, algorithms execute the editorial tasks with even less human involvement, thus, implying the system's alleged neutrality.[13] This incident, although probably exceptional rather than representative, is an illuminating example of how corporate social media, that is, social media as institutions, can operate in similar manner to corporate mass/mainstream media, being gatekeepers of newsworthiness and operating in favor of the platform's, the institution's agenda and interests. In this context, the issue of alleged neutrality of algorithms, which is an argumentative strategy

---

[13] It is questionable, whether Facebook has intended to employ a human editorial team all along. A further option is that the human, intellectual labor conducted by the team was part of the algorithm's development process. That is to say, that the Trending News algorithm was improved by "learning" the decisions human editors made, implementing these into the algorithmic decisions that are now made completely automatically.

common to Internet corporations such as Google, Amazon, and Facebook, will be discussed in Chapter 11.

Yet another "gatekeeper of newsworthiness" on social media platforms is the so-called filter bubble.[14] The term addresses the creation of personalized informational space by adapting the content that the individual—the platform's user—is exposed to in accordance with a variety of objective and subjective parameters about him or her, informational spaces that are tailored to the individual's own opinions, designed to be free of disturbance, and are filled with primarily easy to consume information. Thus the algorithms that constitute the filter bubble are no other than gatekeepers, who filter content according to its "newsworthiness" for the individual, without transparency on the filtering parameters or the filtering itself, but at the same time under the disguise of algorithmic "neutrality."[15] Furthermore, just as with mass/mainstream media outlets, the filter bubble is a gatekeeper that comes to serve the economic interests of the social media platform (as institution)—construct a coherent, free-of-disturbance environment, in which the individual's data and activities are better monetized. When considering social media as alternative for mainstream media and focusing on the effect of the filter bubble, a situation might emerge, in which several parallel "mainstreams" are constructed, all of which have characters of mainstream media for the individuals who use the platform as news source and platform of discussion. A double-edged sword for collective action, since such a situation might bring like-minded activists and movements together, but on the other hand segregates between groups and social networks, posing difficulties on creating a collective and striving to reach broad legitimacy for the movement.

Lastly, there are alternative social media such as diaspora*, Occupii, and N-1. They pose an alternative not in their functionalities or usage (social media as ICT), but rather in their organizational structure (social media as institution). These are platforms that are not part of the corporate social media landscape, are noncommercial and nonprofit oriented. In contrast to corporate social media, whose business model relies on targeted advertising as well as collecting, commodifying, and monetizing users' data, these platforms are collectively owned; thus the control of the practices and algorithms is executed by the immediate users (Fuchs, 2014). However, comparing with corporate social media, such platforms are in disadvantaged position, similarly to alternative media in comparison with corporate mass/mainstream media. They have a significantly smaller circle of users and material resource, so that they, according to the time of writing, do not play a role in reaching the broad public or, for that matter, drawing the attention

---

[14] See Pariser (2011) as well as Chapter 2.
[15] For more on the aspects of neutrality, algorithms, and design of social media platforms see Chapter 11.

of mass/mainstream media. Having said that, deploying these platforms in collective action and/or social movements offers activists the usage of social media (as ICT and media) that are closely connected to the movement, its goals and activists, the construction of spaces of information, communication, and cooperation that are not affected by the interests of corporate social media (social media as institutions). In other words, alternative social media offer movements and activists platforms that are not alienated, platforms in which their activity is not exploited as unpaid digital labor, but rather is meaningful digital work (that is, without the dimensions of alienation and exploitation, which, according to Marxism, distinguish work from labor in capitalist society).[16] The Occupy Wall Street movement, for example, has used such platforms parallel to corporate social media platforms exactly for these reasons.

8.3 CONCLUSIONS

In May 2013, protests sparked in Istanbul after a sit-in in Taksim Gezi Park was violently evacuated. Due to extensive state control over mass media, media coverage of the Gezi Park protests as well as the following protests across Turkey was virtually nonexistent. Twitter, on the other hand, was full of real-time, on-site updates, pictures and videos from the protests, and documentation of police violence using the hashtags *#OccupyGezi* and *#DirenGeziParki*.[17] As Elif Batuman stated in *The New Yorker*: "CNN Turk was broadcasting a food show, featuring the "flavors of Nigde." Other major Turkish news channels were showing a dance contest and a roundtable on study-abroad programs. It was a classic case of the revolution not being televised. The whole country seemed to be experiencing a cognitive disconnect, with Twitter saying one thing, the government saying another, and the television off on another planet. Twitter was the one everyone believed—even the people who were actually on the street" (Batuman, 2013). Similar testimonies of Turkish protesters condemning the lack of media coverage and expressing their distrust in local mass media outlets were also circulating in Twitter parallel to the protests.

In the case of the Gezi Park protests, Twitter was not only an alternative media source, but also one of the few sources for protest-related information. This comes to show, that in some contexts, such as with state censorship and control over mass media, the relation between social media and mass/mainstream media can be less an interplay (as with the previous examples) and more of parallel universes. As the next chapter will show, the deployment of social media in an authoritarian context is a complex issue and aspects of state as well as corporate surveillance in social media are relevant in both authoritarian and democratic societies.

---

[16] To stress this difference, Fuchs (2014) refers to alternative social media as working-class social media.
[17] Turkish for "Resist, Gezi Park."

References

Baldauf, J., Dittrich, M., Rathje, J., Schramm, J., Schwarz, K., 2016. Monitoringbericht zu recht-sextremen und menschenverachtenden Phänomenen im Social Web für 2015/2016. Amadeu Antonio Stiftung. Retrieved from: www.amadeu-antonio-stiftung.de/w/files/pdfs/monitoring-bericht-2015.pdf.

Barthel, M., Shearer, E., Gottfried, J., Mitchell, A., 2015. The Evolving Role of News on Twitter and Facebook. Pew Research Center.

Batuman, E., 2013. Occupy Gezi: Police Against Protesters in Istanbul. The New Yorker. Retrieved from: www.newyorker.com/news/news-desk/occupy-gezi-police-against-protesters-in-istanbul.

Bell, E., 2016. Facebook Is Eating the World. Columbia Journalism Review. Retrieves from: http://www.cjr.org/analysis/facebook_and_media.php.

Facebook, 2016. Get Started on Facebook: Trending. Retrieved from: www.facebook.com/help/1401671260054622.

Fuchs, C., 2014. Digital Labour and Karl Marx. Routledge, New York.

Gamson, W.A., 2004. Bystanders, public opinion, and the media. In: Snow, D.A., Soule, S.A., Kriesi, H. (Eds.), The Blackwell Companion to Social Movements. Blackwell Publishing Ltd, Malden, pp. 242–261.

Garrett, R.K., 2006. Protest in an information society: a review of Literature on social movements and new ICTs. Information, Communication & Society 9 (2), 202–224.

Graeber, D., 2012. Inside Occupy. Campus, Frankfurt.

Jones, S., 2015. Army Revives Chindits as "Facebook Warriors" for Smart Battle. Financial Times. Retrieved from: www.ft.com/cms/s/0/537c7436-a892-11e4-ad01-00144feab7de.html.

Keen, A., 2015. The Internet Is Not the Answer. Atlantic Monthly Press, New York.

Mitchell, A., Holcomb, J., Weisel, R., 2016. State of the News Media 2016. Pew Research Center.

Morozov, E., 2011. The Net Delusion: The Dark Side of Internet Freedom. PublicAffairs, New York.

Naji, D., 2015. The Secret Battle Carried Out over Twitter, Facebook, and WhatsApp. Haaretz. Retrieved from: www.haaretz.co.il/tmr/1.2743568.

Newman, N., Fletcher, R., Levy, D.A., Nielsen, R.K., 2016. Reuters Institute Digital News Report 2016. Reuters Institute for the Study of Journalism. Retrieved from: reutersinstitute.politics. ox.ac.uk/sites/default/files/Digital-News-Report-2016.pdf.

Nunez, M., 2016. Former Facebook Workers: We Routinely Suppressed Conservative News. Gizmodo. Retrieved from: www.gizmodo.com/former-facebook-workers-we-routinely-suppressed-conser-1775461006.

Pariser, E., 2011. The Filter Bubble. Penguin Books, London.

Shirky, C., 2008. Here Comes Everybody: The Power of Organizing without Organizations. Penguin Group, London.

Stocky, T., 2016. Statement on Reports Alleging that Facebook Contractors Manipulated Trending Topics. Retrieved from: www.facebook.com/tstocky/posts/10100853082337958.

Tagesschau, A.R.D., 2016. München - Reaktionen im Netz. Retrieved from: www.tagesschau.de/inland/muenchen-schiesserei-social-media-101.html.

Tucker, N., 2016. The Instructions: No Reporting on Golan Telecom and No Pictures of Daphni Leef. TheMarker. Retrieved from: www.themarker.com/advertising/1.2869502.

CHAPTER 9

Big Brother Is Watching You: Collective Action and Surveillance in Social Media

ABSTRACT

Using social media platforms, individuals are exposed to several dimensions of surveillance—state surveillance on the one hand and corporate surveillance on the other. Especially in authoritarian regimes, surveillance and its implications pose direct threat to activists, social movements, and collective action. Since the Snowden revelation, the dimensions of surveillance in Western democratic regimes are widely known. The business model of corporate social media, which is based on targeted advertising and the commodification of users' data, makes corporate surveillance an immanent part of the platforms' design. This chapter discusses the implications of the different dimensions of surveillance as well as the interplay between them on collective action, social movements, and individuals involved in them.

Keywords: Authoritarianism; Censorship; Corporate surveillance; Five eyes; NSA; Orwellian society; Panopticon; Postpanopticon; Social media; State surveillance; Surveillance.

CONTENTS

In his novel *1984*, George Orwell describes a society in which state surveillance, public manipulation, and thought control prevail. In the book, the written communication of the Citizens of Oceania (one of the world's three superstates) is

133

Collective Action 2.0. http://dx.doi.org/10.1016/B978-0-08-100567-5.00009-8

regularly read and documented by state authorities. Furthermore, they live in the constant presence of two-way telescreens and hidden microphones in their homes, workplaces, and public spaces, through which they can be watched and listened, no imaginary vision considering the surveillance-friendly, data-collecting modern smart-televisions, smartphones, and tablets. The novel popularized the term *Orwellian Society*, which is used to describe a condition of ubiquitous state surveillance, censorship, as well as manipulation of recorded history by a totalitarian or authoritarian state. Hence, *1984* and Orwell are a common allegory when addressing issues of surveillance, both online and offline.

Although this allegory is very instructive when considering authoritarian contexts, in an increasingly connected global society with new technologies, models, and practices of communication, the practices of surveillance and manipulation change as well. New forms and practices of state and corporate surveillance, which emerge with the development of digital information and communication technologies (ICTs)—among them social media, are not reserved to authoritarian states. Furthermore, they are inseparable in the deployment of digital ICTs and of social media, also when it comes to collective action. As the following chapter will discuss, the different kinds of surveillance practices in social media affect in various ways collective action and social movements, who deploy these platforms, sometimes with grave consequences.

9.1 STASI 2.0[1]: STATE SURVEILLANCE AND THE DEPLOYMENT OF SOCIAL MEDIA FOR COLLECTIVE ACTION IN AUTHORITARIAN CONTEXT

By offering a platform that connects otherwise unrelated individuals or groups and supports faster and more efficient organization of collective action for negligible (financial) costs, the deployment of social media for political purposes challenges the balance of power between protesters and the institutions they protest against (first and foremost the governments).

To date, the information overload on the Internet can be of benefit for the organization of these short-term collective actions. Although some actions can be organized very fast, the identification of suspected online behavior, its analysis, and the organization of an institutional reaction to it are time-costly tasks in the sea of information that is constantly created and circulated in social media

---

[1] Stasi 2.0 is a political slogan that emerged around 2007 in Germany. The term expresses protest against the government's legislative plans, which constituted threats to civil and political rights online, for example, computer and network surveillance/eavesdropping, telecommunications data retention, and limitations on net neutrality and freedom of information.

as well as in consideration of the hierarchical structures of state institutions and decision making (Morozov, 2011). Therefore social media can support the organization of instant protests, or protests that seem to be instant ones, such as flash mobs, while keeping the organization and its measures invisible until the moment it breaks out.

Having said that, the deployment of social media, and other online platforms for that matter, offers advantages not only for political activists, but also for the governments they protest against. In other words, the deployment of social media for political or antigovernmental causes in authoritarian regimes has a substantial backfire potential compared with "low-tech" methods of surveillance such as tapping phones and bugging apartments. Not only collective action and activism change in the course of technological development, utilizing new capabilities for their advantage, but also their opponents, in this case, the state, utilize the same tools for their own advantage. To illustrate this notion, Evgeny Morozov gives the film *The Lives of Others*[2] as an example and compares the new surveillance capabilities with the methods used by the Stasi in East Germany during the Cold War, pointing out the degree of difference. Morozov further suggests that the time and human resources saved by the new ICTs are not spared, but rather being converted for amplifying the surveillance capabilities (Morozov, 2011).

Similar to social movements and activists, the deployment of social media makes many new and valuable resources available for authoritarian regimes. However, state authorities "deploy" social media in a very different manner than social movements and activists. As the following examples of the uses and advantages that authoritarian states derive from social media will show, these are resources that were previously not available or even nonexistent, as activists did not tend to keep such a considerable amount of information and evidence regarding their activities and networks in one central place. Furthermore, the information and evidence they did possess could only be gained through physical access to it, unlike social media with its cloud computing feature that makes remote access to the information possible, often without the user's, i.e., the activist's, knowledge[3]:

- Monitoring and cracking social media platforms with emphasis on building and maintaining social networks (e.g., Facebook or its equivalents in other countries, such as the Chinese *Renren* or Russian *VKontakte*) can reveal whole networks of government opponents, human rights activists, or persecuted minorities. This is also true for

---

[2] *Das Leben der Anderen.*
[3] Many of the following aspects are discussed in Morozov (2011).

other services that contain information on the user's social networks, such as email services that contain contacts, correspondences, and mailing lists.

- Cracking activists' email, WhatsApp, or social media accounts with messaging functionalities can reveal relevant correspondences; both the content and the participants of those correspondences are highly valuable information.

- Cross-linking of information such as group memberships in social media platforms, contact (Twitter followers, Facebook "friends," email contacts, etc.), and blog subscriptions can not only reveal existing activist networks but also draw attention to possible future activists.

- Monitoring the location of known activists through their cellphone's network operator and/or (social media and other) Apps that collect their location data. This location data can be used, for example, for alerting any extraordinary group gathering and launching a proactive crackdown on a supposed protest.

- Applying facial recognition systems on protest documentation (which is openly available on social media platforms and later on in the foreign press) and cross-checking the information with social media platforms can help locate activists who were previously anonymous.

- In random or targeted inspections of activists (or uninvolved citizens) and their smartphone/tablet/laptop, authorities can gain access to the data stored on device as well as on platforms these devices have access to (since most people do not regularly logout their accounts).[4]

In other words, the "opportunity to cheaply encrypt their online communications may have made 'professional' activists more secure, but the proliferation of Web 2.0 services—and especially social networking—has turned 'amateur' activists into easier targets for surveillance" (Morozov, 2011, p. 82).

The advantages for the authoritarian state do not stop in the "deployment"[5] of social media in its own interest, but is also evident in the state's power to cut access to them altogether. As happened during the events of the Arab Spring and many other occasions, some regimes impose Internet blackouts, turn off

---

[4] This strategy was deployed by Turkish authorities after the failed coup attempt in 2016 (Aykanat and Langenau, 2016). Furthermore, the journalism blog Bellingcat has gained access to a WhatsApp group chat used by coup participants. Bellingcat's analysis of the conversation, together with cross-references of the messages with photos, videos, and news reports of the events exemplify how realistic the mentioned dangers are (Triebert, 2016).

[5] The terms deployment or usage should be treated with caution in this context, since state authorities do not use social media platforms in a similar manner to activists/movements and in accordance with the system's proclaimed purposes and uses. Rather, they abuse it to gain advantage and uphold the power asymmetry between the state and its citizens.

cellular networks or 3G signals in the areas of unrest, or block the access to certain services (such as Twitter, Facebook, or WhatsApp) during protests and uprisings.[6] As seen in previous chapters, the reliance on social media platforms and other online tools is often central in collective action, thus making these platforms and tools an increasingly crucial infrastructure for activists and movements. Such blackouts and blockings are a deliberate and direct attempt to cut off this crucial infrastructure in the hope this will contribute to suppressing the protest or movement.

Authoritarian regimes being able to "deploy" social media for their advantage is not an aspect of social media's "neutrality" as a tool, which different parties with different, even conflicting, interests can use in similar manner (in accordance with the tool's purposes) but for their own interest.[7] Neither is the social media deployment by activists and state authorities completely unrelated to each other. In fact, these are two sides of the same coin, whereas the deployment by activists and the platforms' design enable the state to use—or abuse—it for its own good. Many of the possibilities that social media platforms offer activists and movements are based on the aggregation of data and their algorithmic analysis, the platforms' location- and time-independent availability, their infrastructural character, and so on. In turn, by using the platforms to profit from these possibilities, activists and movements form the basis for the state's "deployment" of the platforms and tools against them, which is why such deployment has the potential to backfire. On the other hand, not all of these potential dangers are unavoidable technical necessities; much of the data being collected and analyzed are part of the social media's (as institutions) business model, which relies on targeted advertising and monetizing user data. Some of the data could have been left out altogether, whereas other data could have been protected by strong encryption that leaves both the social media institution and the government out. In this manner, the economic interests of the institutions and corporations behind the social media platforms play, even if indirect and presumably unintended, into the hands of authoritarian regimes.

This, in a nutshell, makes social media to a *dual-use technology*, that is, a technology that fulfills several goals (and interests) at the same time. In its political and diplomatic meaning, the term dual-use refers more specifically to technologies, which are used for both peaceful and military goals. As dual-use technologies, corporate social media platforms—other than alternative social media—simultaneously help fulfill the goals of collective action (in many cases a political one), state surveillance/censorship (which often aims at political movements), as well as corporate surveillance and monetization of user data.

---

[6] See, for example, Barbera et al. (2013), Cohen (2011), MISA-Zimbabwe (2016), Stepanova (2011).
[7] For a discussion on this aspect, see Chapter 11.

Most of these aspects do not cause concern for social movements or individuals, who are practicing political protest in democratic states where freedom of expression and freedom of assembly are constitutionally protected. In authoritarian regimes, however, they can have grave consequences for activists, who enjoy the advantages of social media—often taking examples from their counterparts in democratic states—but are unaware of its possible implications. Having said that, in light of the 2013 disclosure of mass surveillance programs operated by the US National Security Agency (NSA) and its counterparts in the so-called Five Eyes (Australia, Canada, New Zealand, the United Kingdom, and the United States), it is apparent that not just the activists in authoritarian states have reasons to be concerned.

9.2 LIVING IN THE POST-SNOWDEN ERA: STATE SURVEILLANCE AND THE DEPLOYMENT OF SOCIAL MEDIA FOR COLLECTIVE ACTION IN DEMOCRATIC CONTEXT

In 2013 the whistleblower Edward Snowden, a former Central Intelligence Agency employee and contractor for the US government and NSA, had contacted the journalists Glenn Greenwald, Laura Poitras, and Ewen MacAskill. Snowden handed the journalists thousands of classified NSA documents over, which reveal numerous mass-surveillance programs on a global scale such as PRISM, XKeyscore, and Tempora. The programs are run by the NSA, its counterparts in the Five Eyes Intelligence Alliance and other European countries, as well as in cooperation of telecommunication companies. Not only telecommunication companies but also information technology, Internet, and social media corporations are suspected of cooperating with these surveillance programs (Greenwald and MacAskill, 2013; Griggs, 2015). The post-Snowden era has begun.

In contrast to authoritarian regimes, the consequences of such surveillance are not as direct and comprehensible for citizens of democratic states, who are accustomed to civil freedoms such as the freedom of assembly and freedom of speech. This, for one, is a central aspect in a surveillance apparatus that is not constructed for immediate censorship, suppression, or crackdowns. The NSA and its counterparts' unsatisfiable hunger for data relies on individuals feeling free to communicate, free to act, free to cooperate, and by doing so, supplying more and more data.[8] Data—more precisely Big Data—that can be aggregated, cross-linked, and analyzed. This has created an enormous informational

---

[8] See, for example, Chapter 2 for the various kinds of data that are collected by social media and online platforms.

advantage in the hand of the state as opposed to the public and the individual citizens. Furthermore, this informational advantage and asymmetry form, at least in theory, the basis for subtler and effective methods of control and manipulation.

It is true that this kind of surveillance might not be a crucial aspect for the organization and even success of a particular social movement or instance of collective action.[9] However, as social media become a standard in the collective action toolbox, this means that the state gains access to comprehensive information about the entirety of social movements and collective action of all scales, comprehensive information on their goals, internal communication, methods of organization, activists networks, etc. An uncomfortable power imbalance, considering the fact that the majority of social movements and collective actions, such as protests, aims to criticize, attack, and change the establishment.

Apart from large-scale mass-surveillance programs of the NSA and its counterparts, also law enforcement agencies in various democratic states are increasingly monitoring social media activity of protesters and activists (Fuchs, 2014; Rawlinson, 2012; Kubovich, 2016; Borchers, 2016). That is, the deployment of social media becomes a double-edged sword for activists in democratic states as well. Similar to the aspects listed earlier, law enforcement agencies can use information gained from social media platforms (both publicly available information as well as by gaining access to activists' social media accounts) to monitor social movements' and activists' activities and communication, prepare for crackdowns on protests, and deploy methods of intimidation (e.g., investigating activists prior to protests) to suppress their activities.

9.3 AIDING THE ENEMY: CORPORATE SURVEILLANCE AND ECONOMIC INTERESTS ON SOCIAL MEDIA

The surveillance on social media platforms does not end, or start, with state surveillance. Corporate surveillance is immanent to corporate, for-profit social media platforms. The business model of corporate social media is based on targeted advertisement, for which the collection and analysis of various kinds of user data is necessary; thus, corporate social media's business model is based on the commodification and monetization of user data. This is the main reason that the social media corporations do not implement strong end-to-end encryption, follow principles of privacy by design and data protection in their

---

[9] Unless, of course, the NSA or its counterparts analyze and hand over information to the respectable government or local police forces. An activity, whose legality and legitimacy in a democracy are highly questionable and, to date, are not known or reported to have taken place.

platforms' design, or delete any information from their servers and databases (even if the user has removed—"deleted"—the content). As mentioned earlier, this business model and resulting practices and technical designs enable, or at least support, state surveillance and its consequences in a variety of contexts.

Furthermore, social movements and activists often act against powerful elites other than the political ones. Many examples of social media deployment by social movements, such as the Israeli social justice protests, the Occupy Wall Street movement, the Spanish 15-M movement, or parts of the events of the Arab Spring, are political movements, whose resistance aims not solely at the political establishment, but rather at economic elites. Ironically, deploying (corporate) social media by social movements or collective action, which targets the economic elites, the capital, or the 1%, serves the interests of the latter; it serves the interests of the movements' self-defined enemies. As Christian Fuchs puts it: "[the] commodification process is irrespective of content: it does not matter for Facebook, YouTube or Twitter if their users talk about world revolution on the one hand or pop songs, movies and new haircuts on the other hand. All of this information is instrumentalized for selling targeted ad space to advertising clients. The revolution cannot be twittered, but it can certainly be commodified. By using Twitter, Facebook, YouTube and other corporate social media, activists help corporations accumulate capital; they advance the profits of the 1% and thereby contradict their own goal of taking wealth away from the 1%" (Fuchs, 2014, p. 345).

In contrast to corporate social media, alternative social media[10] clearly pose an alternative with key advantages for social movements and activists. Since these platforms are noncommercial and they—as well as the data!—are owned by the platform's users, they do not have immanent corporate surveillance to pursue certain business models, so that privacy by design and data protection can be better integrated into the platforms. Furthermore, many of the alternative social media platforms offer data encryption (depends, of course, on the particular functionality), which is an important means against state surveillance. Lastly, when it comes to resistance against economic elites and socioeconomic inequality, deploying alternative social media platforms does not "aid the enemy"; that is, the resistance itself is not being commodified and monetized by privately held corporation.

---

[10] Which are in Christian Fuchs' terms "working-class social media because they are collectively owned and controlled by the immediate users" (Fuchs, 2014, p. 343).

9.4 LIVING IN THE POSTPANOPTICON ERA? CONCLUSIONS

According to the sociologist and director of the Surveillance Studies Center David Lyon, ever since the Snowden revelation, it is clear that mass surveillance practices such as Predictive Policing[11] or No Fly Lists[12] have their technical foundation in Big Data methods from the economic and marketing sector (Lyon, 2014, 2016; Vaidhyanathan, 2004). The transfer of the surveillance-based Big Data and predictive logic from the economic and marketing realm to the national security and intelligence sector is highly problematic.

For one, as media scholar and cultural historian Siva Vaidhyanathan notes, "Data mining presents multiple problems for law enforcement that go beyond civil libertarian discomfort. To serve commercial purposes, they only need to furnish mostly accurate (rather that completely accurate) information to justify the investments in the [...] The difference between Food Lion and the U.S. Department of Justice is that the government can imprison you" (Vaidhyanathan, 2004, p. 177). False positives and false negatives in no fly lists are one prominent example of how this exchange of surveillance logic and methods can go wrong; it is one thing to predict a person buying a product he or she does not want, it is a different thing to falsely predict her building a bomb or committing a crime.

Second, this marks a change in the thinking and logic of law enforcement and intelligence agencies. Instead of a "divine sight" that exerts its power by observing—or surveilling—individuals and society, there is a shift toward forecasting future behavior based on data, patterns, analytics, and statistics (Lyon, 2014, 2016). This change is part of a bigger paradigm change in surveillance (and consequently, in surveillance theory). Lyon describes this paradigm change in surveillance theory by exploring the central role of the panopticon in these theories and the slow advancement toward a post-panopticon (Lyon, 2006). Alongside George Orwell's *1984*, Jeremy Bentham model of the panopticon as well as Michel Foucault's subsequent analysis of the panopticon[13] were constitutive

---

[11] The deployment of predictive methods in law enforcement to identify potential criminal activity. These methods are based on a variety of mathematical, statistical, analytical techniques.

[12] No Fly Lists are lists of individuals who are suspected of terrorist activity and are prohibited from boarding commercial flights for travel across national borders. No Fly Lists are widely criticized due the phenomenon of "false positives" (an individual who is not on the No Fly List but his or her name matches or is similar to a name on the list) and "false negative" (terrorist, who are familiar with the criteria the law enforcement authorities use to identify data, use stolen identities, false documents, stolen credit cards, or off-shore venders).

[13] Jeremy Bentham as an architectural model for a prison designed the Panopticon. Michel Foucault later used the Panopticon for theorizing surveillance, disciplinary power, and self-discipline in modern society. See also Bentham (1843), Foucault (1995).

in modern research and theories of surveillance. The panopticon theories and research include aspects such as the ability of extensive and penetrative observation (surveillance) of individuals, the power imbalance that results from the different positions of the observer and the observed, and the internalization of control and censorship and further effects on the individual (and, in turn, on the collective). A postpanopticon notion in the research of surveillance, and, of course, in surveillance practices, methods, techniques, and politics themselves, however, includes further aspects that go beyond the instructive but limited notions that evolve the panopticon. To name a few examples:

- Panopticommodity regards how capitalist corporations and institutions use consumers, rather than workers, to increase productivity and generate revenues; to insure this happens consumer surveillance is needed.[14]
- Although many panopticon surveillance theories are modern in terms of relating to the nation-state, bureaucracy, technologic and political economy, postmodern theories of surveillance "tend to focus on the ways in which digital technologies 'make a difference'" (Lyon, 2006, p. 10). Furthermore, "Post-panoptic surveillance is deterritorialized as well as rhizomic and as such resists exclusionary control strategies […] The soul-training of the panopticon with its moulded subjects gives way to flexibly modulated hybrid subjects, suited to varying circumstances" (Lyon, 2006, p. 13).
- In addition, postpanopticon approaches consider aspects of surveillance such as the cultures of surveillance, the contexts in which surveillance occurs, and the interaction between the technologies and technological artifacts with the subjects (instead of focusing on the artifacts themselves) (Lyon, 2006).
- Lastly, not "self-repression but self-expression characterizes this surveillance, which, importantly, is on the terms of the watched, not the watcher" (Lyon, 2006, p. 15). Byung-Chul Han, for example, considers this a shift from a society of negativity to a society of positivity. It is characterized by narratives such as "you can" or "yes we can" instead of "you should" or "you must"; motivation instead of compulsion and control; change in the economy of attention (the pressure to multitask, hyperattention, or the rapid change of focus between tasks and information sources); and the feeling of freedom instead of being controlled (Han, 2010, 2012).[15]

---

[14] This notion is discussed not only in the context of social media, but also in terms of watching commercial television and labor. See Andrejevic (2004), Fuchs (2014) and Lyon (2006).

[15] Furthermore, Han shows how in modern capitalism, address this shit is directed in to voluntary self-exploitation. Instead of being subjected to external control and disciplinary mechanisms (as in Foucault's theory of disciplined society), the individual (the subject) in the achieving society is subjected to quasi self-suppression (Han, 2010, 2012).

Orwell's intellectual counterpart (and friend) Aldous Huxley described in his novel *Brave New World* a different type of dystopia, of political regime, than the panopticon-like *1984*. In this world—a sharp criticism of modern capitalism—society is controlled by constant consumption, maximization of pleasure and fulfillment of desires, minimization of time spent alone by individuals, and sexual promiscuity, technology and scientific progress being efficiently exploited for these aims. In such a reality, critical thought becomes scarce. Furthermore, in contrast to an Orwellian, panopticon society, individuals (and collectives) are much less likely to politicize (among others by their repression) and grow resistance. Evgeny Morozov criticizes the common "rigidity of thought suggested by the Orwell–Huxley coordinate system" (Morozov, 2011, p. 79) that considers the two works at the opposite ends of a spectrum, on which regimes can be placed. Instead, Morozov pleads for an examination of how elements of both systems are incorporated in both authoritarian and democratic regimes, the NSA's surveillance being a striking example of this combination.

Postpanopticon approaches offer us the frameworks needed to overcome the "Orwell–Huxley coordinate system" and consider surveillance in its complexity, especially when considering social media deployment and the variety of contexts in which it takes place. Although surveillance in social media can be part of a panopticon-like surveillance (for example, in authoritarian states), a postpanopticon approach is much more instructive for understanding it in its complexity. Surveillance in social media platforms is a mélange of postpanopticon aspects of surveillance: the business models and the capitalist system in which they operate; the individual's interaction with the platforms, not only communication and interaction using the platform, being a central source of surveillance data; the surveillance's reliance on the individuals' perception of freedom (to communicate, to express, to act) and the platforms' affordance of constant self-expression, self-representation, and communication; the multinational character of the surveillance in social media as most platforms (excluding some local versions that focus on a rather national user circle) have users from different countries, regions, cultures, languages, religions, etc.; and the mechanisms of control (such as the filter bubble) being more positivistic, subtle, and context related rather than repressive, total, and (self-)violent.

The theory I offer is that living in a postpanopticon era, the dangers that surveillance poses collective action and social movements are becoming indirect and intangible. Panopticon surveillance relates to rather direct methods of repression and control such as censorship, crackdowns, locating and arresting activists, etc. In the postpanopticon world, in contrast, there will be a shift toward predictive prevention using, for example, big data analysis, user profiling, and statistical methods; behind the scene manipulation, control, and construction of opinions within the individuals' digital informational spaces (such as social media platforms) to prevent the emergence of critical, resisting collectives; the construction of filter bubbles, in which deviant opinions are not silenced, but do not exceed the boarder of the filter bubble; and the commodification and monetization of resistance itself. Thus weakening and preventing collective action and social movements with goals not in the interests of those who are in power without using violent or even perceivable methods of control.

On the other hand, it is not collective action per se that is in danger, since many instances of collective action and their goals may stay unaffected from such trends. Furthermore, in a postpanopticon reality, in which resistance (or any other form of collective action for that matter) that deploys social media actually serves the interests of economic and political elite as well as of the surveillance system itself, collective action can even become a wanted activity, as long as it does not pose an existential threat, so that the goals of surveillance and control may be not to prevent resistance (in this case, in the form of collective action and social movements), but rather to channel it, to choreograph it, to keep it in unthreatening dimensions while using it in the system's own interest (i.e., collecting, analyzing, and commodifying data).

Of course, the surveillance abilities that come together with technological development and postpanopticon methods and practices of surveillance can be used for direct repressive methods hitherto related to panopticon surveillance (or an Orwellian society). However, the shift toward a postpanopticon is not only in the manner in which we research and understand surveillance, but also in the self-understanding and the politics of surveillance itself and the methods that are, in turn, deployed to exert control.

This theory does not come to draw a dystopian notion of collective action in a future that is increasingly connected and digital, neither does it argue for the rejection of social media deployment—or of ICT in general—in collective action. We have seen the deployment of social media for collective action with different goals—from political uprisings in totalitarian regimes, to consumer boycotts, to social justice protests in many countries, to refugee aid, to expressions of solidarity, to discussions on gender, sexism, and abortions etc.—comes with a variety of advantages and disadvantages. The important message is that by deploying social media, individuals (as well as the collectives they construct) need to be aware not only of the promises, but also of the dangers these tools bring with them, one of which is the danger of surveillance. To continue profiting from the advantages that social media has to offer as well as to counteract and reduce the disadvantages and dangers, or even to revolutionize social media itself, it is crucial not only for activists, but also for the broad public to take necessary measures. Such measures can be the deployment of alternative and noncorporate social media platforms, using encryption, reflecting if social media (and which one) is the right tool for the specific task, pressing for better privacy legislation, posing the question regarding ownership on (user generated) data, resisting state and corporate surveillance, etc.

Several parts of the book have touched upon how social media contribute to mobilization, which is crucial for collective action and social movements to gain momentum and relevance. The following chapter will complement these discussions by addressing the often-overlooked danger of demobilization. Being a central issue of collective action and social movements, social media and its impact on mobilization (or demobilization) becomes a double-edged sword for collective action.

References

Andrejevic, M., 2004. Reality TV: The Work of Watching. Rowman and Littlefield, New York.

Aykanat, D., Langenau, L., 2016. Nach dem Putschversuch: Wer nicht für den Präsidenten ist, verschanzt sich und schweigt. Süddeutsche Zeitung. Retrieved from: www.sueddeutsche.de/politik/nach-dem-putschversuch-wer-nicht-fuer-erdoan-ist-verschanzt-sich-und-schweigt-1.3087113.

Barbera, P., Metzger, M., Tucker, J.A., 2013. A Breakout Role for Twitter in the Taksim Square Protests? Al Jazeera. Retrieved from: www.aljazeera.com/indepth/opinion/2013/06/201361212350593971.html.

Bentham, J., 1843. The Works of Jeremy Bentham, Vol. 4 (Panopticon, Constitution, Colonies, Codification). W. Tait.

Borchers, D., 2016. Social Media in der aktiven Polizeiarbeit. Heise. Retrieved from: www.heise.de/newsticker/meldung/Social-Media-in-der-aktiven-Polizeiarbeit-3249962.html.

Cohen, N., 2011. Egyptians Were Unplugged, and Uncowed. New York Times. Retrieved from: www.nytimes.com/2011/02/21/business/media/21link.html?_r=0.

Foucault, M., 1995. Discipline and Punish: The Birth of the Prison. Vintage Books, New York.

Fuchs, C., 2014. Digital Labour and Karl Marx. Routledge, New York.

Greenwald, G., MacAskill, E., 2013. NSA Prism Program Taps in to User Data of Apple, Google and Others. The Guardian. Retrieved from: www.theguardian.com/world/2013/jun/06/us-tech-giants-nsa-data.

Griggs, B., July13, 2015. Report: Microsoft Collaborated Closely with NSA. CNN. Retrieved from: edition.cnn.com/2013/07/12/tech/web/microsoft-nsa-snooping/.

Han, B.-C., 2010. Müdigkeitsgesellschaft. Matthes & Seitz, Berlin.

Han, B.-C., 2012. Südkorea - Eine Müdigkeitsgesellschaft im Endstadium. Matthes & Seitz Berlin. Retrieved from: http://www.matthes-seitz-berlin.de/artikel/byung-chul-han-suedkorea-eine-muedigkeitsgesellschaft-im-endstadium.html.

Kubovich, Y., 2016. The Facebook Squad: How Israel Police Tracks Activists on Social Media. Haaretz. Retrieved from: www.haaretz.com/israel-news/.premium-1.701662.

Lyon, D., 2006. The search for surveillance theories. In: Lyon, D. (Ed.), Theorizing Surveillance: The Panopticon and beyond. Willan Publishing, Cullompton, Devon, pp. 3–20.

Lyon, D., 2014. Surveillance, Snowden, and big data: capacities, consequences, critique. Big Data & Society 1–13.

Lyon, D., 2016. Keynote Conversation: Anxious to Secure. Transmediale. Retrieved from: 2016. transmediale.de/content/keynote-conversation-anxious-to-secure.

MISA-Zimbabwe, 2016. MISA-Zimbabwe Statement on Disconnection of WhatsApp – MisaZim. Retrieved from: www.misazim.com/misa-zimbabwe-statement-on-disconnection-of-whatsapp/.

Morozov, E., 2011. The Net Delusion: The Dark Side of Internet Freedom. PublicAffairs, New York.

Rawlinson, K., 2012. Activists Warned to Watch What They Say as Social Media Monitoring Becomes "Next Big Thing in Law Enforcement". The Independent Online. Retrieved from: www.independent.co.uk/news/uk/crime/activists-warned-to-watch-what-they-say-as-social-media-monitoring-becomes-next-big-thing-in-law-8191977.html.

Stepanova, E., 2011. The Role of Information Communication Technologies in the "Arab Spring". PIR Center. Retrieved from: pircenter.org/kosdata/page_doc/p2594_2.pdf.

Triebert, C., 2016. "We've Shot Four People. Everything's fine." the Turkish Coup through the Eyes of its Plotters. Bellingcat. Retrieved from: www.bellingcat.com/news/mena/2016/07/24/the-turkey-coup-through-the-eyes-of-its-plotters/.

Vaidhyanathan, S., 2004. The Anarchist in the Library: How the Clash between Freedom and Control Is Hacking the Real World and Crashing the System. Basic Books, New York.

CHAPTER 10

Sharing Is Caring? Social Media and Demobilization

ABSTRACT

Mobilizing individuals and/or collectives to participate is one of the central concerns and challenges facing collective action and social movement activists. Although social media often support mobilization, they also bring about demobilization. Such forms of demobilization are also known as *slacktivism* and, to a certain extent, *clicktivism*. Not only slacktivism, but also the structural elements of social media platforms are factors that encourage demobilization.

Keywords: Clicktivism; Demobilization; Mobilization; Slacktivism; Social media.

CONTENTS

Mobilizing individuals and/or collectives to participate is one of the central concerns and challenges facing collective action and social movement activists. Clay Shirky gets to the heart of the dilemma, stating that "[h]aving a handful of highly motivated people and a mass of barely motivated ones used to be a recipe for frustration. The people who were on fire wondered why the general population didn't care more, and the general population wondered why those obsessed people didn't just shut up" (Shirky, 2008, pp. 181–182).

As discussed in previous chapters, mobilization requires creation of common ground around grievances and demands, aggregation and utilization moral and cultural resources, successful framing, increasing shared awareness, etc. Social media can support these processes of mobilization in a variety of ways. Among other things, social media can lower the hurdles of participation and enable individuals, who may sympathize the cause at hand but do not feel great obligation toward it, to participate and contribute in a smaller manner. By creating a more casual context of participation, which motivates individuals to be effective without becoming activists themselves, more individuals can be reached and by aggregating their (minor) participation an effect on collective action is possible. These "microcontributions" (Garrett, 2006) also have the potential to lead to a greater sense of individual obligation. In this manner a participation distribution that statistically resembles a long tail distribution is created (Shirky, 2008). On the other hand, some scholars warn from the demobilizing effect this can have on collective action, a warning that was confirmed by the experience of activists and movements.

10.1 A LONG TAIL OF SLACKTIVISM

Although participating in collective action in its more traditional manner was attached to taking actions on-site, actions that extend beyond the borders of social media platforms, digital/online activism offers participation without leaving the comfort of one's home. But when it comes to mobilization for more concrete and less 'digital" actions, the participation seems to decrease dramatically (Hesse, 2009; Morozov, 2011).

Already in 2011, during the peak of inflated expectations regarding social media and collective action, Evgeny Morozov has warned from what he terms as *Slacktivism*: pseudoactivism, which serves the calming of a person's self-conscious and the maintenance of one's (online) identity and image more than the engagement in influential activism (Morozov, 2011).

With digital activism on social media platforms, such as being a member of a group promoting a certain cause, sharing movement-related information, or signing and sharing online petitions, people tend to calm their social conscious without having to invest much effort. The online support of a cause can satisfy people just as writing letters to their elected representatives, participating in demonstrations, or organizing a boycott, but without having the effect the latter might have.

On social media platforms, group memberships, pictures, linked information, etc. are a part of the construction of one's (online) identity. As Morozov explains: "they believe that the kinds of Facebook campaigns and groups they join reveal more about them than whatever they put in the dull 'about me' page" (Morozov, 2011, p. 186). So that—cynical as it may be—the support of different causes, instances of collective action, and social movements on social media becomes part of self-marketing and self-presentation, which are an integral part of online and social media communication. In contrast, although sharing on-site collective action documentation (e.g., pictures and videos from a demonstration) can also serve the construction of one's online identity, it is more likely to contribute to the mobilization of one's friends (one's social network).

The downside of microcontributions and their aggregation is that the whole does not always exceed the sum of its parts. As the number of participants increases, the social pressure on each participant diminishes, with the possible result of inferior outcomes. In other words, when everyone in the group performs the same tasks, it is impossible to evaluate individual contributions and people inevitably begin "slacking off" (Morozov, 2011); that is, take the least painful sacrifice (e.g., donating $1 instead of $10, signing an online petition instead of writing letters to their elected representatives, or sharing a demonstration's Facebook event instead of participating in it). For example, in its campaign Likes Don't Save Lives, the United Nations Children's Fund (UNICEF) Sweden confronted slacktivism, urging people to do more than like UNICEF's causes on social media. As Petra Hallebrant, UNICEF Sweden Director of Communications, explained: "We like likes, and social media could be a good first step to get involved, but it cannot stop there […] Likes don't save children's lives. We need money to buy vaccines for instance" (Murphy, 2013).

Furthermore, the ease of raising money over the Internet and social media may result in shifting the primary focus of social movements to pursue monetary objectives (instead of political ones, for example). The resource mobilization theory successfully acknowledges that not in every case money (although tangible, proprietary, and fungible) is the suitable means for solving the problem at hand and other resource types always play a major role. So that shifting the focus of social movements' objectives or dismissing people from taking meaningful on-site action after making a donation can result with the contraproductive effect of demobilization. Although this might not apply for UNICEF's plea, it is unavoidable for social movements that deploy social media and online tools to reflect on these issues as well.

Collective action has much more complex and multifaceted processes than opening a Facebook group. Starting a social movement as a Facebook group (without taking the needed actions and strategies to extend it beyond Facebook's borders) or having a Facebook group as a social movement has very low chances to succeed. Therefore most of the groups of the sort fail to take the next step after mobilizing individuals to show support of their cause.[1] On the other hand and as discussed in previous chapters of the book, the utilization of platforms as part of a social movement's strategy, combined with other actions, can be proved more efficient.

---

[1] See also Chapter 7.

10.2 DEMOBILIZATION AND THE STRUCTURAL ELEMENTS OF SOCIAL MEDIA

To understand the demobilizing effect that social media can have on collective action, considering it through the lens of slacktivism is not sufficient. Some structural elements of social media as well can prove to cause demobilizing effects:

- the filter bubble,
- information overload,
- social media literacy, and
- institutional aspects.

Following the discussions of the filter bubble in Chapters 2, 8, and 9, its demobilizing effect lays in its control and segregation of information flow. Although a good functioning filter bubble may show movement-related information to like-minded people, thus convincing the convinced, it hinders the information from reaching other individuals and groups. In this manner, the filter bubble poses an obstacle in a movement's/collective action's way of reaching and mobilizing further milieus. Thus opaque filter bubble algorithms and their classification of individuals, groups, and milieus—classification that serves the marketing and economic interests and the social media institutions—influence how individuals and groups can reach out and mobilize each other.

Apparently, people begin to internalize the discourse constructed by the filter bubble, avoiding the discussion of topics that might cause dissents within their social media friends and followers (their social networks within social media). As the PEW Research Center study Social Media and the "Spiral of Silence" (Hampton et al., 2014) shows, individuals were less likely to discuss the Snowden National Security Agency revelations over social media than in person, especially if they thought their social media contacts would disagree with them. Although the "spiral of silence" phenomenon is neither new nor unique for social media, the study shows that social media actually reproduce, rather than reduce it. Not a surprising conclusion for platforms, for informational environments, which, due to the interests of the corresponding institutions, are designed to be convenient, disturbance-free environments and to contain mainly positive echo. Thus the suppression of discourse on controversial topics also suppresses political discussions, interferes with finding like-minded individuals, stands in the way of mobilization, prevents individuals from sharing movement or collective action–related information, etc., all of which have a demobilizing effect on collective action.

In contrast to the filter bubble stands the phenomenon of information overload that people experience online and therefore, also in social media platforms. Due to the ease of dissemination of information over social media, a person might confront situations of being overwhelmed from the quantity of movement-related information one receives (e.g., causes, fund-raisings, invitations for demonstrations and sit-ins, press releases, or friends sharing their opinion on the issue) and/or the quantity of movements and causes one receives information from. An overload can be both mentally and emotionally stressful so that, as a reaction, the person would resort to slacktivism or plain disinterest. Having said that, a person's social networks and the filter bubble significantly influence this aspect as they are decisive for the flows of information within the social media platform.

Social media literacy,[2] that is, the repertoire of competencies that enable individuals to use social media—perceive, evaluate, and analyze information they receive over social media, produce and communicate over social media, as well as the needed technical expertise—may also be a source of demobilization. When social media become central tools, even infrastructure in the exercise of collective action and participation in social movements, individuals who lack the needed competencies to use social media may feel left out or unable to participate. Furthermore, as mentioned in Chapter 6, when social media deployment becomes a source of legitimacy for social movements and/or in the participation in collective action, these individuals may also doubt the legitimacy of their own participation, thus resulting in a demobilizing effect on possible sympathizers. This is a major challenge for social movements, that is, to prevent that the tools, which can be inclusive in many ways and for many individuals, would become exclusive to others.

Lastly, also the institutional aspect of social media may have a demobilizing effect. For one, certain clauses in a platform's terms of use may compound difficulties on activists. This is the case with Facebook's strict real name policy, which led to the deletion of the Chinese activist's Michael Anti (ne Zhao Jing) profile (Chen, 2011a). The real name policy also makes it difficult, even impossible, for individuals and activists to anonymously join collective action using pseudonyms. This is especially problematic in repressive regimes and was highly criticized during the events of the Arab Spring (Chen, 2011b). Furthermore, as discussed in the previous chapter, issues of privacy, data collection, and corporate surveillance, which are related to such policies and clauses in corporate social media's terms of use, may have demobilizing effects on activists both in authoritarian, repressive regimes and in democratic ones.

To state yet another example, Facebook has repeatedly blocked the Israeli activist Tali Koral who administrates the Facebook page When He Pays[3] (as

---

[2] Which is a dimension of information of media literacy, however, with specific characteristic that concern the usage of social media platforms.
[3] www.facebook.com/When-He-Pays-953331571347707/.

well as the corresponding tumblr-Blog,[4] which is the activist's main platform) (Yaron, 2016). The page publishes prostitution customers'—often explicit and violent—descriptions of their encounters with female sex workers, which are published in online groups and forums. Thus the page aims to fight prostitution and its customers by raising awareness to the verbal and physical violence against sex workers, their working conditions, and how prostitution customers treat them as mere objects or "products." On the basis of the platform's policy restricting sexual content, Facebook has blocked Koral's account and deleted several posts from the page, although the page's content exposes the original (but anonymized) quotes of real prostitution costumers in order to fight prostitution rather than promote it.

10.3 SHARING IS CARING? CONCLUSIONS

On World Peace Day 2016,[5] Facebook has released a new feature for the occasion—when users use the "love" reaction (an extension of the "like" button), the heart will be animated as a presentation of love over the social media platform. Although using the feature surely serves Facebook's purpose of linking the platform to a positive feeling—"love"—and having users with good conscience, it is questionable whether this campaign has a greater contribution to world peace than, for example, offering a function make a donation for civilians in the Syrian civil war, a function to send letters to local elected officials protesting arms exports, increasing the social media reach of peace movements and nongovernmental organizations, or providing information on nearby antiwar demonstrations.

Although not used by Facebook on World Peace Day, the phrase "sharing is caring" has been experiencing a renaissance since social media. From simple information and questions, to social causes, to fundraisings, to political issues, the phrase often appears in posts that aim to achieve some kind of mobilization. The statement that by sharing the issue at hand, one would prove that he or she also cares about the issue, implies that sharing it over the social media platform is an actual action in favor of the cause. However, this usage of the notion of "sharing is caring" on social media turns the concept of sharing into an empty phrase. Unlike sharing resources one has (e.g., money, political and/or social power, living space, time, labor), "sharing" on social media is more like disseminating.[6] Although sharing also means making a sacrifice for

---

[4] when-he-pays.tumblr.com.

[5] September 21, 2016.

[6] Having said that, one of the few resources that can actually be shared by "sharing" on social media is one's social network, by, for example, giving a social movement or collective action cause access to this network. See also Chapter 5.

someone else's or a common good, "sharing" on social media requires little or no sacrifice.

This, in itself, is not reprehensible, but the equation of sharing is caring—sharing equals caring—is no other than a solicitation for slacktivism: by "sharing," you will prove and exhibit (to your complete social network!) that you care; no need for further actions. Hence, disseminating—liking, retweeting, and posting—is indeed a way to exhibit sympathy toward certain causes and issues; but real sharing, in terms of nonslacktivist activism, is caring.

References

Chen, A., 2011a. Chinese Activists Less Welcome on Facebook than Mark Zuckerberg's Dog. Gawker. Retrieved from: www.gawker.com/5780385/chinese-activists-less-welcome-on-facebook-than-mark-zuckerbergs-dog.

Chen, A., 2011b. Why Facebook Should Do More to Help Egypt's Protesters. Gawker. Retrieved from: www.gawker.com/5752904/why-facebook-should-do-more-to-help-egypts-protesters.

Garrett, R.K., 2006. Protest in an information society: a review of literature on social movements and new ICTs. Information, Communication & Society 9 (2), 202–224.

Hampton, K.N., Rainie, L., Lu, W., Dwyer, M., Shin, I., Purcell, K., 2014. Social Media and the "Spiral of Silence". Pew Research Center, Washington, DC.

Hesse, M., 2009. Facebook Activism: Lots of Clicks, but Little Sticks. Washington Post. Retrieved from: www.washingtonpost.com/wp-dyn/content/article/2009/07/01/AR2009070103936.html.

Morozov, E., 2011. The Net Delusion: The Dark Side of Internet Freedom. PublicAffairs, New York.

Murphy, T., 2013. UNICEF Asks People to Stop "liking" Things on Facebook & Send Money. Humanosphere. Retrieved from: www.humanosphere.org/basics/2013/04/unicef-sweden-wants-your-money-not-your-likes/.

Shirky, C., 2008. Here Comes Everybody: The Power of Organizing without Organizations. Penguin Group, London.

Yaron, O., 2016. Facebook Blocks Anti-prostitution Activist's Account. Haaretz. Retrieved from: www.haaretz.co.il/captain/net/1.3067911.

CHAPTER 11

The Right Tool in the Wrong Hands: Neutrality, Values, and Biases of Social Media Deployment

ABSTRACT

Not only social justice protests, refugee aid, and political resistance to authoritarian regimes are successful in their deployment of social media, but also causes such as terrorism, right-wing extremism, mobbing, and anorexia. The neutrality of social media, however, is not measured by its deployment to "positive" or "negative" causes. Social media are tools whose design is value laden due to preexisting, technical, and emergent biases and values. These biases and values are affected by the institutions and individuals who build and operate the platforms, the context in which the platforms are used, and the individuals who use them. In turn, the platforms' design comes along with affordances that affect how and in which contexts they are deployed as well as the consequence of their deployment.

Keywords: Biases in technology; Neutrality thesis; Social media; Technocentrism; Technodeterminism; Technoutopianism; Value-sensitive design; Values in technology.

CONTENTS

Throughout the book as well as in general discourse regarding the social media deployment by social movements and/or for causes of collective action, the discussion mostly goes along the lines of progressive, emancipatory, and democratic case studies. This, of course, has a rhetorical value of framing such social media deployment in positive terms, which, in turn, contributes to the positive perception of social media themselves as well as of the institutions and corporations that stand behind them, as was the case during the 2009

Collective Action 2.0. http://dx.doi.org/10.1016/B978-0-08-100567-5.00011-6

Iranian elections and the events of the Arab Spring.[1] On the other hand, many reported cases of social media deployments by movements and activists serve causes that are anything but progressive, emancipatory, or democratic—from promoting anorexia among teenage girls, to terror organizations such as ISIL,[2] to Neo-Nazi and extremist right-wing movements, to the practice of shaming,[3] to school/workplace mobbing.

Is social media in these cases "the right tool in the wrong hands," as proponents of the neutrality thesis—arguing technology is neutral and can be used for both positive and negative causes—would argue? Or are there other aspects to consider before concluding which kind of social media deployment is "wrong" or, alternatively, declaring social media to be the "right tool"?

11.1 THE WRONG HANDS? NEGATIVE CAUSES, FRAMING, AND SOCIAL MEDIA

In his book *Here Comes Everybody* (Shirky, 2008), Clay Shirky discusses the example of Pro-Ana (proanorexia) girls, who used the bulletin board of YM[4] to exchange tips and encourage each other in their anorexia, a phenomenon that exists in social media platforms of all kinds, from WhatsApp groups, to blogs, to Instagram (Juarascio et al., 2010; Krättli, 2015; Naue, 2016). In the argument leading to his conclusion that the "gathering of the Pro-Ana girls isn't a side effect of our social tools, it's an effect of those tools" (Shirky, 2008, p. 207), Shirky acknowledges that social media platforms help individuals, groups, and causes that are deemed negative in society, be it by law, social conventions, or norms, come together. However, by only deploying the theory of information cascades ["lowered transaction costs have made gathering together so simple that anyone can do it" (Shirky, 2008, p. 207)] Shirky fails to sufficiently explain and situate the issue in its specific, cultural context and/or in complexity of the relation between social media and collective action.[5]

---

[1] See Chapter 3.

[2] Islamic State of Iraq and the Levant (ISIL), which is also known as *Islamic State of Iraq and Syria* (ISIS), *Islamic State* (IS), and its Arabic acronym *Daesh*.

[3] Public humiliation of a person as a form of vigilantism using social media platforms. See also Ronson (2015).

[4] The website of the teen girl magazine *Young Miss* (renamed later *Your Magazine*).

[5] Evgeny Morozov extends this to a fundamental criticism of the rational choice and information cascades theories: "It's no wonder that Clay Shirky can explain the behavior of anorexic girls, open-source communities, revolutionaries in East Germany, and rebellious teenagers in Belarus through one clean theory of information cascades. It's a theory that can explain everything—but in its generality and disregard for details, it actually ends up explaining nothing. [...] there's more to political behavior than just incentives and opportunities" (Morozov, 2013, p. 41).

This is a theoretical void that was tackled in previous chapters, by situating the discussed case studies in their cultural, political, economic, etc. contexts parallel to examining each of them through the application of a different theoretical framework; this while acknowledging that the application of different theoretical frameworks to each case study would only contribute for a holistic understanding of the collective action/social movement at hand. Having said that, this chapter aims to fill a different theoretical void left unexplained: in what terms the deployment of social media by movements and/or for causes that are socially deemed as negative can be conceptualized. Consider the following examples:

- Propaganda and recruitment by terror and/or extremist Islamist movements,
- Neo-Nazi and right-wing extremist agitation.

Following the outbreak of the Syrian civil war, a militant fundamentalist group named ISI delegated in 2011 a mission to Syria, to participate the war. The group, hitherto based in Iraq and has its origins in an alliance with al-Qaeda, later changed its name to ISIL (also known as ISIS). During 2013–4, ISIL gained worldwide attention as it drove Iraqi government forces out of important cities as well as conquered Syrian territories (fighting both government and rebel forces), while massacring and raping civilians, destroying historical and cultural heritage, and appropriating oil deposits. ISIL also stood out and gained prominence due to its deployment of media, among others social media for propaganda and recruitment. Using pictures and messages, which went viral on social media platforms, and by "hijacking" trending hashtags and accounts on Twitter and Facebook, ISIL achieved awareness for its goals and actions, disseminated its ideas and ideology, recruited sympathizers around the world, and raised funds (Berger, 2014; Keen, 2015; Norland, 2014). Furthermore, ISIL also released an Arab-language Twitter App called *Dawn* (Dawn of Glad Tidings), in which "users must agree to turn over a surprising amount of personal data and — whether they realize it or not — give ISIS the power to send tweets from that individual's account" (Stone, 2014). Eventually, however, social media corporations such as Twitter and Facebook have begun confronting such extremist propaganda, not only ISIL's, by removing accounts and content related to terror organizations (Abutaleb and Volz, 2016; Haaretz and Reuters, 2016).

In recent years, a variety of scholars have pursued the application of social movement theory frameworks to analyze Islamist and/or terrorist groups such as al-Qaeda, claiming that "Terrorism is a form of contentious politics, analyzable with the basic social movement approach of mobilizing resources, political opportunity structure, and framing" (Beck, 2008). This approach acknowledges the dominance of Western scholars in the social movement theory, which led to the neglect of non-Western movements. Thus applying the social movement theory to the research of terrorism and/or Islamist movement (as one form of non-Western movements) is both insightful for the research itself and can help fill theoretical voids in the respective social movement theories (Bayat, 2005; Beck, 2008; Metzger, 2014; Wiktorowicz, 2004).

Against this background and while acknowledging not all of ISIL's social media methods are common for social movements with democratic legitimation, the effective deployment of social media by ISIL, as well as other Islamist and/or terrorist groups, is not surprising. The advantages that other social movements can draw from social media deployment and were discussed throughout the book apply also for movements such as ISIL. For example, ISIL was successful in framing its actions as resistance to Western hegemony, constructing Wahhabi Sunni Muslim group-identity with an "us against them" stance, mobilizing resources, and undertaking organizational tasks within the organization (also using encrypted communication).

In his critical book *The Internet Is Not the Answer*, Andrew Keen argues that "ISIS's effective use of social media highlights the core problem with the Internet. When the gatekeeper is removed and anyone can publish anything online, much of that 'content' will be either propaganda or plain lies" (Keen, 2015, p. 142). However, the problem with Keen's notion, which is a rejoinder to Shirky's *Here Comes Everybody*, is that it also falls short of delivering a sufficient notion of social media usage in this context. Although criticizing Shirky's notion, Keen explains ISIS social media deployment in just the same terms of information cascades, without taking the social, political, and economic context in which this deployment takes place into consideration and without deploying an extensive theoretical framework (such as the social movement theory).

Yet another example for successful but alarming social media deployment is by Neo-Nazi and right-wing extremist groups. According to Julia Schramm from the project *no-nazi.net* (part of the German *Amadeu Antonio Stiftung*), Neo-Nazi movements in Germany use social media in three ways:

- closed communication via WhatsApp, chats, and instant messaging for the strategic planning as well as coordination of violent actions;
- closed communication channels offered by social media platforms such as closed Facebook groups and private Twitter accounts; and
- open agitation using Facebook groups and pages, Twitter, etc. (Köver and Schramm, 2015).

Social media help right-wing extremist movements and political parties to break the borders of a scene that was hitherto closed, segregated (e.g., through movement specific clothing, music, bars, and symbolic), and predominantly marginalized in society. The social media deployment consists of deliberately taking on a victim role of being marginalized in society as well as connecting racist, anti-Semitic, and nationalist narratives from the right-wing ideology with grievances and worries in society. For example, the diminishing trust in mainstream media, decreasing wages, unemployment, immigration, the sudden arrival of refugees, etc. are commented and framed in terms of nationalist identities and conflicts. Thus these movements reach many individuals with (and without) right-wing tendencies, who are susceptible to these messages, and succeed in mobilizing many of them (e.g., to participate in demonstrations, join movements, vote for parties such as the NPD[6] or AfD,[7] or even take part in violent attacks on refugee accommodations) (Baldauf et al., 2016; Köver and Schramm, 2015). Characteristic for the social media deployment of right-wing movements is that it relies greatly on cultural, identity, and emotional aspects in their social media strategy (regarding agitation and mobilization outside the Neo-Nazi scene); these aspects vary from music, to fashion, to photography, to feminism, to religion, to vague concepts of "German" or "European" culture and identity, to critique of capitalism (with anti-Semitic notions), etc. (Baldauf et al., 2016; Karig, 2016). Such an accentuation in social media deployment was discussed—using a case study that could not have been more different—in Chapter 4.

As in the case with terrorism, social media corporations such as Facebook and Twitter react to hate speech and other right-wing/Nazi content, which is reported by users. However, in light of increasing right-wing and hate speech-related violence, which show relation to hate speech and right-wing propaganda online and on social media, the insufficient engagement of these corporations against hate speech becomes a source of controversy.

Right-wing movements' framing of their own (national) identities and cultures as superior values or offering their own interpretation to anticapitalism, ISIL's own framing as resistance to Western hegemony, or the claim that what one views as "terror" might be "warfare" in the view of another (and vice versa) come to show a crucial point: the definition of which movement's causes and goals are "positive" or "negative" is a flexible one, which depends on the subjective positions of the individual and/or collective as well as a matter of social and political discourse. Having said that, this does not necessarily apply to the means for achieving those goals. To state yet other examples: Hamas' framing of its actions as resistance to Israeli occupation or PKK's[8] framing as resistance to Turkish oppression of Kurdish minorities, both, in turn, framed by Israel or

---

[6] *Nationaldemokratische Partei Deutschlands* (National Democratic Party of Germany), a far-right ultranationalist political party in Germany.
[7] *Alternative für Deutschland* (Alternative for Germany), a right-wing populist and Eurosceptic political party in Germany.
[8] Partiya Karkerên Kurdistanê?, the Kurdistan Workers' Party. The PKK is involved in a long-standing armed conflict with the Turkish state.

Turkey as terror organizations; or left-wing and/or social justice movements such as Occupy Wall Street, the Israeli social protests of 2010, and the Spanish 15-M being framed by their opponents as communists and anarchists.

In light of the discussed examples, proponents of the neutrality thesis would argue to prove their point—technology, in this case social media platforms, is neutral; it can be used for causes deemed both positive and negative in the eyes of the beholder (or the user). Deploying this line of argumentation, however, is barking up the wrong tree. The alleged neutrality of a hammer is not measured by its deployment to hammer black, green, or red nails; neither by its ability to hammer metallic or wooden ones. But rather, it is measured by the hammer's affordance and deployment to, for example, hit another person in the head or smash a window while committing a breaking and entering in comparison with its explicit usage, hammering nails.

As the following section will show, due to social media platform's complexity as information and communication technology (ICT)/as Tools as well as their unique character as Institutions, applying this analogy to social media is somewhat more complex.

11.2 THE RIGHT TOOL? VALUES AND BIASES IN SOCIAL MEDIA

Chapter 2 offered a discussion of the span between the neutrality thesis and technological determinism. In this discussion, three kinds of biases and/or values that are embedded in social media were presented (Brey, 2010; Friedman and Nissenbaum, 1996):

1. *Preexisting biases/values:* both individual biases/values resulting from the values of those who design the system and societal ones resulting from organizations, institutions, and the general culture that constitute the context in which the system is developed. For example, Western norms, capitalist interests, and the political worldview of the platform founders/owners.
2. *Technical biases/values,* which arise from technical constraints or considerations. For example, bandwidth and limited computing abilities and also restrictions such as the 140 characters limitation in Twitter, the algorithms that constitute the "filter bubble," or social media's reliance on expensive broadband Internet connection and end devices.
3. *Emergent bias/values* arise when the social context in which the social media platform is used is not the one intended by its designers (the social media institutions), such as the above-mentioned examples.

The question remains, how do these biases and values affect collective action, when deploying social media?

On the one hand, one could argue that values such as free speech that are manifested in the design of social media platforms promote their deployment in collective action, especially in political context. On the other hand, as discussed in Chapter 9, censorship and surveillance also take place in social media platforms and pose a threat to collective action and/or activists. Furthermore, Chapter 10 has shown how preexisting biases embedded in the social media platform's policies, such as Facebook real name and sexual content policies, can have demobilizing effects. And Chapter 8 has shown how the political orientation of the owners of social media platforms can affect the curation of journalistic content on certain issues, in turn affecting collective action that develops or might have developed surrounding these issues.

Furthermore, corporate social media are platforms that are developed and used in a capitalist context; they are not the product offered by these institutions, but rather their means of production—their product being the platform users' data that are commodified and monetized using advertising. This preexisting bias is manifested in a technical bias, favoring—hence affording—surveillance, data collection, construction of personal profiles, etc. By implication, this preexisting bias is also the reason for the technical bias against end-to-end encryption, data minimization, privacy by design, and anonymity.

Under these conditions, corporate social media can never be neutral, since they are biased toward the financial interests of the institutions behind the platform. By favoring these interests, the platforms are designed to promote certain values and to afford certain uses that serve these interests. This is where the filter bubble algorithms[9] come into play. These algorithms shape the informational environments that are constructed within the social media platform, to influence how individuals use the platform and how they feel while using it.

Social media deployment by social movements and in collective action on the one hand[10] and data accumulation and monetization on the other—these two uses of social media (as tools or ICT) derive from the preexisting biases surrounding social media platforms and are expressed by their technical design and the affordances that come along with it. The stress ratio between these two uses can be considered in terms of their use-value and exchange-value[11]:

> The personal data and information that is collected by social media
> platforms, search engines, advertising companies, and other third-parties
> is rarely deployed for satisfying social needs, such as promotion of social

---

[9] See Chapters 2, 8, and 9 as well as Pariser (2011).

[10] Or in terms of Christian Fuchs' TripleC model—social media's use for cognition, communication, and corporation. See Fuchs (2014b), Fuchs and Trottier (2014) as well as Chapter 2.

[11] In terms of Marx's definition of commodity character and the differentiation between the commodity's use-value and exchange-value.

justice and equality, but rather for serving the economic interests of those who are in control of the information. The information's value is thus an exchange-value; a function of the collection, storage, and deployment costs as well as the profits that (can) derive from it. This does not mean that information isn't perceived by its use-value; nor that informational spaces (such as social media platforms or search engines) cannot be used for ends that promote social progress. Both do. But also such uses of information (uses primarily for the information's use-value or promoting social progress by, for example, organizing social protests over social media) serve the economical interests of the institutions and stakeholders who are in control of the informational spaces—they take place within the commercial informational spaces (which, in turn, serve as means of production), hence they are monitored, protocolled, analyzed, sold, and deployed to generate profit. Thus, the economic or exchange-value of information prevails.

Spier (2016, p. 392)

Another problem of preexisting biases, which in practice becomes a technical bias, is the alleged neutrality of algorithms. Information technology companies, among others Google and Facebook, consistently argue that their algorithms are neutral and only reflect what is going on online and/or within the platform.[12] Consider the following examples:

- Flickr's algorithm for automatically tagging of uploaded photos labels pictures of black men as "animal" or "ape" (Hern, 2015);
- A risk assessment software used to predict future criminals in the United States is biased against black individuals (Angwin et al., 2016);
- Google search queries that contain black-sounding names are more likely to serve up advertisements suggestive of a criminal record than white-sounding names (MIT Technology Review, 2013);
- Although the percentage of women Chief Executive Officers (CEOs) in the United States is 27%, in Google images only 11% women are shown for the query "CEO" in the top 100 search results; the first female CEO being CEO Barbie (Kay et al., 2015; Langston, 2015; Miners, 2015)!

These examples come to show that biases and values in society are cemented in algorithms, which are propagated as being neutral. Algorithms present us biased information as if it were an unbiased, accurate reflection of "reality," thus making it harder to reveal and prove discrimination and injustice. In turn, in the belief of algorithmic neutrality, decisions of all kinds—insurance policies and prices, creditworthiness, business decision, stock transactions, newsworthiness of journalistic content, criminality statistics, etc.—are increasingly based on the results of algorithms or even are taken by algorithms.

---

[12] In his book *To Save Everything, Click Here* Evgeny Morozov discusses this notion as well as the interests behind it at great length, proving the notion of algorithmic neutrality to be false. See Morozov (2013)

For collective action, the reliance on tools and platforms with biased/value-laden algorithms but whose owners—the social media institution—promote as neutral, means that the tools might manipulate, discriminate, and affect what activists and movements do with these tools, for better or for worse. Although social media platforms do not manipulate the content of movement-related information itself (e.g., manipulate a post, a tweet, a shared photo or video), most social media platforms would present individuals who, according to their algorithms, might be sympathizers or opponents a different picture regarding the intensity or even the existence of the movement/collective action; they would construct a digital presentation of "reality" that matches the user's own worldview, thus suppressing the emergence of relative deprivation and limiting the user's autonomy; they would cluster like-minded individuals in their own filter bubbles;they will interfere with the emergence of shared awareness; they would remove movement-related content that are incompatible with their values; they would show you information that might not be meant for you but its algorithms "discriminatorily" decided to be relevant for you (e.g., feminist content for women, antiracist content to black persons), etc.

Similar to corporate social media, alternative social media such as diaspora*, Riseup, GNU social, Friendica, Ocupii, N-1, and Ello also have biases and values. However, these are partially different from those of corporate social media. The preexisting biases/values of alternative social media are usually based on being collectively owned and/or noncorporate, therefore not profit oriented. This, in turn, affects their technical design, which is biased against surveillance and commodification of data and toward privacy by design and encryption. This causes a fundamental difference in the algorithms of the platforms, which may have similar functionalities as corporate social media on the surface, but different algorithms, functions, structures, principles, and values that serve as the basis of these functionalities underneath the surface. For example, alternative social media platforms also might calculate the relevance of certain content to certain users to prevent potential information overload. However, unlike the filter bubble, these algorithms will have other basic assumptions and other values implemented within them than the economic interests of a social media corporation.

On the other hand, some technical biases/values apply both for corporate and alternative social media, biases and values that are not related to the institutional aspect of social media. Such a purely technical bias is that social media platforms being advanced computer systems, their usage relies on expensive (mobile) end devices and access to (mobile) broadband Internet, and requires a considerable level of (information, media, and social media) literacy. Having said that, these platforms are easier to use—hence, more accessible—than many previous online technologies (e.g., curating a website). As discussed in Chapters 5 and 6, these technical biases are embodied in discriminatory access to social media as well as unequal power relations in their deployment, thus unintentionally preferring individuals and collectives with higher income, better access to education and to technology, etc., as well as discriminating in the legitimacy that individuals, collectives, or movements derive from the usage of social media. This was, for example, evident in the 2010 Israeli social justice as well as in parts of the Occupy Wall Street movements, which were perceived as predominantly young, white, and middle-class movements.

Lastly, emergent biases/values arise when social media platforms are used in contexts other than the ones intended by the social media institutions behind the platform. As Philip Brey notes, "[i]n this context, the system may not adequately support the capabilities, values or interests of some user groups or the interests of other stakeholders" (Brey, 2010, p. 50). Considering the above-mentioned examples—terror organization, extremist Islamist movements, and right-wing extremist movements and parties—the deployment of social media in these contexts was not intended by Facebook or Twitter. Hence, the emergent values that arise from these uses stand in contradiction and conflict with the (preexisting) values and interest of other—the majority of—platform users, with social media's marketing as "promoting democracy," and with the institutions' financial interests (keeping the platforms safe and disturbance-free spaces, thus supporting consumption as well as commodification and monetization of data).

On the one hand, corporate social media are "unbiased" to the extent that they are able to commodify and monetize almost any activity on their platform, even terrorist and right-wing extremist ones. However, as such emergent biases and values arise through the deployment of social media in such contexts, the latter poses a threat on social media platforms and institutions; it poses a threat on their image, marketing, and financial interests. Therefore it is not surprising that when this threat becomes obvious (for example, by wide debates in media and politics regarding the accountability of the social media institutions), social media corporations begin to react to these uses, trying to suppress them.

Moreover, social media's design and usage as tools for data accumulation, commodification, and monetization by the social media institutions can be a source for emergent biases and values. As discussed in Chapter 9, due to social media's bias toward data accumulation and corporate surveillance, social media can be effectively used in the context of state surveillance, thus placing social media in a context other than the one intended by their developers. In this context, an emergent bias toward state surveillance and suppression arises, since the more individuals and movements use social media, the easier it is for state surveillance to gather information about them. This emergent bias is anything but supportive of the values and interests of the platforms' users, let alone of political activists and movements, dissidents, and protesters, who deploy social media.

In other words, the characteristic of social media as dual-use technologies is inherently contradictory. Whereas the use of social media for one aim profits from the counterpart's use of the same technology (e.g., state surveillance profits from activists leaving information trails in online platforms or the plain commodification and monetization of every action and interaction); using social media for another aim necessarily comes along with the support of the counterpart, "the opponent," to gain other benefits (e.g., organizing movements and protests while being subjected to corporate and/or state surveillance). Thus, social media as dual-use technologies reinforce existing power relations in society.

In conclusion, the discussion offered in this chapter shows that the neutrality of social media is not measured by their deployment to "positive" or "negative" causes, since these definitions are a matter of framing, socialization, political opinion, subjective interests, etc. Social media are tools whose design is value laden due to preexisting, technical, and emergent biases and values. These biases and values are affected by the institutions and individuals who build and operate the platforms, the context in which the platforms are used, and the individuals who use them. In turn, the platforms' design comes along with affordances that affect how and in which contexts they are deployed as well as the consequence of their deployment.

11.3 THERE IS NO RIGHT LIFE IN THE WRONG ONE? CONCLUSIONS

During the 1960s in the United States, the Vietnam War resistance movement deployed music and culture as means of protest and mobilization.[13] The philosopher and member of the Frankfurter School Theodor W. Adorno warned the student movements of the time from expressing antiwar sentiments using pop music, since it gives the atrocious a commodity-character, making it consumable:

> Actually, I believe that attempts to bring political protest together with popular music –that is, entertainment music – are doomed for the following reason. The entire sphere of popular music, even there where it dresses itself up in modernist guise is to such a degree inseparable from "Warencharakter", from amusement, from the cross-eyed transfixion with consumption, so that attempts to outfit it with a new function remain entirely superficial. When somebody sets himself up, and for whatever reason accompanies maudlin music by singing something about Vietnam being unbearable, then I find exactly this song unbearable. By making the horrendous somehow consumable, it ends up wringing something like consumption-qualities out of it![14]

---

[13] A trend that is connected to the emergence of the cultural turn and new social movement in the study of collective action and social movements, as discussed in Chapter 4.
[14] English translation of a televised interview with Theodor W. Adorno, cited in (Gil and Nesci, 2012, p. 187).

This, for Adorno typical critique of modern culture should be read in its context—written in US exile, under the shock of National Socialist and fascist terror, and baffled by the US cultural and medial reality. Furthermore, as is the case with the cultural critique expressed in other Adorno works, this does not come to deny the usage of culture as means of resistance and protest per se, but rather of culture in its commodified form.

Can it be that, in Adorno's terms, social media with its absolute commodification of all activities and actions, even of protest and resistance itself, and with its built-in corporate surveillance, which is biased toward state surveillance as well, is actually the wrong tool? The "wrong one" in which the "right" collective action, the "right" social values, the "right life" cannot prevail? This question, this fundamental Adorno-istic notion, leads back to the stress ratio between the two main uses of social media (as tools or ICT) and their expression in use-value and exchange-value:

- Cognition, communication, and cooperation by individuals and collectives as use-value on the one hand; and
- data accumulation, commodification, and monetization by institutions as exchange-value on the other.

Christian Fuchs suggests to "think about the media in social movements in contradictory terms: Media do not have one-dimensional, clear-cut effects on social movements, but rather can have multiple effects that contradict each other. There are both commercial media and alternative media, and one needs to have a look in what relationship these media stand to each other" (Fuchs, 2014a, p. 341). This notion, addressing mainstream, mass, and alternative media,[15] can be applied to social media as well. As the discussion throughout the book has shown, the deployment of social media is not "good" or "bad" for collective action and social movements; it has a variety of aspects and effects, rather than clear-cut ones. In many cases, this variety of effects stands in contradiction to each other—mobilization versus demobilization, political resistance versus surveillance and suppression, free speech versus corporate/state censorship, promotion of social justice and anticapitalist causes versus the commodification and monetization of resistance itself, etc. Therefore thinking of social media in their complexity, in their contradictory effects and relations, helps overcome technological determinism and centrism, be it utopian or dystopian ones.

Regarding the question of social media being "the right tool in the wrong hands?", as is the case with many other tools, being in "the wrong hands" is not completely avoidable for social media platforms as well. Although the

---

[15] See Chapter 8.

discussion regarding which causes and uses are indeed "wrong" or "negative" is a broad social discussion, avoiding many of these uses (such as the ones discussed in this chapter) is not an issue of social media itself, but rather of society—fighting the causes for terror, right-wing extremism, etc. It is, however, also a matter of social, political, and media discourse to examine how we use new forms of communication and organization offered to us by our technologies, to reach social progress rather than violence, populism, and alienation.

As to the role of social media institutions, it is crucial to begin implementing value sensitive design (VSD) (Brey, 2010; Flanagan et al., 2008; Friedman et al., 2006), based on this discourse. That is, emphasizing ethical values in the platforms' design, values that are part of a larger context and discourse, rather than the outcome of the social media institution's own financial interests and political agenda.[16] A first step in this direction is for social media institutions to acknowledge that their platforms, their algorithms are neither neutral nor "just a tool"; to acknowledge the power they possess and exert through decisions of design. One platform, although not a predominantly social media platform, that acknowledged these issues is Airbnb.[17] After facing criticism on the ability to discriminate potential renters based on race, age, gender, or other factors, Airbnb launched an intern review (Benner, 2016). The results, published in a special report (Murphy, 2016), were untypical for the industry: Airbnb did not resort to the classical defense, claiming algorithms to "neutrally" represent the existing realities on the rental market and Airbnb solely being a "neutral" intermediary, but rather rejected this, somewhat helpless, narrative. Instead, Airbnb, acknowledging its power as a value-laden platform, implemented a VSD approach and consulted a variety of stakeholders (hosts, victims of discriminations, employees, civil rights organizations, regulatory agencies, elected officials, travel and tourism executives, and expert consultants) on how to change the platform's design and terms of use to prevent both intentional and unintentional discrimination.

As for being "the right tool," the answer is that it is time to consider—corporate as well as alternative—social media platforms as just another tool in the collective action/social movement toolkit and repertoire. When deploying it in an effective, informed, reflected, and well-balanced manner while being aware of the positive and negative aspects of the deployment, social media can definitely be the right tool, but it does not have to be the only tool. In contrast, deploying social media for the sake of using social media just because it is said to be "the right tool," while neglecting the complex, negative, and in part dangerous aspects of this deployment, might often backfire.

---

[16] Evgeny Morozov (2013), Eli Pariser (2011) give recommendations on how principles of VSD can be implemented in online platforms, apps, and digital technologies.
[17] An online platform, which enables people to list and rent vacation rooms, apartments, as well as their own apartments.

Having said that, neither VSD, as is the case with Airbnb, nor the well thought out deployment of corporate social media, as seen in the case studies throughout the book, would solve the stress ratio between the two main uses of corporate social media, the stress ratio between their use- and exchange-values. The rejoinder to the Adorno-istic notion of the commodification of collective action—the commodification of cognition, communication, and cooperation—would be to take the latter out of the sphere of commercialism and consumption. That is, to strengthen alternative social media that offer activists, movements, as well as private individuals in their everyday, nonactivist communication and cooperation a sphere that is outside of corporate and state surveillance, a sphere in which their communication, their action, and their data stay private, encrypted and uncommodified, owned by the users themselves and not by corporations. Because, in the words of philosopher and media scholar Marshall McLuhan, "the medium is the message" (McLuhan, 1994). And using a medium, which is inherently—that is, in its technical design as well as social-organizational structures—noncommodified, noncommercial, private by design, and encrypted, confers the message—that is, the processes of cognition, communication, and cooperation—dimensions that are by contemporary terms revolutionary; a revolutionary message that would be embodied in contexts, which go beyond the specific collective action itself.

This is the challenge we are facing, before reaching a real emancipatory and social media.

References

Abutaleb, Y., Volz, D., 2016. Twitter, Facebook Move Quickly to Stem Celebrations of Nice Attack. Reuters. Retrieved from: www.reuters.com/article/us-europe-attacks-socialmedia-idUSKCN0ZW00Z.

Angwin, J., Larson, J., Mattu, S., Kirchner, L., 2016. Machine Bias. ProPublica. Retrieved from: www.propublica.org/article/machine-bias-risk-assessments-in-criminal-sentencing.

Baldauf, J., Dittrich, M., Rathje, J., Schramm, J., Schwarz, K., 2016. Monitoringbericht zu rechtsextremen und menschenverachtenden Phänomenen im Social Web für 2015/2016. Amadeu Antonio Stiftung. Retrieved from: www.amadeu-antonio-stiftung.de/w/files/pdfs/monitoringbericht-2015.pdf.

Bayat, A., 2005. Islamism and social movement theory. Third World Quarterly 26 (6), 891–908.

Beck, C.J., 2008. The contribution of social movement theory to understanding terrorism. Sociology Compass 2 (5), 1565–1581.

Benner, K., 2016. Airbnb Adopts Rules to Fight Discrimination by Its Hosts. The New York Times. Retrieved from: www.nytimes.com/2016/09/09/technology/airbnb-anti-discrimination-rules.html?_r=0.

Berger, J.M., 2014. How ISIS Games Twitter. The Atlantic. Retrieved from: www.theatlantic.com/international/archive/2014/06/isis-iraq-twitter-social-media-strategy/372856/.

Brey, P., 2010. Values in technology and disclosive computer ethics. In: Floridi, L. (Ed.), The Cambridge Handbook of Information and Computer Ethics. Cambridge University Press, Cambridge, pp. 41–58.

Flanagan, M., Howe, D., Nissenbaum, H., 2008. Embodying values in technology: theory and practice. In: van den Hoven, J., Weckert, J. (Eds.), Information Technology and Moral Philosophy. Cambridge University Press, Cambridge, pp. 322–353.

Friedman, B., Nissenbaum, H., 1996. Bias in computer systems. ACM Transactions on Computer Systems 14 (3), 330–347.

Friedman, B., Kahn, P.H., Borning, A., 2006. Value sensitive design and information systems. In: Zhang, P., Galletta, D.F. (Eds.), Human-computer Interaction and Management Information Systems: Foundations. M. E. Sharpe, New York, pp. 348–372.

Fuchs, C., 2014a. Digital Labour and Karl Marx. Routledge, New York.

Fuchs, C., 2014b. Social Media: A Critical Introduction. Sage, London.

Fuchs, C., Trottier, D., 2014. Theorizing social media, politics, and the state: an introduction. In: Fuchs, C., Trottier, D. (Eds.), Social Media, Politics and the State: Protests, Revolutions, Riots, Crime and Policing in the Age of Facebook, Twitter and YouTube. Routledge, New York, pp. 3–38.

Gil, I.C., Nesci, C., 2012. Plots of War: Modern Narratives of Conflict. De Gruyter, Berlin.

Haaretz, Reuters, 2016. Twitter Shuts Down 125,000 Accounts for Promoting Terrorism, Most Linked to ISIS. Haaretz. Retrieved from: www.haaretz.com/world-news/1.701678.

Hern, A., 2015. Flickr Faces Complaints over "offensive" Auto-Tagging for Photos. The Guardian. Retrieved from: www.theguardian.com/technology/2015/may/20/flickr-complaints-offensive-auto-tagging-photos.

Juarascio, A.S., Shoaib, A., Timko, C.A., 2010. Pro-eating disorder communities on social networking sites: a content analysis. Eating Disorders 18 (5), 393–407.

Köver, C., Schramm, J., 2015. Julia Schramm von no-nazi.net erklärt die Social-Media-Strategien der Rechten. Wired. Retrieved from: www.wired.de/collection/life/julia-schramm-von-no-nazi-net-erklart-die-social-media-strategien-der-rechten.

Karig, F., 2016. Die neuen rechten Mädels nutzen das Netz. Jetzt. Retrieved from: www.jetzt.de/was-ist-rechts/junge-rechtsextreme-frauen-nutzen-das-netz-fuer-propaganda.

Kay, M., Matuszek, C., Munson, S.A., 2015. Unequal representation and gender stereotypes in image search results for occupations. CHI '15 Proceedings of the 33rd Annual ACM Conference on Human Factors in Computing Systems 3819–3828.

Keen, A., 2015. The Internet Is Not the Answer. Atlantic Monthly Press, New York.

Krättli, N., 2015. Im Anorexie-Chat: Wenn Mädchen sich und ihren Körper hassen. Der Schweizerische Beobachter. Retrieved from: www.beobachter.ch/familie/jugend-pubertaet/artikel/im-anorexie-chat_wenn-maedchen-sich-und-ihren-koerper-hassen/.

Langston, J., 2015. Who's a CEO? Google Image Results Can Shift Gender Biases. Univesity of Washington. Retrieved from: www.washington.edu/news/2015/04/09/whos-a-ceo-google-image-results-can-shift-gender-biases/.

McLuhan, M., 1994. Understanding Media: The Extensions of Man. MIT Press, Cambridge.

Metzger, T., 2014. Social movement theory and terrorism: explaining the development of Al-Qaeda. Inquiries Journal/Student Pulse 6 (09).

Miners, Z., 2015. The First Woman CEO to Appear in a Google Images Search is… CEO Barbie. PC World. Retrieved from: www.pcworld.com/article/2908592/the-first-woman-ceo-to-appear-in-a-google-images-search-is-ceo-barbie.html.

MIT Technology Review, 2013. Racism Is Poisoning Online Ad Delivery, Says Harvard Professor. MIT Technology Review. Retrieved from: www.technologyreview.com/s/510646/racism-is-poisoning-online-ad-delivery-says-harvard-professor/.

Morozov, E., 2013. To Save Everything, Click Here: Technology, Solutionism, and the Urge to Fix Problems that Don't Exist. Allen Lane, London.

Murphy, L.W., 2016. Airbnb's Work to Fight Discrimination and Build Inclusion: A Report Submitted to Airbnb. Airbnb. Retrieved from: blog.airbnb.com/wp-content/uploads/2016/09/REPORT_Airbnbs-Work-to-Fight-Discrimination-and-Build-Inclusion.pdf?3c10be.

Naue, J., 2016. Instagram als Plattform für Frauen mit Essstörung. Heise. Retrieved from: www.heise.de/newsticker/meldung/Instagram-als-Plattform-fuer-Frauen-mit-Essstoerung-3287352.html.

Norland, R., 2014. Iraq's Sunni Militants Take to Social Media to Advance Their Cause and Intimidate. The New York Times. Retrieved from: www.nytimes.com/2014/06/29/world/middleeast/iraqs-sunni-militants-take-to-social-media-to-advance-their-cause-and-intimidate.html.

Pariser, E., 2011. The Filter Bubble. Penguin Books, London.

Ronson, J., 2015. So You've Been Publicly Shamed. Riverhead Books, A Member of Penguin Group, New York.

Shirky, C., 2008. Here Comes Everybody: The Power of Organizating without Organizations. Penguin Group, London.

Spier, S., 2016. From culture industry to information society: how Horkheimer and Adorno's conception of the culture industry can help Us examine information overload in the capitalist information society. In: Kelly, M., Bielby, J. (Eds.), Information Cultures in the Digital Age: A Festschrift in Honor of Rafael Capurro. Springer VS; Wiesbaden, pp. 385–396.

Stone, J., 2014. ISIS Attacks Twitter Streams, Hacks Accounts to Make Jihadi Message Go Viral. International Business Times. Retrieved from: www.ibtimes.com/isis-attacks-twitter-streams-hacks-accounts-make-jihadi-message-go-viral-1603842.

Wiktorowicz, Q., 2004. Islamic Activism: A Social Movement Theory Approach. Indiana University Press, Bloomington.

PART

Epilogue

CHAPTER 12

On the Verge of the Plateau: Epilogue

ABSTRACT

This chapter, the book's epilogue, offers a closure of the discussion in both parts of the book, coming full circle back to the issues mentioned in the introduction and throughout the book. Additionally, prospects for related research topics, which are outside the book's scope, are sketched. Such research topics are, to name a few: digital "waste disposal" labor, shaming, resistance *within* social media platforms and their communities, and challenges of digital democracy and socially adapting to new forms of communication.

Keywords: Collective action; Digital democracy; Digital labor; Hype cycle; Online communities; Shaming; Social media; Social movement; Social movements theory.

CONTENTS

In the book's introduction, the examples of telephone and mailing lists, leaflets, *samizdat*, fax machines and photocopiers, radio, and Internet websites were mentioned to stress the notion that throughout the history of technological and social development, information and communication technologies (ICTs) of different kinds have played a central role in collective action. Despite this central role, ICTs in general and social media in particular tend to be underrepresented in the scholarly literature and discourse, thus creating a void in the theoretical framework to research the role of ICT in collective action. Furthermore, the fact that since "the 1980s the field of social movement studies has been characterized by an eclecticism with many theoretical strands but without a dominant paradigm(s)" (Benski et al., 2013, p. 557) had also contributed to this void in the scholarly literature; despite the fact that the resource mobilization approach enjoys a rather dominant stand in some circles. A surprising change in this trend occurred around 2009–2011, years of major social protests worldwide. Beginning with the 2009 protests in

173

Iran, following the events of the Arab Spring and reaching social movements in Greece, Spain, Israel, the United States, Chile, and more, a discourse surrounding the deployment of social media platforms in these movements have emerged, a discourse that, as argued in the introduction, took the shape of a hype cycle discourse. Thus for a certain period, ICTs took the center stage.

With or without noticing, the discussion in the book took the shape of the hype cycle discourse as well. The book began with a discussion of "what is social media?" in Chapter 2, describing the Technological Trigger, and worked its way toward the Peak of Inflated Expectations in Chapters 3–6, discussing the ways in which social media effectively integrates in various models and theoretical frameworks of social movements and collective action, at the same time acknowledging first problems, dangers, and failures that emerge in relation to these models. Then, the discussion slowly ascended by posing critical questions on the relations between algorithms and actions as well as mass/mainstream and social media, reaching the Trough of Disillusionment with aspects of state surveillance, corporate surveillance, commodification of collective action, and demobilization. Subsequently, it touched upon the biases, values, and (alleged) neutrality of social media platforms, addressing ethical and moral aspects in regard to its deployment in collective action and social movements, and trying to answer the question of social media being "the right tool," leading the way to the Slope of Enlightenment.

Thus we are now standing on the verge of the Plateau of Productivity. As said in the previous chapter, it is time to consider—corporate as well as alternative—social media platforms as just another tool in the collective action/social movement toolkit and repertoire, not as the revolution itself. Deploying social media in an effective, informed, reflected, and well-balanced manner while being aware of the positive and negative aspects of the deployment is the very essence of reaching the plateau of productivity, but it is only one half of the story. Discussing this deployment without resorting to technological centrism and determinism, without framing collective action and social movements in terms of the tools they deploy—in terms of "Twitter revolutions" or "Facebook protests"—while neglecting the crucial social and political contexts in which they take place, and without ignoring the inherent contradictions of corporate social media, this is the second half, without which we will continue drifting back and forth between the peak of inflated expectations and trough of disillusionment. One of the book's primary objectives is to offer theoretical frameworks, with which social media can be studied as part of the historically continuous reciprocal relation between ICT and collective action (as well as beyond this relation), as well as to dispel common myths regarding this relation. But hopefully, the book's contribution would not be purely to academic, but also to social and activist discourse surrounding social media, to reach the plateau of productivity in its fullness.

Having said that, several related subjects were left out of the book's scope. To name a few of these subjects, consider:

- digital "waste disposal" labor,
- shaming,
- the role of social media in the notion of "smart-cities,"
- resistance *within* social media platforms and their communities, and
- digital democracy and socially adapting to new forms of communication.

Digital "waste disposal" labor is conducted by workers in the Philippines, who keep social media platforms such as Facebook, Twitter, Instagram, or Tinder clean from explicit content—from decapitations, to child abuse, to violence as well as other, less explicit content that social media institutions do not want their users to see. These jobs include contracts with draconian secrecy clauses threatening the workers and considerable psychological strains due to the constant exposure to such content (Chen, 2014; Kaul and Riesewieck, 2016). Furthermore, as a research of the German newspaper *Süddeutsche Zeitung* has revealed, since 2015 Facebook operates in Berlin a center for such "waste disposal" through the contractor Avarto. Also here, employees report bad working conditions, intensive exposure to explicit materials (often several hundreds, even thousands posts daily), psychological implications of this exposure, and threatening secrecy clauses (Krause and Grassegger, 2016a,b). This, however, is not merely a question of working conditions and transparency. In democratic societies, the legislature, the executive, and the judiciary are democratically elected, controlled, and of course separated. In the case of digital "waste disposal" on corporate social media platforms, neither the rules and laws for deletion (or for the exclusion of persons who do not obey the rules) nor the decisions or their execution are known to the public or being developed and executed as part of a democratic social and political process. Although these platforms constitute spaces, in which public discourses and processes take place, they increasingly become an infrastructure of social processes, such as collective action. This issue, however, has been hitherto covered by several investigative journalists without much public, political, or academic attention.

The term *Shaming* articulates the practice of public humiliation of a person as a form of vigilantism using social media platforms (Ronson, 2015). Shaming is often, but not always, used as vengeance against a person, whose victims are powerless against him in traditional/institutional justice systems (e.g., victims of sexual harassments being powerless in the justice system against a highly ranked politician or manager). This practice is essentially an act of collective action that poses many ethical dilemmas such as the act of vigilantism, the reaction to power relations in society, proportionality, the "collateral damage" caused to people surrounding the subject of shaming, etc.

In recent years, the notion of "smart-cities" enjoys growing attention in politics, academia, and the (IT) industry. Smart-city refers to an urban development with a vision of using big data, Internet of things, and further information technologies to improve the management of the city's assets and processes (e.g., public service, public transportation, waste disposal, or energy and water supply) as well as develop means of e-participation (online citizen participation). Thus, using real-time data, cities should become more efficient, productive, environment-friendly, and not only with better quality of life but also with an increased surveillance of public as well as private urban spaces. Especially in terms of citizens participation, which is a form of collective action, there are many projects and examples worldwide of social media being part of these processes.

However, the challenges and open questions regarding smart-cities show similarities to those regarding social media such as: how can individuals be protected from surveillance and profiling (especially considering the examples discussed in Chapter 9 and the notion of post-panopticon)? how can a further commodification of public, hitherto noncommercial spaces be avoided? how should the infrastructures be designed, to avoid the commodification and monetization of the collected data? In this regard, alternative social media offer initial approaches and ideas which need to be developed in the context of urban spaces and smart-cities.

Resistance as collective action, which takes place *within* social media platforms and their communities, is a special form of social media–related collective action. As such, it has many singularities worth of particular analytical attention. For example, in July 2015, Reddit users protested the dismissal of Reddit's director of Talent and popular employee in the Reddit community, Victoria Taylor. These protests joined a growing dismay toward Reddit executive Ellen Pao, due to her harsh policies against harassment on the platform, and peaked as large sections of the platform were set to private, virtually paralyzing the platform. Eventually, Ellen Pao has resigned (Katz, 2015; Nguyen, 2015; Süddeutsche Zeitung, 2015).

The new and changing forms of communication, in which social media play a central role, profoundly affect the political sphere. Among others, as the following examples will show, they change how discourses in Western democracies function. Chapter 8 touched upon issues such as the spread of rumors, lies, and further unwanted effects of the diminishment of gatekeepers, the filter bubble, and the increasing speed of communication. In 2016, these effects revealed their full power, as the successful Brexit[1] campaign on the one side

---

[1] United Kingdom European Union membership referendum, held on June 23, 2016.

of the Atlantic Ocean and the Donald Trump US presidency campaign on the other have spawned the notion of a "post-fact era," "post-factual politics," or even "post-truth politics." In these campaigns, the structures of the digital sphere and especially social media—the speed of communication, lack of gate-keepers, filter bubbles serving as segregators and amplifiers—have set optimal conditions for populism to win over facts (Jaishankar, 2016; Viner, 2016), thus having grave political consequences not only on the outcomes of the Brexit referendum or the political discourse in the United States, but on an international scale as well. Furthermore, the fact that Donald Trump's election and (to a certain extent) the Brexit referendum's success was publicly perceived as a shock is the outcome of democracy in times of the filter bubble; when everybody—including the media—see what they want to see, reality comes as a shock.

But it does not end there—during the 2016 US presidential campaign, social media bots (artificial software agents that spread information over social media, as if they were "real" users, that is, human agents) were massively interfering with the social media communication during the elections. For example, between the first two presidential debates, one of three pro-Trump tweets and nearly one of five pro-Clinton tweets were placed by such bots (Shiroma, 2016; Guilbeault and Woolley, 2016). Thus, algorithms and computer programs use big data methods to influence public discourse and even (mobilization for) collective action, which take place over social media platforms, in turn, influencing democratic processes and their outcomes. These are, on the one hand, worrying finding especially from the point of view of social media deployment in collective action. On the other hand, this might pose a fascinating supplement for the discussion on algorithms and actions from Chapter 7.

As with other case studies of social media deployments, focusing on technology, that is, social media, alone is insufficient. It is crucial to address these issues in terms of social media's role and effect within the specific social, cultural, political, historical, and economic context. For example, what are the economic, social, and religious conditions that make the Philippines—or Berlin—optimal for digital "waste disposal" labor (Kaul and Riesewieck, 2016)? Or what are the historical and political conditions and realities in the United States, Britain, and the European Union, in which populism finds a fertile ground to grow and reach what is termed as "post-factual" or "post-truth politics?"

Furthermore, issues such as digital democracy and its role in the emergence of the so-called "post-factual politics," shaming, workplace/school mobbing carried out over social media, right-wing extremists' usage of social media, and many further examples are not just intriguing topics of academic research. But rather, these are warning signals for us, as society, to learn and socially adapt to the new forms of cognition, communication, and cooperation that digital technologies in general and social media in particular enable us. Learn and adapt as to how we design our tools as well as how we, in turn, use these tools, to reach social progress in terms of inclusion, (fact based) democratization, tolerance, social justice, and peace, rather than violence, populism, and alienation. This too, is crucial for us to reach and stay on the plateau of productivity, instead of being lost in the trough of disillusionment.

These are academically fascinating and socially crucial issues, to which I hope the book will make a contribution.

On a personal note, writing these words symbolizes an end of a journey; a journey that began on that Mayday 2010 in Berlin, continued as I have written my thesis on the subject at the Humboldt University of Berlin, and ended with the completion of this book. During this journey, I had the pleasure of participating in movements and protests that not only were indeed academically intriguing, but also moved me as an individual with grievances and anger as well as hopes and dreams. I had the pleasure of protesting, debating, being inspired, exchanging ideas, and coworking while protesting together with activists claiming social justice in Israel, where I grew up; while blocking Neo-Nazi marches in Berlin, my home town in the past decade; and while engaging in refugee aid, often losing sense of time and space as locals—with and without migration background—meet refugees from around the world and build collectives I hitherto never thought possible. Writing this book would have never been possible without all these people.

References

Benski, T., Langman, L., Perugorría, I., Tejerina, B., 2013. From the streets and squares to social movement studies: What have we learned? Current Sociology 61 (4), 541–561.

Chen, A., 2014. The Laborers Who Keep Dick Pics and Beheadings Out of Your Facebook Feed. Wired. Retrieved from www.wired.com/2014/10/content-moderation/.

Guilbeault, D., Woolley, S., 2016. How Twitter Bots Are Shaping the Election. The Atlantic. Retrieved from www.theatlantic.com/technology/archive/2016/11/election-bots/506072/.

Jaishankar, D., 2016. Brexit: The First Major Casualty of Digital Democracy. The Huffington Post. Retrieved from: www.huffingtonpost.in/dhruva-jaishankar/brexit-the-first-major-casualty-of-digital-democracy/.

Katz, B., 2015. Ellen Pao and Victoria Taylor Find Themselves on Opposite Ends of the Great Reddit Revolt. The New York Times. Retrieved from: nytlive.nytimes.com/womenintheworld/2015/07/08/ellen-pao-and-victoria-taylor-find-themselves-on-opposite-ends-of-the-great-reddit-revolt/.

Kaul, M., Riesewieck, M., 2016. Müllentsorger in Sozialen Netzwerken. Taz. Retrieved from: www.taz.de/Muellentsorger-in-Sozialen-Netzwerken/!5295220/. Krause, T., Grassegger, H., 2016a. Inside Facebook. Süddeutsche Zeitung. Retrieved from: international.sueddeutsche.de/post/154513473995/inside-facebook.

Krause, T., Grassegger, H., 2016a. Inside Facebook. Süddeutsche Zeitung. Retrieved from international.sueddeutsche.de/post/154513473995/inside-facebook.

Krause, T., Grassegger, H., 2016b. Im Netz des Bösen. Süddeutsche Zeitung. Retrieved from www.sueddeutsche.de/digital/inside-facebook-im-netz-des-boesen-1.3295206.

Nguyen, M.D., 2015. Reddit Users Turn on Interim CEO Ellen Pao. NBC News. Retrieved from: www.nbcnews.com/news/asian-america/reddit-users-turn-interim-ceo-ellen-pao-n377226.

Ronson, J., 2015. So You've Been Publicly Shamed. Riverhead Books, A member of Penguin Group, New York.

Shiroma, S., 2016. Trump's Twitter Debate Lead Was 'Swelled by Bots'. BBC. Retrieved from http://www.bbc.com/news/technology-37684418.

Süddeutsche Zeitung, 2015. Rücktritt von Reddit-Chefin Ellen Pao: User-Revolution in der Internet-Goldgrube. Retrieved from: www.sueddeutsche.de/digital/ruecktritt-von-reddit-chefin-ellen-pao-user-revolution-in-der-internet-goldgrube-1.2561692.

Viner, K., 2016. How Technology Disrupted the Truth. The Guardian. Retrieved from www.theguardian.com/media/2016/jul/12/how-technology-disrupted-the-truth.

Index

'*Note:* Page numbers followed by "f" indicate figures.'

181